FAMILY AND DISABILITY ACTIVISM

EDITED BY
PAMELA BLOCK, ALLISON C. CAREY,
AND RICHARD K. SCOTCH

FAMILY AND DISABILITY ACTIVISM

Beyond Allies and Obstacles

TEMPLE UNIVERSITY PRESS
Philadelphia • *Rome* • *Tokyo*

TEMPLE UNIVERSITY PRESS
Philadelphia, Pennsylvania 19122
tupress.temple.edu

Cover description: A painting depicting a cyborg infant in a green bassinet. Birds have entered the room through an open window. They have toppled a potted plant that lies beside the cradle. A yellow canary stands on the floor below a child's growth chart. It appears to be looking into a closet in which an empty cradleboard is just visible in the shadows. Three pictures of flowers decorate the wall above the cradle. A dream catcher hangs from a curtain rod above the cradle from which is also draped a white lace curtain. One of the birds, a brown-headed cowbird, pulls on the wires attached to the infant's arm. This painting is displayed on the cover of this book.

Library of Congress Cataloging-in-Publication Data

Names: Block, Pamela, editor. | Carey, Allison C., editor. | Scotch,
   Richard K., 1951– editor.
Title: Family and disability activism : beyond allies and obstacles /
   edited by Pamela Block, Allison C. Carey, and Richard K. Scotch.
Description: Philadelphia : Temple University Press, 2025. | Includes bibliographical
   references and index. | Summary: "This book collects accounts of people with disabilities
   and the relationship between their activism and their family. Insofar as the disability
   rights movement is at odds with allied parent activism, especially as regards the goal of
   independence, this dynamic changes across different disabilities and across families of
   different cultures"— Provided by publisher.
Identifiers: LCCN 2024053708 (print) | LCCN 2024053709 (ebook) | ISBN
   9781439923887 (cloth) | ISBN 9781439923894 (paperback) | ISBN
   9781439923900 (pdf)
Subjects: LCSH: People with disabilities—Family relationships. | People
   with disabilities—Political activity. | People with disabilities—Social conditions.
Classification: LCC HV1568 .F35 2025 (print) | LCC HV1568 (ebook) | DDC
   362.4—dc23/eng/20250312
LC record available at https://lccn.loc.gov/2024053708
LC ebook record available at https://lccn.loc.gov/2024053709

The manufacturer's authorized representative in the EU for product safety is
Temple University Rome, Via di San Sebastianello, 16, 00187 Rome RM, Italy
(https://rome.temple.edu/).
tempress@temple.edu

CONTENTS

Acknowledgments

As with our first book together, this book is the product of decades of conversation and scholarship on disability activism as it emerges, intersects, and sometimes resists other forms of disability activism. Over time, many people have contributed to the formulation of our ideas. We would first like to acknowledge Ryan Mulligan, our editor at Temple University Press, the Temple University Press team, and the peer reviewers who provided direct commentary on portions of the manuscript. We are deeply grateful for the time and perspectives shared by the chapter authors, and we are also grateful for their activism and contributions to transforming the world and opening opportunities for disabled people. We are immensely grateful to the Ford Foundation U.S. Disability Rights Program for providing a grant that allowed us to pay chapter authors from outside tenured academia and increase access to this volume by lowering the price. More broadly, we are grateful to the activists and scholars who push the boundaries of justice in all contexts—in the streets, in classrooms, on the stage, at kitchen tables, online, etcetera . . . In particular, we are grateful to activists and scholars such as Sara M. Acevedo, Patty Berne, Lydia X. Z. Brown, Susan Burch, Kerima Çevik, Rebecca Cokely, Nirmala Erevelles, Michele Friedner, Shayda Kafai, Petra Kuppers, Leroy Moore, Akemi Nishida, Leah Lakshmi Piepzna-Samarasinha, Margaret Price, Jasbir Puar, and Alice Wong, who have pushed us to go further and do better. We also wish to thank Western University undergraduate students Aaliya Stoman and Kim-Cheree Mcpherson and graduate students Matthew Resendes Medeiros and Lucas Riboli Besen as well as Shippensburg graduate student Katie Spengler for editorial assistance in the final stages of preparing this manuscript for peer review.

Pam adds the following acknowledgments. I wish to thank my coauthors and coeditors, Allison and Richard, for these years of fun. Here is to many more! I wish to thank Joan Headley and Brian Tiburzi at Post Polio International and Julie Maury for their guidance and assistance with the Aging Out of Children's Hospitals and Health Systems project. I thank Helen Ries, Siblings Canada, Liv Mendelsohn, and the Canadian Centre for Caregiving Excellence for helping expand my understanding of activism and complex care relationships beyond the binary of parents and disabled children to consider siblings, young caregivers, and other kin, including chosen family. I thank Western University, the Social Sciences and Humanities Research Council, and the Azrieli Foundation for financial support for current and future research endeavors. I am continually grateful for my colleagues and staff in the Anthropology Department at Western University for simply existing and allowing me to be among them. They are the best coworkers anyone could ask for anywhere. I praise the memory of Nick Dupree, Carrie Ann Lucas, Stacey Milbern, Gini Laurie, Barbara Kilcup, Neil Marcus, and other disability activist ancestors. I am grateful for my friends Jackie Yeo and Laura Schwartz, who comfort and cheer for me every day. I am grateful to my family—my husband, Matthew Lebo, and my children, Shoshana, Isaac, and Harrison Lebo—for their love and sarcasm. I am forever grateful to my sisters, Hope Block, Karen Block, and Kerry Edwards, for bringing me joy and understanding jokes no one else does. I am thankful to my Stepmother Dale, Aunt Marty, and the rest of the cousins, aunts, uncles, stepfamily, in-laws, and chosen family who have provided so much loving care for me and my family and to whom I will forever be Pammy.

Richard adds the following personal acknowledgments. I would like to thank my colleagues Allison C. Carey and Pam Block for their helpful and thoughtful encouragement and support throughout the creation of this volume. As always, I am grateful to Jenny Keller and Grace Keller Scotch for all they have given me and continue to share.

Allison echoes the deep appreciation already shared and gives an additional word of thanks to Richard and Pam and the process of collaboration, which fostered many rich conversations and new insights. Shippensburg University and my colleagues have been a tremendous source of support, and I appreciate the flexibility they have provided to work on projects I consider important. Finally, I am profoundly grateful to my colleagues, friends, and family for all of their love and support.

FAMILY AND DISABILITY ACTIVISM

INTRODUCTION

PAMELA BLOCK, ALLISON C. CAREY, AND RICHARD K. SCOTCH

I n *Allies and Obstacles: Disability Activism and Parents of Children with Disabilities*, published in 2020, we examined tensions and convergences between the activism of disabled people and the activism of parents of disabled children. Building on this work, *Family and Disability Activism* further explores families, parent activism, and complex historical and contemporary relationships between organizations led by parents and organizations led by disabled people, expanding the populations under discussion, focusing on the experiences of family and disabled people who identify as BIPOC and/or LGBTQIA2S+, and elevating the voices of activists.

For readers unfamiliar with *Allies and Obstacles: Disability Activism and Parents of Children with Disabilities*, it developed four case studies focused on parent activism related to intellectual disability, autism, mental illness, and physical disabilities to document unique histories of parent activism as well as specific points of alliances and contestation between parents and disabled activists. We then explored issues that cut across these populations, such as life-course experiences and transitions, policy, social movements strategies, and rights narratives. To summarize our key arguments, we found that, although parent activism is highly diverse, parent activists tend to share a commitment to the perceived well-being of their child and frame activism in terms of disability rights. From the perspective of disabled activists, parental priorities are at times misplaced, as some parents frame controversial decisions such as institutionalization and medicalized treatments intended to erase disability *as* disability rights. In contrast, disabled activists frame disability rights in terms of access, inclusion, and empowerment. The political arena includes a complex field of social movement organizations, some led by parents and others led by disabled people, promoting different and competing visions of disability rights. Furthermore, disabled activists point out that parents' claims to authority and expertise often undermine their own expertise and perspective. Imbalances of power heighten these tensions. While neither parents nor disabled activists wield much power in relation to the capitalist, state, and cultural forces shaping disability experience in the United States, parents tend to have greater social and economic capital, and several parent-led (or historically parent-led) organizations carry tremendous weight in disability politics. On a more micro level, formal and informal systems of power give parents disproportionate power over the lives of their disabled children, even as children become adults. Thus, alliances between disabled activists and parents are often fraught, leading sometimes to powerful synergies creating positive change and other times to division and direct conflict.

Building on *Allies and Obstacles*, this new volume seeks to respond to calls for greater representation of marginalized populations in disability scholarship and expand the conversation in several ways.[1] First, this volume introduces populations unexplored or underexplored in *Allies and Obstacles*— including people who are blind, Deaf, or Deafblind, those who have complex medical conditions, and disabled parents. Across these populations, chapter authors consider central themes of kinship, biological and chosen family, activism, and alliances and tensions between family and disabled activists within additional populations and different kin relationships. Second, we prioritize scholarship examining intersectionality and authors with personal experience with these identities. Chapter authors chronicle the pathbreaking advocacy of activists with intersectional experiences and of family members. They examine why and how parents, siblings, and other kin organize and engage in legal and political advocacy and explore the complex and often tense relationships between family and disabled activists as well as between white and nonwhite families, adoptive and birth families, and disabled activists. Chapter authors consider complex identities and relationships at the intersections of race, ethnicity, sexuality, birth and adoptive family ties, and cross-disability activism. They reveal how people of different backgrounds understand care and rights; confront systemic issues of segregation, institutionalization, and access to special education services depending on ethnic and racial identities; create narratives of rights versus justice; and experience tensions and connections between parents and disabled activists.

To achieve these goals, *Family and Disability Activism* includes authors with diverse backgrounds as activists and scholars; they share their own narratives and explore a range of disability and family experiences and views of current and historical disability social movement activism not available in our first volume. Aware that nonacademic writers need to be paid, we sought and were awarded a Ford Foundation Narrative Change grant focused on changing the narrative of how disabled people are perceived in society and what they can achieve in professional and personal life. This funding provided stipends to all authors who did not have stable employment that supports the creation of written scholarship. It also allowed Temple University Press to reduce the cost of the book to increase access, and it will fund the development of associated materials.

By presenting a richer, more complex landscape of experiences of family advocates and disabled activists within intersectional and historical contexts, we both reinforce and expand the findings of *Allies and Obstacles*. As in the first volume, these chapters show that family activism cannot be reduced to one side, or even both sides, of an ally/obstacle dichotomy. Families face challenging choices and trade-offs in promoting perceived best interests of their child and family, and these interests do not always align. The outcomes of choices and trade-offs are shaped by variations in policies, types of impairments and the social responses to those impairments, intersectional identities and contexts, professionalization, and political opportunities or barriers.

Greater attention to new populations and to intersectionality expands contributions to scholarship of the family, rights, and social movements. This collection centers intersectional identities and cross-disability organizing that have often been obscured or erased within totalizing accounts of parent advocacy and disability activist movements. In scholarship, family is often represented as a key site for exercise and pursuit of rights.[2] However, as *Allies and Obstacles* found, the relationship between parents and disabled activists may be tenuous and even hostile. Parent organizations may position themselves as promoting the well-being of members' children, but they may do so through the pursuit of rights, cure, care, or some combination initiating from positions of privilege held by white and middle-class parent organization leaders.[3] In this volume, chapter authors further consider the intersection of activism across families and children experiencing different social, racial, and ethnic identities and the resulting intersectional activism of disabled people and their families. With this intersectional focus, we find new understandings of the relationships, collaborations, and tensions between and within parent organizations and disability activist organizations.

Decisions that seem antithetical to disability activism—such as institutionalization, medical treatment, and sterilization—are promoted by some parents as "rights" that support the welfare of individual and family. Whereas rights rhetoric may suggest some rights are inalienable, not all families have access to these rights, and even the most privileged families deal in relational compromises where sacrifice is expected. They often see care, safety, and even convenience or fit with family needs as priorities that outweigh civil and human rights of disabled family members. While some parents advocate for these things, others may be coerced into accepting them against their will through structures of systemic racism and disadvantage—leading to a mistrust of even potentially helpful state interventions. Parents are held accountable for their child's health and well-being by numerous bureaucracies that pressure and surveil them to comply with medicalized and professionalized understandings of disability and race, which for some groups put children in danger of interactions with foster care and criminal justice systems.[4] Through generations of systemic abuse and exclusion, marginalized communities have continued or developed alternative systems of mutual aid where family, for better or worse, may play a central role in care.[5]

This different perspective is not simply a matter of diverse beliefs; we must consider the issue of power. In the family, parents typically hold power to decide which rights are supported and which ignored, even when a disabled child becomes an adult. Organizationally, parent groups may have greater social, economic, and political capital than disability activist groups.[6] This distance is compounded when parent organizations and organizations of disabled activists from racialized communities come into conflict with organizations controlled by white parents and white disabled activists.[7] This imbalance of power exacerbates tension not just between parents and disabled activists but along lines of race and other social identity categories (including experiences of disability activists who are LBGTQ2S+ or adopted).[8] Disability activist organizations, disproportionately led by white people from financially secure backgrounds, have a legacy of accepting and reproducing racist exclusions present in broader society.[9] This legacy of racism and exclusion then creates and perpetuates hostility toward disability rights organizations in BIPOC communities. In the twenty-first century, disability justice activists—led by disabled, LGBTQA2S+, and BIPOC leaders—question the disability rights framework that leaves so many behind and provide an alternative approach to collective access.[10] This new generation of disabled activists is distrustful of established organizations, those led by parents and those led by disabled people. This situation further complicates sometimes productive and sometimes tense alliances to achieve political and social goals and often leads to the development of political divides, hesitation, and distrust, preventing groups from fully allying with each other.

As we consider family, power, and intersectionality, gender emerges as a central factor. Much parent activism is performed by mothers; this expectation is even embedded in the ideology of intensive motherhood. Mothers of disabled children often describe themselves as warriors fighting against individual-level stigma and systemic exclusions that threaten their children and families.[11] While many women feel pressure and blame if they are deemed inadequate as a mother, the expectations, responses, and consequences of intensive motherhood vary. For women marginalized by race, class, disability, and sexuality, stereotypes of incompetence and deviance undercut their societal valuation as mothers.[12] They are less likely to have the economic, political, and cultural capital required for success as warrior mothers, and when they engage in activism, they are often met with discrimination and resistance on multiple fronts.[13] Cultural variations in patriarchal expression may also valorize different models of motherhood, contrasting with white expectations. Although marginalized women may have less access to, desire to, or success in enacting the warrior mother archetype, caregiving remains a largely gendered phenomenon, with minority women disproportionately providing (poorly) paid care for white families while struggling to provide care for their own families.[14]

Intersectional identities and struggles also broaden the social movement arena, as disabled activists of color, for example, consider how and whether to bridge disability organizations and organizations committed to racial and ethnic justice. Cross-organizing for rights and justice can yield powerful alliances, but disabled activists may feel excluded when disability organizations ignore issues of race and sexuality and other movements ignore disability.[15] Tension between white and nonwhite family and disabled activists allows us to further explore the meanings of rights and justice in a relational world in which needs and abilities vary. The tension can be examined on multiple levels. First, we consider the tension between the social model and individualistic model of rights. The social model of disability as articulated by disability justice activists calls us to recognize interdependence and relational obligations to create conditions of collective access; this approach conflicts with the traditional model of rights, which is individualistic and involves operating within and accepting existing governmental structures. This tension plays out directly within families on the micro level and within the macro politics of family, as families and society construct which rights are inalienable and individual (for some) and which are negotiable within the private sphere of the family (for some). Second is the tension between public and private spheres. Families are social units seen as operating in the private sphere, but the public sphere is intricately interwoven into the family. Families of children with disabilities actively seek services and supports from the public sphere,[16] but the public sphere of professionals and policies then comes to wield increasing power over their family lives; in the case of BIPOC individuals and families, this power is often punitive.[17] Laws and policies that construct relations of power and determine which rights are seen as inalienable and which are left to parental or familial discretion are enacted differently in white versus nonwhite families. Policy seeks to govern some families and preserve autonomy for others; a tension that BIPOC families of children with disabilities experience powerfully. This disparity may also lead to faith in the importance of family as private and free from state intervention, which can offer protection from state abuses but heighten the power of families to deliver or negate disability identities and rights.

Greater attention to intersectionality also contributes to the social movement literature. Many books have discussed the growth of the disability rights movement as a civil rights movement and the ways it draws on the African American civil rights movement.[18] We contribute in two ways. First, parent activism is very rarely discussed in a macro way, and existing scholarship privileges whiteness. Most studies of parent activism look at issues of identity, motivation, strategy, and framing but not necessarily with an intersectional lens. We look at parent activism as it creates organizations in the disability activist *field* of social movement organizations and the effect of these organizations on other groups and movements. Second, we take up the issue of alliance but focus on contentious allies, more in line with studies of white activism within the African American civil rights movement and recent critiques of disability rights and disability studies leveled by disability justice activists.[19] What does alliance mean when one's allies have more power than you and are situated in and privileged by the very power structure you are challenging? Access to the "inside" is critical to success, yet threats of cooptation, tokenism, and paternalism loom. In disability politics, we add into the equation the possibility of lifelong needs fulfilled by that power structure that you are challenging. How is alliance most fruitful in the midst of resisting power inequality and preserving life-long relationships within systems of power?

Perhaps most importantly, *Family and Disability Activism* engages activists and scholars in conversation, coalition, and community building. We see our volumes working together to serve a vital practical function: encouraging dialogue and building understanding across diverse disability and disability-allied communities who might work together but too often fight against each other.

To begin this volume, Tsao explores the often-overlooked history of Asian American social justice activism and its relationship to disability rights movements centered on whiteness. She delves into her own experiences, the results of a survey of eight disabled Asian activists, and oral history data collected from disabled Asian activists to discuss family relationships and the ways activists have been supported by or come in conflict with their families. Because disability and mental health issues are so heavily stigmatized in Asian cultures, the relationship between disabled Asian Americans and their families may be fraught with complications while also offering support and care, a complex dynamic Tsao describes as "beautiful, chaotic, and broken simultaneously."

Torres closely discusses her family's disability experiences across generations, including how her mother's disability influenced Torres growing up and the ways disability is viewed in Latinx contexts. Torres describes cultural factors that may have influenced choices made in her family across generations and that certainly fueled Torres's decision to engage in activism with disabled Latinx people. Ellis, whose "autie"-ethnographic portrait graces the cover of this book, uses visual arts to explore their experiences as an Indigenous autistic and disabled adoptee with rich, meaningful relationships with both their birth and adopted families and communities. Utilizing an interview format and based in their art, this chapter is richly grounded in the themes of *Allies and Obstacles* while bringing innovative insight into the cultural dynamics of disability and family.

Chapters by Rouse and Najarian Souza look at the experiences of Deafblind and Deaf children and their families. Both chapters consider the experiences of these children and their families at the intersections of race, citizenship, immigrant experience, belonging, and experiences of racism. Rouse considers her parents' experiences navigating services systems and advocating for her as well as her own experiences as a child and teen. Rouse describes the decision she faced as a very young child of whether to have a cochlear implant and how her decision impacted her life and activism. She decided not to undergo implantation, and her parents respected her wishes. Najarian Souza places Deafblind activism and family into a broader context, providing a review of organizational websites and memoirs. She finds that parents of Deafblind children exist in a complicated space between Deaf and blind activist communities, which agree on some matters but disagree on others, while the national Deafblind organization offers little outreach to parents.

Like Rouse, Liang provides a personal history that focuses on the intersections of ethnic, autistic, and LGBTQ identity intersecting with Asian heritage and community. Whereas both Rouse and Liang's parents were confronted with medical advice regarding their disabled children, Liang's parents (unlike Rouse's) decided to follow medical advice to engage in surgery on their young child for aesthetic reasons, and Liang discusses the trauma this choice caused. Liang compares the mentorship and support of LGBTQ professionals and communities with the lack of support and even hostility emanating from the autistic community controlled by clinicians and parents.

Pamela Block brings in children with complex medical conditions, providing a historical contextualization of how these children have been understood and discussed throughout the twentieth and early twenty-first centuries. She looks at how disabled survivors of the polio epidemic and their families (including families of those who did not survive) changed policy and practice to enable disabled polio survivors to live, love, work, and learn in their communities. In particular, Block describes the motivations of activist and sibling Gini Laurie and the impact she and others like her had, as well as tensions between nondisabled family activists and organizations led by disabled people. Block describes how the United States changed policies and practices to accommodate a large influx of newly disabled people. Technology has extended the lives of people with complex medical conditions past childhood, but policies have not changed accordingly, leading to limits and dangers for this population as they age.

Block's chapter is followed by Stone et al. who describe the Little Lobbyists movement, which directly takes up issues described in Block's chapter. Little Lobbyists was formed to support children and emerging adults with complex medical conditions and ensure their needs are supported by U.S. policymakers. Though this organization was formed by parents, these parents have positioned themselves as mentees and allies of disabled activists and have constructed an intersectional movement that reflects the values of disabled activists and acts in concert with them. Compton and Compton are a mother-daughter team discussing self-advocacy for youth with intellectual disabilities, taking a strong stance against broad use of parental guardianship and discussing how parents can support their children to make their own decisions and choices. Their approach is similar to the approach discussed by Stone et al., in which child activists' preferences are centered in the processes of Little Lobbyist.

In sum, we hope we have succeeded in drawing together a range of insightful, innovative, and underrepresented voices that expand the contributions of *Allies and Obstacles*, moving further from artificial binaries such as parent versus child or disabled versus nondisabled activist leaders. This book shares stories by sometimes disabled, sometimes nondisabled or ambivalently abled activists and seeks to understand kinship and disability beyond parents and children to include the complexities of siblings, cousins, grandparents, step- and adoption-mediated kinship as well as chosen kin. We consider how children who may or may not be disabled engage in complex care relationships with their disabled parents. There are still many more stories to tell about disability, kinship, and activism, and we are excited to contribute this volume to this vital, ongoing conversation.

NOTES

1. Kerima Çevik, "Autistic while Black: The Erasure of Blacks from Histories of Autism," *InterSected* (blog), January 22, 2016, http://intersecteddisability.blogspot.com/2016/01/autistic-while-black-erasure-of-blacks.html; Shayda Kafai, *Crip Kinship: The Disability Justice & Art Activism of Sins Invalid* (Vancouver: Arsenal Pulp Press, 2021); Akemi

Nishida, *Just Care: Messy Entanglements of Disability, Dependency, and Desire* (Philadelphia: Temple University Press, 2022); Leah Lakshmi Piepzna-Samarasinha, *Care Work: Dreaming Disability Justice* (Vancouver: Arsenal Pulp Press, 2018); Sami Schalk, *Bodyminds Reimagined: (Dis)ability, Race, and Gender in Black Women's Speculative Fiction* (Durham, NC: Duke University Press, 2018); Sami Schalk, *Black Disability Politics* (Durham, NC: Duke University Press, 2022); Alice Wong, *Disability Visibility: First-Person Stories from the Twenty-First Century* (New York: Vintage, 2020); Alice Wong, *Year of the Tiger: An Activist's Life* (New York: Penguin Random House, 2022).

2. Allison C. Carey, Pamela Block, and Richard K. Scotch, *Allies and Obstacles: Parents of Children with Disabilities and Disability Rights* (Philadelphia: Temple University Press, 2020); Barry Jones, *Childhood Disability in a Multicultural Society* (London: CRC Press, 2004); Lanita Jacobs, Mary Lawlor, and Cheryl Mattingly, "I/We Narratives among African-American Families Raising Children with Special Needs," *Culture, Medicine, and Psychiatry* 35 (2011): 3–25; Jennifer A. Reich, *Calling the Shots: Why Parents Reject Vaccines* (New York: New York University Press, 2016).

3. Allison C. Carey, *On the Margins of Citizenship: Intellectual Disability and Civil Rights in Twentieth-Century America* (Philadelphia: Temple University Press, 2009), 15; Jennifer N. Fink, *All Our Families: Disability Lineage and the Future of Kinship* (Boston: Beacon Press 2022); Jones, *Childhood Disability in a Multicultural Society*; Laura Mauldin, *Made to Hear: Cochlear Implants and Raising Deaf Children* (Chicago: University of Minnesota Press, 2016).

4. Liat Ben-Moshe, Chris Chapman, and Allison C. Carey, eds., *Disability Incarcerated: Imprisonment and Disability in the United States and Canada* (New York: Palgrave Macmillan, 2014); Liat Ben-Moshe, *Decarcerating Disability: Deinstitutionalization and Prison Abolition* (Chicago: University of Minnesota Press, 2020); Nirmala Erevelles, "Thinking with Disability Studies," *Disability Studies Quarterly* 34, no. 2 (2014); Nirmala Erevelles and Andrea Minear, "Unspeakable Offenses: Untangling Race and Disability in Discourses of Intersectionality," *Journal of Literary & Cultural Disability Studies* 4, no. 2 (2010): 127–45, https://doi.org/10.3828/jlcds.2010.11; Michael Gill and Nirmala Erevelles, "The Absent Presence of Elsie Lacks: Hauntings at the Intersection of Race, Class, Gender, and Disability," *African American Review* 50, no. 2 (2017): 123–37, https://doi.org/10.1353/afa.2017.0017.

5. Piepzna-Samarasinha, *Care Work*; Nishida, *Just Care*.

6. Carey, Block, and Scotch, *Allies and Obstacles*; Hannah B. Rosqvist, Charlotte Brownlow, and Lindsay O'Dell, "'An Association for All': Notions of the Meaning of Autistic Self-Advocacy Politics within a Parent-Dominated Movement," *Journal of Community and Applied Psychology* 25, no. 3 (2015): 219–31.

7. Jennifer L. Erkulwater, "How the Nation's Largest Minority Became White: Race Politics and the Disability Rights Movement, 1970–1980," *Journal of Policy History* 30, no. 3 (July 2018): 367–99, https://doi.org/10.1017/S0898030618000143; Leroy F. Moore Jr., Talila A. Lewis, and Lydia X. Z. Brown, "Accountable Reporting on Disability, Race, and Police Violence: A Community Response to the 'Ruderman White Paper on the Media Coverage of Use of Force and Disability,'" May 16, 2016, https://docs.google.com/document/d/117eoVeJVP594L6-1bgL8zpZrzgojfsveJwcWuHpkNcs/; Wong, *Year of the Tiger*.

8. Corbett Joan O'Toole, *Fading Scars: My Queer Disability History* (Fort Worth, TX: Autonomous Press, 2015); Jaclyn Ellis, "Tàcharan: An 'Autie'-Ethnographic Examination of the Biopolitics of Changelings and Cyborgs," in *Family and Disability Activism*, ed. Pamela Block, Allison C. Carey, and Richard K. Scotch (Philadelphia: Temple University Press, 2024); Bridget Liang, "Empathy Deficits among Neurotypicals," in *Family and*

Disability Activism, ed. Pamela Block, Allison C. Carey, and Richard K. Scotch (Philadelphia: Temple University Press, 2024); Wong, *Year of the Tiger*; Eli Clare, *Exile and Pride: Disability, Queerness, and Liberation* (Durham, NC: Duke University Press, 1999); Leah Lakshmi Piepzna-Samarasinha, *The Future Is Disabled* (Vancouver: Arsenal Pulp Press, 2022).

9. Çevik, "Autistic while Black"; Nishida, *Just Care*; Piepzna-Samarasinha, *The Future Is Disabled*; Wong, *Disability Visibility*; Wong, *Year of the Tiger*.

10. Patty Berne, "Disability Justice—A Working Draft by Patty Berne," *Sins Invalid: An Unshamed Claim to Beauty in the Face of Invisibility* (blog), June 10, 2015, https://www.sinsinvalid.org/blog/disability-justice-a-working-draft-by-patty-berne; Mia Mingus, "Access Intimacy, Interdependence and Disability Justice," *Leaving Evidence* (blog), April 12, 2017, https://leavingevidence.wordpress.com/2017/04/12/access-intimacy-interdependence-and-disability-justice/.

11. Linda Blum, *Raising Generation Rx: Mothering Kids with Invisible Disabilities* (New York: New York University Press, 2015); Sharon Hays, *The Cultural Contradictions of Motherhood* (New Haven: Yale University Press, 2011); Amy C. Sousa, "From Refrigerator Mothers to Warrior-Heroes: The Cultural Identity Transformation of Mothers Raising Children with Intellectual Disabilities," *Symbolic Interactionism* 34, no. 2 (2011): 220–43; Glenda Wall, "Mothers' Experiences with Intensive Parenting and Brain Development Discourse," *Women's Studies International Forum* 33, no. 3 (2010): 253–63.

12. Blum, *Raising Generation Rx*; Dionna Cheatham, "Unpacking the Social and Economic Disparities among Disabled Black Mothers," *McNair Scholars Journal* 19, no. 1 (2015): 18–25; Angela Frederick, "Between Stigma and Mother-Blame: Blind Mothers' Experiences in USA Hospitals Post-natal Care," *Sociology of Health and Illness* 37, no. 8 (2015): 117–41; Kelly Fritsch, "Contesting the Neoliberal Affects of Disabled Parenting: Toward a Relational Emergence of Disability," in Michael Rembis *Disabling Domesticity* (New York: Palgrave, 2017), 243–67.

13. Amber M. Angell and Olga Solomon, "'If I Was a Different Ethnicity, Would She Treat Me the Same?': Latino Parents' Experiences Obtaining Autism Services," *Disability and Society* 32, no. 8 (2017): 1142–64; Jacobs, Lawlor, and Mattingly, "I/We Narratives among African-American Families"; Summer L. G. Stanely, "The Advocacy Efforts of African American Mothers of Children with Disabilities in Rural Special Education: Considerations for School Professionals," *Rural Special Education Quarterly* 34, no. 4 (2015): 3–17.

14. Nishida, *Just Care*.

15. O'Toole, *Fading Scars*.

16. Valerie Leiter, *Their Time Has Come: Youth with Disabilities Entering Adulthood* (New Brunswick, NJ: Rutgers University Press, 2012).

17. Ben-Moshe, *Decarcerating Disabiliy*; Erevelles, "Thinking with Disability Studies"; Erevelles and Minear, "Unspeakable Offenses"; Gill and Erevelles, "The Absent Presence of Elsie Lacks."

18. Doris Fleischer and Freida Zames, *The Disability Rights Movement: From Charity to Confrontation* (Philadelphia: Temple University Press, 2011); Richard K. Scotch, *From Good Will to Civil Rights: Transforming Federal Disability Policy* (Philadelphia: Temple University Press, 1984).

19. Moore Jr., Lewis, and Brown, "Accountable Reporting on Disability, Race, and Police Violence"; Wong, *Year of the Tiger*; Piepzna-Samarasinha, *The Future Is Disabled*.

1

Familial Relationships in Asian American Disability Advocacy and Activism

Grace Tsao

Introduction

Asian Americans are situated between the black and white binary of American society. There is an erasure of Asian Americans in many spaces, and when they are included, they are often seen as a model minority or as invisible and silent. In comparison, needs and issues affecting people with disabilities, despite being the largest minority in the United States, are usually an afterthought. Even if the focus is on diversity, equity, and inclusion (DEI), disabled people are left out of the conversation. Over thirty years have passed since the passage of the Americans with Disabilities Act (ADA), yet there is still so much to be realized regarding the rights of disabled people. Asian Americans with disabilities occupy a unique space within this framework in society and may feel draped in invisibility. Recently, the global coronavirus pandemic brought issues affecting disabled people and Asian Americans to the forefront. COVID-19 disproportionately affects the disabled community, and concerns like medical rationing and vaccine inequity were frequently reported in the media. Stories covering disability have increased in mainstream media, while the incredible number of incidents of Asian hate highlights the struggles Asian American communities have faced for years.

In this chapter, I explore the history of Asian American social justice activism. I then discuss the experiences of Asian Americans in disability advocacy and activism and their role in disability rights and disability justice movements centered on whiteness. There are firsthand accounts from disabled Asian American activists about their relationships with their immigrant families and experiences within disability advocacy and movements. I also delve a bit into my own experiences. Because disability and mental health issues are heavily stigmatized in Asian cultures, the relationship between disabled Asian Americans and their families may be fraught with complications. There are difficulties as they straddle divergent realties. But where there are troubles, there is also support and care. The relationship between Asian American disability activists and their families is not a dichotomy; it is much more complicated. It can be beautiful, chaotic, and broken simultaneously. This complexity is also true of the experiences of disabled Asian American activists in disability rights advocacy spaces.

Asian American Activism: History

I want to give a brief history of Asian American activism that fueled calls for action in the United States before discussing the experiences of disabled Asian American advocates and activists in the context of family dynamics and the disability rights movement as a whole. I think this context is important because many people do not know anything about Asian American history because it is not taught in schools. Hopefully this will change; in 2021, my home state of Illinois became the first in the country to require Asian American history be taught in public schools.[1] This change comes at a critical time when conservatives in the United States are attacking DEI efforts and critical race theory in an effort to whitewash history and maintain white supremacy. It is especially significant because most people have stereotypes of Asian Americans as a quiet, submissive group that does not challenge the status quo. Stereotypes and tropes of the meek and emasculated Asian man and docile and submissive Asian woman are harmful to Asian American communities.

Despite stereotypes like the model minority myth and common misconceptions that Asian Americans do not rock the boat, make noise, or engage politically, the contrary is true. Asian Americans have a long history of social justice activism in the United States. The model minority myth relies on the color-blind perception that all people are completely in charge of their own destiny—that anyone regardless of race or socioeconomic background can be successful if they try hard enough. It is the epitome of the elusive American dream, screaming of rugged individualism and ignoring systemic oppression: if people who are culturally, visually, and linguistically different can achieve, so can you, and if you do not, it is your own fault and not that of embedded racism, ableism, and other isms built in the foundation of our society that prevent Black, Brown, working class, disabled, and trans people and other groups from moving up. These stereotypes are especially detrimental to disabled Asian Americans, who face a double burden coming from a collectivist culture that may view our supposed limitations as a negative, thinking we cannot contribute fully to society, while simultaneously subjecting us to stereotypes of the hegemonic society. It also ignores the fact that Asian Americans are a diverse group and that many Asian American groups live in extreme poverty and have little opportunities, such as the Burmese population.

Asian Americans are often seen by mainstream hegemonic white society as the acceptable, compliant, "good" minority. Unfortunately, many people in the Asian American community have come to believe this view as well. White supremacy, individualism, and capitalism pit Asian Americans against other BIPOC groups. Asian Americans may adopt this mentality and view groups like Black, Indigenous, and Latinx people through this lens, causing other people of color to have negative views of Asian Americans and vice versa. According to scholar and writer Elaine H. Kim: "In a society held together by hierarchical arrangements of power and the privileging of competitive individualism, it is difficult for groups of color to deal with each other on an equal basis, without falling into competition, ranking, and scrambling around hierarchies of oppression."[2] Unfortunately, there is still a lot of anti-Blackness in the Asian American community, especially among the older immigrant generation. More education and outreach are needed to remind the older generation that white supremacy is the enemy and that communities of color should not be pitted against each other. We see this dynamic playing out right now as Asian Americans were used as a wedge and weapon against affirmative action in cases regarding policies at Harvard and the University of North Carolina that have reached the Supreme Court.[3] In June 2023, in a 6–3 decision, the conservative majority Supreme Court dismantled affirmative action in higher education admissions that will result in long-term detrimental effects for diversity and equity in college and universities across the nation.[4]

Marginalized communities need to unite and build coalitions to fight racism, ableism, misogyny, homophobia, transphobia, and other isms, phobias, discrimination, and policies instituted by the hegemonic society. Many groups do not have the perspective that all oppression is intertwined, and although groups may experience varying degrees of oppression, their oppression comes from the same roots and foundation built by dominant male, straight, white, cisgender society. Women and Black, Indigenous, Latinx, Asian American, LGBTQ, and disabled people should care about issues that affect each other's community; although on the surface, others' issues may not seem to concern you, we are all oppressed by the same agents. We will never change structural and systemic policies designed to keep us down if we are battling one another instead of the dominant culture that is oppressing us. We are all more powerful together.

The 1960s was a hotbed of activism in the United States, with many social movements occurring simultaneously, including the civil rights movement. It is no surprise that Asian American activists built on this momentum. We saw the fruits of coalition building in the 1960s. Filipino farmworkers were instrumental in the fight for labor rights that Caesar Chavez is mostly credited with. It was Larry Itliong, a Filipino farmworker who initially organized Filipino grape farmworkers to strike in 1965, who asked Chavez and Mexican farmworkers to join the strike. This ultimately led to the formation of the United Farm Workers Union.[5] In the 1960s, Emma Gee and Yuji Ichioka, students at the University of California at Berkeley, created the category "Asian American" as a way to harness political and social power by joining the forces of diverse Asian groups. Their organization, Asian American Political Alliance (AAPA), was part of a multiracial coalition of student organizations at San Francisco State University called the Third World Liberation Front, which included the Black Student Union and participated in the longest student strike in the nation and the birth of the College of Ethnic Studies. The strike was such a success that Berkeley students organized another strike at their university. We have these students to thank for ethnic studies at colleges and universities throughout the country.[6] During the civil rights movement in the 1960s, Dr. Martin Luther King Jr.'s philosophy was influenced by Gandhi's notion of peaceful, nonviolent protest, whereas the Black Panther Party took a more radical approach. Revolutionaries like Grace Lee Boggs, Yuri Kochiyama, and Richard Aoki were Asian Americans who joined their Black brothers and sisters in the fight for equality. Aoki was a field marshal in the Black Panther Party and the only Asian American to be a leader in the group.[7] Kochiyama worked closely with Malcolm X and was part of his group, the Organization for Afro-American Unity.[8] Lee Boggs, along with her husband, James Boggs, were prominent activists in the Black Power Movement.

In 1973, Chol Soo Lee, a Korean immigrant, was arrested and wrongfully convicted of murder due to white eyewitnesses misidentifying him because of the "all Asians look alike" stereotype. This conviction led thousands of Asian Americans of various backgrounds protesting to get justice for Lee and push back against stereotypes. Lee was granted a new trial in 1979 and found not guilty in 1982. A documentary chronicling Lee's life and the movement to free him, titled "Free Chol Soo Lee," debuted at the Sundance Film Festival in early 2022.[9] The year 2022 also marked the fortieth anniversary of the death of Vincent Chin. Chin was a twenty-seven-year-old Chinese American man out celebrating his upcoming wedding with friends in Detroit in the summer of 1982 when he got into an altercation with two white men, Ronald Ebens and his stepson, Michael Nitz. Ebens and Nitz, laid-off auto workers who blamed Japanese cars for their plight, yelled racist slurs at Chin and beat him to death. They received probation and a small fine as the result of their plea deals, but Asian American activists successfully lobbied for a federal civil rights case to be opened. It became the first such case for an Asian American in the nation's history. Nitz was acquitted, and Ebens was convicted but had his conviction overturned. The two served no time in jail for the killing.[10] I first heard of the killing of Vincent Chin as a college student in the 1990s, an important time in my life when I was delving into my identity as an Asian American and learning more about the history I had not learned while growing up. It really resonated with me, the cruelty, hatred, and damaging effects of racial stereotypes.

There has been tension between Asian and Black communities because of misconceptions and because white supremacy pits our communities against each other. We saw a high point of this tension with the Los Angeles riots thirty years ago. More recently, during the pandemic, the media was complicit in drawing attention to this perceived conflict highlighting hate crimes committed by Black perpetrators toward Asian victims. This gave the impression that most incidents of hate against Asians are committed by other people of color; the reality is that more than 75 percent of Asian hate incidents have white perpetrators.[11] Younger generations are actively trying to create change by being better allies and accomplices. We can see how Asian Americans came out to support Black people during the Black Lives Matter protests against systematic racism and police brutality. And the Black community has come out in support of Asians during the wave of anti-Asian violence caused by the pandemic. Black-Asian solidarity has occurred throughout history. At the Bandung Conference, held in Indonesia in 1955, Asian and African nations discussed their histories of colonization, strategies to end poverty, and other pressing issues.[12] The Immigration and Nationality Act of 1965, which many Asian immigrants have benefited from, was won because of the civil rights movement and Black activists' difficult fight. The disability rights movement was influenced by the civil rights movement. Disabled Asian Americans have rights because of Black people.

Fueled by blame directed at China for having spread coronavirus in the 2020 COVID-19 pandemic, racism against Asians is through the roof. The vile and harsh rhetoric directed at Asian Americans Pacific Islanders (AAPIs) because of the pandemic has made them targets for an alarming number of violent hate crimes and incidents throughout the nation. Anti-Asian violence and hate became widespread during the pandemic, making it clear that racism against Asians is very much alive. Trump and his supporters fed this violence using racist rhetoric and calling the coronavirus the "China Virus" or "Kung Flu." According to the group Stop AAPI Hate, there were

11,500 incidents of hate against AAPIs between March 19, 2020, and March 31, 2022.[13] The Stop Asian Hate movement has taken off as a result, calling for an end to racism and xenophobia with rallies across the United States. The Unity March was a march of Asian American groups and their allies in Washington, DC, in June of 2022.[14] Groups like Asian Americans Advancing Justice hold bystander intervention trainings for allies and accomplices who want to help root out hate. In 2012, seven Sikhs were killed at a mass shooting at a Sikh temple in Wisconsin. The murder of six Asian women in Atlanta in 2021 was a result of racist misogyny and fetishization. Anti-Asian sentiment is not new; the United States has a long history of othering Asian Americans and treating them as yellow peril or perpetual foreigners. From the Chinese Exclusion Act to Japanese internment during WWII to the profiling and targeting of Muslims after 9/11, Asian Americans have been used as scapegoats, just like they have been blamed for the coronavirus pandemic.

Asian American Disability Activism

Why does the history of Asian American activism in the United States belong in an essay on relationships between disabled Asian American activists and their families? I think this history means everything, because when we think Asian and we think disabled, we do not often think of fighters. Instead, we conjure images of people who are quiet and helpless. We need to explore the rich history of Asian American activism and the legacy it brings to disabled Asian American advocates and activists. The goal of my essay is not to write a traditional academic paper but rather to reflect on some of my own experiences while drawing from input from disabled Asian American activists and advocates with disabilities. It is not a large study aiming to draw blanket conclusions or findings or a formal study with a great sample size but rather an informal survey with a few participants sharing experiences. The purpose is not to make assumptions but rather to allow participants to express their perspectives.

I created an informal survey through Google Forms and received eight responses from people with different disabilities and ethnic backgrounds. I asked them about how their advocacy affects their relationships with their families, how they perceive their involvement in disability activism, and whether their family participates in advocacy. There were a variety of questions, including some regarding how respondents got involved in activism and how they felt as Asian Americans in the disability rights and disability justice movements and as members of the Asian American community. Eight people completed the survey: three of Korean descent, two Chinese Americans, one Pakistani American, one of Filipino/Spanish descent, and one of mixed race (Asian and white Jewish background). They have a variety of disabilities from physical, developmental, to visual and mental health.[15] Three participants wished to rename anonymous, so Joyce, Julie, and Kelly are pseudonyms. However, no other identifying information like age, ethnicity, or disability were changed, with participant consent. Age information has been updated since the initial survey.

Despite their long history and presence in the United States, Asian Americans are often silent, invisible, ignored, overlooked, unseen members of society. Disabled people share many of these experiences. The intersection of race and disability can complicate things further. When we factor in disability, issues are amplified, and the needs and concerns of disabled Asian Americans often fade into the background. Many of us have our physical needs met by family, since our cultures are supportive in this respect, but aspects regarding quality of life and mental well-being are ignored. Joyce, a forty-year-old Korean woman with cerebral palsy, stated that she received "more physical support, less emotional/moral support" from her family.[16] This stems from the collective nature of Asian communities and how they care for family and community members. Some Asian American families feel shame asking for help and have low advocacy skills, which can hurt their disabled children, who may not receive the services they need.[17] Collectivism, familism, relational orientation, and family obligation are cultural values that shape how AAPI families and group members interact with one another.[18] The stigma of disability prevalent in Asian cultures may cause conflicts, and there can be tension concerning disabled family members in Asian American families. Disability and mental illness have been taboo topics in most Asian cultures, with many elders still believing in superstitions that disability is a consequence of bad karma. These topics are seldom discussed or acknowledged in many of our families. It is a more complicated matter when we go beyond basic survival and into the realm of disability acceptance and pride.

I focus on Asian Americans and not Pacific Islanders because the groups are so different even if categorized under one umbrella category. The experiences of Pacific Islanders and Native Hawaiians are very different. Asian Americans are not a monolith; they consist of distinct groups with their own cultures and languages. According to the Pew Research Center, there are twenty-two million people of Asian descent from over twenty countries in the United States who belong to the Asian American community. We have many shared values and experiences but so many more cultural and linguistical differences.[19] There are over 1.3 million people with disabilities who are of Asian descent in the United States, according to the U.S. Census Bureau.[20] The actual figure may be much higher due to some Asian Americans choosing not to identify as disabled because of factors including stereotypes and cultural stigma.[21]

Role in the Disability Rights Movement and Disability Advocacy

The disability rights movement, like many other movements in society, is largely white and often fails to represent people of color. Our voices are frequently unseen and unheard. Asian Americans are ignored or not included, even if the feedback of people of color is sought out. For disabled Asian Americans who are immigrants, there are also linguistic and cultural barriers; those working or advocating for disability rights need to address these issues. There is frustration among Asian Americans with disabilities that they are usually the only Asian American face in a given space and are expected to represent their entire community. They are dismayed at the lack of leadership roles not just for Asian Americans but for people of color in general within the disability rights and independent living movement. When asked whether they feel they belong or are accepted in the disability rights and/or justice movement as an Asian American, Jae Jin, a fifty-five-year-old South Korean man with epilepsy and visual disability, responded:

> My answer changes depending on context. In my local community. In Chicagoland, IL, yes, to some extent I feel connected and belong in the disability community. A large part of that is I have found, met and connected with other Asian disabled folks. Outside in the larger disability justice movement, I don't see much representation of BIPOC, let alone Asian folks with disabilities. I can name those that count on one hand who are outside of IL. The other struggle I deal with is to fight the feeling I have to be the Asian voice or rep at larger disability events when there so few Asian folks at events. It's tiring.[22]

Julie, a fifty-year-old Chinese American woman with muscular dystrophy, stated: "I guess? I feel tokenized and can tell anytime a disability rights event wants to be 'intersectional' they'll ask me to be involved which I find tiresome. I also believe strongly in centering the experiences of Black, Latinx, and Indigenous disabled people, not just Asians and East Asians in particular." Kelly, a thirty-four-year-old second-generation Korean American born legally blind, felt that: "For the most part, yes. However, I often feel I lack knowledge/confidence to take on more of a leadership role within the movement."[23]

A group of disability activists felt the need to center its own experiences in a movement that has largely ignored the needs of marginalized communities including BIPOC and LGBTQ groups. In 2005, a group of activists called the Disability Justice Collective, which included Leroy Moore, Eli Clare, disabled Korean American women Mia Mingus and Stacey Milbern, and others, created the disability justice movement. Disability justice focuses on issues and concerns of disabled BIPOC and LGBTQ people from their own perspective and leadership. It recognizes the complexities of intersectional identities when it comes to disability.[24]

In addition to Milbern and Mingus, there are many prominent Asian American activist leaders in the disability rights and disability justice movements. I will highlight a few. Japanese American Yoshiko Dart, wife of Justin Dart, the architect of the Americans with Disabilities Act (ADA), was a partner in activism and instrumental in the passage of the ADA. Her role has been largely unrecognized.[25] Sandy Ho is a queer, disabled Asian American woman and founder of the Disability and Intersectionality Summit.[26] Leah Lakshmi Piepzna-Samarasinha is a queer, disabled writer and activist of South Asian and European descent; she wrote the book *Care Work: Dreaming Disability Justice*.[27] Alice Wong is a disabled Chinese American woman and founder of the Disability Visibility Project, which amplifies the voices and perspectives of diverse disabled people. She is the editor of *Disability Visibility: First-Person Stories from the Twenty-First Century*.[28] Mia Ives Rublee was an organizer for the inaugural Women's March in 2017 and created the Women's March Disability Caucus; she is the current director of the Disability Justice Initiative at the Center for American Progress.[29] Chella Man is a deaf, trans actor and LBGTQ activist of Chinese and Jewish descent and the author of *Continuum*.[30] Lydia X. Z. Brown is a nonbinary, autistic, transracial, and transnational adoptee, founder of the Autistic People of Color Fund, and director of Public Policy at the National Disability Institute.[31] This is just a handful of Asian American people who have contributed greatly to the disability rights and disability justice movements by bringing unique and diverse perspectives from intersectional backgrounds as transnational adoptees, queer, mixed race, immigrant, and other identities and disabilities. Countless Asian American disabled advocates and activists at the grassroots level are fighting for rights every day in communities across the nation.

In "Growing up Asian American with a Disability," I wrote:

> It is important to examine aspects of race and culture as it relates to disability because racial and ethnic minorities are already at a disadvantage in the dominant white society, but factor in a disability and the disadvantages and problems increase greatly. It is significant to examine the experience of being a person with a disability from a cultural context. Asian Americans who feel alienated from the dominant culture often find solace in their own communities. But people with disabilities, even if they are members of a minority in-group, often feel alienated from their own cultural group because of the stigma attached to an obvious disability. So, there is often no sense of belonging for many Asian Americans with disabilities.[32]

Many disabled Asian Americans feel disconnected from the various communities they belong to. Noah Petashi, a thirty-five-year-old with physical, developmental, and mental health disabilities of Japanese, Hawaiian, Korean, and white Jewish background, commented: "I think it affected the way to mask/switch the code depends on where I am surrounding. In other words, sometimes, there is nowhere that I could 'fit into' by just being myself."[33] People who are members of multiple marginalized communities often do not know which part of their identity contributes to the prejudice, discrimination, and stereotypes they experience.

Aubrie Lee, a thirty-one-year-old Chinese American with infantile-onset facioscapulohumeral muscular dystrophy, responded:

> It's common for Asian Americans to say they don't fit into either world; they are outsiders both in Asia and in America. But being Disabled and Asian American affects me in another way. I feel much closer to the Disability community than to the Asian American community. Still, when I'm in Disability spaces, those spaces are mostly white. In those rooms, I'm still a racial minority. . . . I sometimes wonder how much people reduce my personhood due to my being a Disabled Chinese American woman. Disabled people are infantilized, East Asian women are stereotyped as submissive, and women are sexualized. I have certainly gotten disgusting comments online, but I'm not sure which aspects of me (and which aspects of the commenters) lead to those comments.[34]

Still others do not feel welcomed or accepted as a part of the larger Asian American community regardless of disability. Brown Asian Americans like Filipinos, South Asians (including Indians and Pakistanis), and Southeast Asians (including Cambodians and Laotians) are frequently overlooked when discussing issues affecting Asian Americans. We often think of fair-skinned people of East Asian descent such as Chinese, Korean, and Japanese people when bringing up concerns that affect Asian Americans. As in many communities of color, colorism is a factor that leads the needs and voices of darker-skinned people to be ignored even within Asian American spaces. There is often an erasure and marginalization of Brown Asian Americans,[35] who feel treated like they are second-class Asians or not Asian enough.[36]

Jessica, a forty-year-old woman with myasthenia gravis and five other illnesses, stated:

> I used to do a lot more Asian American advocacy especially related to mental health. Gradually over time I started to realize that the AAPI community does not treat all ethnicities equally. . . . I don't feel like

I belong in the AAPI community. Whether consciously due to colorism or unconsciously, Filipinos tend to be left out of AAPI discussions. Or they are an afterthought. I stopped considering myself "Asian" a few years ago. I think of my illnesses and disabilities as more part of my identity than my race. However, with the hate crimes, now I can't not think about my ethnicity/race.[37]

Disability issues and rights have been important to me for most of my life. Like most disabled people, I first forayed into disability advocacy as a self-advocate. At a young age, we learn that in order to survive in this world, we have to constantly struggle to get the things we need, whether it be accessibility in education, healthcare and insurance, durable medical equipment (DME), transportation, travel, work, or social settings. The list is endless, and the need to advocate is as well. A lot of respondents became involved in activism out of necessity, first to advocate for their own needs and then growing from there. For Noah, it began as they fought to leave the institution they lived in and received assistance from a center for independent living.[38] Julie echoed similar sentiments: "It happened gradually as I became politicized in my identities as both Asian American and disabled. Advocating for myself as a young person transitioned into broader, systemic approaches. It took me a while to figure out what I cared about and what I want to do. Nowadays most of my activism takes place in online spaces."[39]

As a student in the 1990s growing up in the suburbs of Chicago, I was a member and officer of a high school student organization created to combat stereotypes and racial tension among our student population. It is then that I really began to care about issues of diversity, inclusion, equity, justice, and intersectionality, and it really shaped my worldview. My experiences as a disabled Asian American girl led me to perceive things through an intersectional lens at an early age. I have been involved in issues of race and disability through school, work, organizations, and service on advisory committees and boards, but I did not get involved at the grassroots level through protests or rallies until Donald Trump became president in 2017. As a multiply marginalized member of society, I could not sit idly by. There was too much at stake.

Family Dynamics

I have a complicated relationship with my mother when it comes to advocacy. There have been times in my life where she felt I was not doing enough, and at other times she thinks I do too much. She is supportive to a certain extent, but I often feel like the things I do have to be on her terms or what she deems right. For example, she has obsessed for years that I should write a book, and because I have not, she is disappointed. Never mind that doing so may not be my dream, although I will never say never. In all likelihood, she would probably not approve of topics I am interested in. My mother is a very private person who likes to save face. Saving face is a concept that is very important in many Asian cultures, especially in Chinese culture. It involves preserving others' respect for you and escaping shame and stigma from the community, often at great cost to people or at the expense of mental health, all in the name of looking good to people on the outside. It involves hiding important problems and experiences and can create a very lonely existence for many Asians, likely leading to the high suicide rate among people of Asian descent. My mother would not be comfortable with me sharing too much of what goes on in our family and often criticizes people who share too much through social media or even in personal conversation. She is contradictory at times. She believes certain topics should never be discussed in public, in a large group or audience, or outside family. I wrote something about a sensitive topic that I published online using a pen name because of my mother and fear of her criticism. She often googles my name; she has told me so. For the most part, I am very open with my mother about my beliefs and openly debate her on things about which we disagree, but there are still times when I revert to being a little girl seeking my mother's approval.

I used to get very embarrassed or annoyed with my mother when I was younger because she would tell strangers about my accomplishments, seemingly at random and out of context, like at a shopping mall or grocery store. I thought it was some kind of tiger mom situation or how some Asian parents can be very competitive. But as I have gotten older, I realize that it was her way of trying to combat stereotypes about me as a person with an obvious disability. I was bullied incessantly in middle school, and I remember my parents meeting with school staff to get them to intervene. That was one bit of advocacy I recall my parents being involved in. Unfortunately, their efforts were futile because whenever a group of kids were stopped from bullying me, another group would begin, continuing throughout my middle school years.

As I grew, my parents attended my IEP meetings, but they were often at odds with teachers and counselors who supported my need for independence. I was an independent spirit. While I sought my parents' approval, I did not always feel like I needed it. In general, I have done what I want in life regardless of what my parents think is best for me, and they have not prevented me from doing so. Respondents Joyce, Kelly, and Jae Jin reported that IEP meetings were the one area where their parents participated in advocating for them.[40] For Kelly, language barriers limited her parents' ability to advocate for her. She stated: "Advocating on my behalf was extremely challenging for my parents due to lack of language access. There came a point during middle school through high school where I was translating my IEP meetings for the school. Needless to say, I grew to resent the district for making me go through that hardship."[41] Jae Jin discussed his parents' involvement in advocating for him when he was growing up: "My parents were involved with my special ed teachers and did follow through with what I needed, be it, glasses, magnifiers, med, etc. with little push back. I am grateful for that. Though we didn't talk about my feelings about disability, they did support me in getting the adaptive aids, and services I needed."[42] According to one study, when rated on assertiveness and other self-advocacy skills, Asian American parents of children with developmental disabilities scored much lower than their non–Asian American counterparts.[43] Aubrie was the only respondent who replied that a family member participated in advocacy beyond their childhood years. Her father, a doctor, was inspired by her activism and created a disability group along with a disabled colleague at his hospital, where her mother is also a doctor. She was invited to be a guest speaker there.[44]

Asian parents have a reputation for not showing emotion and affection toward their children, but I have not had this experience. My mother is very warm and affectionate and shows her love for her children and our friends, but she is fiercely overprotective. When I attend protests and rallies in rainy and cold weather, she worries about me getting sick. During the past few years, I have been involved with the Statewide Independent Living Council of Illinois. I can feel her apprehension with my involvement because it often requires me to go to Springfield, which is three hours away. She was happy that we met on Zoom during the pandemic, and now that we are back to a hybrid Zoom or in-person option, she pushes me to do Zoom. Despite my mother's pressure, I still do what I feel is right for me, as I have throughout my life. Her constant concerns stem from her worry that I will become sick or hurt. Aubrie's grandfather worries for her safety in a different way. She responded: "Upon learning of my activism, my grandfather expressed concern, saying he hopes I won't make enemies."[45]

Disabled Asian Americans often have a complicated relationship with their family and community. When we think of disability in the context of Asian communities, we think of shame, stigma, and unacceptance. While there is truth to this perception, the actuality is much more complex. The experiences respondents described having with their parents and families are vast and varied, with some feeling great support for their endeavors, others having little to no support or understanding, and everything in between. Also, as with many immigrant families, the focus is placed on survival rather than nurturing and valuing mental health and emotional well-being. When I asked respondents about how their parents view their involvement in disability advocacy and activism, I received a variety of responses running the gamut of feelings from pride, inspiration, and support to lack of understanding or uncertainty and disapproval. The majority of respondents felt that Asian culture has affected their family's view and involvement in advocacy and activism in both positive and negative ways. According to Kelly, "I actually think Asian culture has prompted my parents to decrease their involvement in advocacy and activism. They care but not enough to challenge the status quo. I have to push them to support the causes I am passionate about."[46] Joyce responded: "They wouldn't even make their home accessible for me, as it would 'decrease the property value' and felt I need to adjust to their needs."[47] Her response echoes the notion of collectivism in Asian cultures, which places more value on the good of the family than of the individual.[48]

Nafia Khan, a thirty-five-year-old Pakistani American woman with depression, anxiety, PTSD, ADHD, and asthma, stated:

> I've been able to create a culture in my own home and in mostly South Asian circles that challenges a lot of what my mother's generation was taught. Even if at times my willingness to challenge those thoughts and behaviors can be a struggle for some family members in my extended family who don't actually bother to question what they have learned, I have been able to remain my authentic self around the family I trust the most and they understand my need to be transparent and critical of unhealthy and sometimes, quite toxic patterns, especially ableism.[49]

Conclusion

My survey had a small number of participants and was not a large social scientific study, so I am careful not to make any overarching conclusions. That being said, I am part of the Asian American disability community and have friendships with people from this group, so I come from a place of personal experience. There are a vast number of things I did not address, such as how other intersecting identities like gender, sexual orientation, generation, religion, mixed-race identity, and more affect an individual's experience. I acknowledge this limitation and know that there are many complexities that affect people's experiences, viewpoints, and relationships with their families and involvement with advocacy and activism. I wanted to cover as much ground as I could but had limitations in a short essay. The experiences of Asian Americans with disabilities are as diverse as the group itself. But we also share many similar experiences and perspectives. I want to make a note that I use both person-first and identity-first language because that is how I identify. Disability is both a source of pride and a part of me, but it is not my entire identity, so I use both interchangeably. People are complex and intersectional, and there are so many layers of their identities that factor into their experiences, perspectives, and values.

NOTES

1. Deepa Shivaram, "Illinois Has Become the First State to Require the Teaching of Asian American History," *NPR*, July 13, 2021, https://www.npr.org/2021/07/13/1015596570/illinois-has-become-the-first-state-to-require-the-teaching-of-asian-american-hi.

2. Elaine H. Kim, "'At Least You're Not Black': Asian Americans in U.S. Race Relations," *Social Justice* 25, no. 3 (1998): 3–12.

3. Kimmy Yam, "Led by AAPI Scholars, Thousands of Academics Tell Supreme Court They Support Affirmative Action," *NBC News*, August 4, 2022, https://www.nbcnews.com/news/asian-america/led-aapi-scholars-thousands-academics-tell-supreme-court-support-affir-rcna41412.

4. Nina Totenberg, "Supreme Court Guts Affirmative Action, Effectively Ending Race-Conscious Admissions," *NPR*, June 29, 2023, https://www.npr.org/2023/06/29/1181138066/affirmative-action-supreme-court-decision.

5. Adam Janos, "How Cesar Chavez Joined Larry Itliong to Demand Farm Workers' Rights," *History*, January 22, 2021, https://www.history.com/news/chavez-itliong-delano-grape-strike.

6. Anna Purna Kambhampaty, "In 1968, These Activists Coined the Term 'Asian American'—And Helped Shape Decades of Advocacy," *Time*, May 22, 2020, https://time.com/5837805/asian-american-history/.

7. "Richard Aoki, Activist Born," African American Registry, 2023, https://aaregistry.org/story/richard-aoki-brilliant-panther/.

8. "May 19, 1921: Yuri Kochiyama Born," Zinn Education Project, 2023, https://www.zinnedproject.org/news/tdih/yuri-kochiyama-was-born/.

9. Dennis Harvey, "'Free Chol Soo Lee' Review: Remembering a Cause Célèbre of Korean-American Activism," *Variety*, January 21, 2022, https://variety.com/2022/film/reviews/free-chol-soo-lee-review-1235156892/.

10. Paula Yoo, *From a Whisper to a Rallying Cry: The Killing of Vincent Chin and the Trial That Galvanized the Asian American Movement* (New York: Norton Young Readers, 2021).

11. Kimmy Yam, "Viral Images Show People of Color as Anti-Asian Perpetrators. That Misses the Big Picture," *NBC News*, June 15, 2021, https://www.nbcnews.com/news/asian-america/viral-images-show-people-color-anti-asian-perpetrators-misses-big-n1270821.

12. Wondam Paik, "The 60th Anniversary of the Bandung Conference and Asia," *Inter-Asia Cultural Studies* 17, no. 1 (2016): 148–57, http://doi.org/10.1080/14649373.2016.1150246.

13. Aggie J. Yellow Horse and Theresa Chen, "Two Years and Thousands of Voices: What Community-Generated Data Tells Us about Anti-AAPI Hate," Stop AAPI Hate, 2022, https://stopaapihate.org/wp-content/uploads/2022/07/Stop-AAPI-Hate-Year-2-Report.pdf.

14. "About," Unity March, n.d., accessed December 20, 2023, https://www.unitymarch.com/en/about.

15. Grace Tsao, *Familial Relationships in Asian American Disability Advocacy and Activism* (Des Plaines, IL: Google Forms survey, 2022).

16. Ibid.

17. Weihe Huang, David A. Delambo, Ricky Kot, Ineko Ito, Henry Long, and Karen Dunn, "Self-Advocacy Skills in Asian American Parents of Children with Developmental Disabilities," *Journal of Ethnic and Cultural Diversity in Social Work* 13, no. 1 (2004): 1–18, http://doi.org/10.1300/J051v13n01_01.

18. B. W. K. Yee, J. Su, S. Y. Kim, and L. Yancura, "Asian American and Pacific Islander Families," in *Asian American Psychology: Current Perspectives*, ed. N. Tewari and A. N. Alvarez (New York: Taylor & Francis, 2009), 295–315.

19. Abby Budiman and Neil G. Ruiz, "Key Facts about Asian Americans, a Diverse and Growing Population," Pew Research Center, April 29, 2021, https://www.pewresearch.org/fact-tank/2021/04/29/key-facts-about-asian-americans/.

20. United States Census Bureau, "2019: ACS 1-Year Estimates Subject Tables: Disability Characteristics," 2023, https://data.census.gov/table/ACSST1Y2019.S1810?q=S0201.

21. Amy Fong, "Disability Data Snapshot: Asian Americans and Pacific Islanders," *U.S. Department of Labor* (blog), July 12, 2022, https://blog.dol.gov/2022/07/12/disability-data-snapshot-asian-americans-and-pacific-islanders.

22. Tsao, *Familial Relationships*.

23. Ibid.

24. Leah Lakshmi Piepzna-Samarasinha, *Care Work: Dreaming Disability Justice* (Vancouver: Arsenal Pulp Press 2018).

25. "An Interview with Japanese American Disabled Historian Selena Moon," Asian American Organizing Project, July 26, 2022, https://aaopmn.org/2022/07/26/national-disability-independence-day-2022-an-interview-with-japanese-american-disabled-historian-selena-moon/.

26. Alice Wong, "Disability & Intersectionality Summit: Interview w/ Sandy Ho," Disability Visibility Project, June 14, 2016, https://disabilityvisibilityproject.com/2016/06/14/disability-intersectionality-summit-interview-w-sandy-ho/.

27. "About," Leah Lakshmi Piepzna-Samarasinha, 2023, https://brownstargirl.org/about/.

28. "About," Disability Visibility Project, 2023, https://disabilityvisibilityproject.com/about/.

29. "Mia Ives-Rublee: Director, Disability Justice Initiative," Center for American Progress, 2023, https://www.americanprogress.org/people/ives-rublee-mia/.

30. "About," Chella Man, n.d., accessed December 20, 2023, https://chellaman.com/About.

31. "About," Lydia X. Z. Brown: Building and Sustaining Love, Liberation, and Justice, n.d., accessed December 20, 2023, https://lydiaxzbrown.com/about.

32. Grace Tsao, "Growing up Asian American with a Disability: 10 Years Later," *TASH Connections* 35, no. 2 (2009).

33. Tsao, *Familial Relationships*.

34. Ibid.

35. Kevin L. Nadal, "The Brown Asian American Movement: Advocating for South Asian, Southeast Asian, and Filipino American Communities," *Asian American Policy Review* 29 (2019): 2–11.

36. Kevin L. Nadal, Kara M. Vigilia Escobar, Gail T. Prado, E. J. R. David, and Kristal Haynes, "Racial Microaggressions and the Filipino American Experience: Recommendations for Counseling and Development," *Journal of Multicultural Counseling and Development* 40, no. 3 (2012): 156–73.

37. Tsao, *Familial Relationships*.

38. Ibid.

39. Ibid.

40. Ibid.

41. Ibid.

42. Ibid.

43. Huang et al., "Self-Advocacy Skills in Asian American Parents of Children with Developmental Disabilities."

44. Tsao, *Familial Relationships*.

45. Ibid.

46. Ibid.

47. Ibid.

48. Barbara W. K. Yee, Jenny Su, Su Y. Kim, and Loriena Yancura, "Asian American and Pacific Islander families," in *Asian American Psychology: Current Perspectives*, ed. Nita Tewari and Alvin N. Alvarez (New York: Taylor & Francis, 2009), 295–315.

49. Tsao, *Familial Relationships*.

2

LEARNINGS FROM MY MOTHER'S COUCH CORNER

Becoming a Latina Disability Activist

LISETTE E. TORRES

This chapter is a critical autoethnography informed by LatDisCrit[1] and intersectionality.[2] It explores my lived experience as a disabled Latina mother scholar and my path to becoming a disability activist, cofounding and helping lead the National Coalition for Latinxs with Disabilities (CNLD).[3] It is a deeply personal story of how I learned about disability by observing my mother's struggle with internalized ableism in relation to her progressive blindness and the stigma of disability in the Latino/a/x community.

Having acquired a disability myself as an adult,[4] I reflect on my mother and discuss how I began to explore the disability rights movement with my cultural lens, noting tensions between U.S. activists' promotion of independence and self-advocacy and Latino/a/x emphasis on family. With an estimated 62.1 million Latinos in the United States,[5] up to 11.8 million of whom identify as having some type of disability,[6] I conclude the chapter by highlighting the need for intersectional, culturally appropriate interventions and programming that remove stigma, enhance individual agency, and welcome active participation of Latino/a/x parents in the movement.

> We, the disabled, the chronically ill, and the Mad carry within us archives. We are intergenerational memory banks filled with the labor, organizing, and artmaking of our radical disabled, queer of color contemporaries, elders, and ancestors. We carry stories of resilience and unearth legacies of colonialism and nondisabled supremacy.[7] (Shayda Kafai)

According to the National Eye Institute (NEI) of the National Institutes of Health (NIH), retinitis pigmentosa is a group of rare eye diseases affecting the retina, the light-sensitive layer of tissue in the back of the eye.[8] It is a genetic condition that causes the retina to break down over time, leading to irreparable vision loss. Symptoms such as loss of night and peripheral vision often start during childhood. Other symptoms include sensitivity to bright lights and loss of color vision. As disintegration of the retina progresses, the field of vision narrows until individuals are left with little to no central vision, resulting in tunnel vision and loss of most or all sight. Such a sterile description does not capture the emotional and psychological impact of living with this impairment.

My earliest memory related to my mother's retinitis pigmentosa is from when I was about five years old. I am playing with a brown dollhouse made in the 1970s in our Victorian living room. Laying on my tummy with a doll in hand, I look up in the dimly lit room to see my mom walking straight toward me. She is unaware of the fact that I am on the floor with a large dollhouse. I call out to warn her—"Mommy . . ."—but it is too late. She plants her foot right on the roof, collapsing the entire structure. She becomes enraged, and I am swiftly admonished for leaving my toys on the floor. "I was playing. Didn't you see me?" I tentatively ask, scared of the wrath that might follow. "You shouldn't be playing with all your toys in the middle of the floor anyway," she responds in a huff, walking away. I cry, picking up the shattered dollhouse walls.

I wish I could say I had a disabled role model in my family, a crip doula[9] to guide me when I acquired my impairment and to teach me everything I would subsequently learn as a disabled Latina scholar-activist. That is not the truth. Instead, I observed my mother's struggle to come to terms with her disability, the way society treated her, and the way she saw herself. My mother's lived experience as a "legally" blind Latina is one of the driving forces behind my activism and advocacy through CNLD.[10] I have witnessed so much self-loathing as well as stewing in pity and shame, amplified by ableism and racism in society. I have noted things I do not want to do or be, and I have tried my best to do the opposite.

This chapter is my reflection on lessons I have accrued observing my mom over the past thirty-five years. It is a collage of interconnected stories involving four generations of Latino/a/xs (myself, my mom, my grandfather, and my children) and the creation of a disability activist organization dedicated to disabled Latino/a/xs and their families (CNLD). Though this work is focused on my memories of disability and disablement, it is also highly influenced by my familial relationships and my family's experiences of disability.

Given my identity as a Boricua/Latina woman and mother, my recollections and analysis are informed by intersectionality[11] and LatDisCrit.[12]

The term "intersectionality" was coined in 1989 by Kimberlé Crenshaw, a leading critical race theory (CRT) scholar, to challenge dominant logics within the legal system and reveal how Black women experience intersecting forms of privilege and marginalization, often rendering them invisible. LatDisCrit is an integration of the theoretical frameworks of LatCrit theory[13] and DisCrit[14] within a broader CRT lineage. Both LatCrit and DisCrit interrogate the interplay of race/ethnicity, diasporic cultures, historical sociopolitical factors, and disability. LatDisCrit in particular honors and complicates the multifacetedness of Latino/a/x identities, acknowledging the "waves and wakes of converging diasporas" (Alexis Padilla, personal communication, 2022) and historic and contemporary manifestations of coloniality. It highlights how trans-Latino/a/x identities are construed as "other" by dominant groups. LatDisCrit aims to enact rightful presence,[15] rejecting inclusion as an extension of rights that perpetuates guest/host relationships rather than disrupting and altering the status quo. Lastly, LatDisCrit privileges alternative modes of intersectional, subaltern knowing and doing.[16]

Much like my memory, the chapter is a bit disjointed; each vignette illustrates my attempt to understand disability in relation to the tacit knowledge I absorbed by viewing my mother's disability identity development (or lack thereof). It is my attempt to ensure that her bodymind story, which is interconnected with mine, is not erased by "writ[ing] ourselves *in* despite being told that we do not matter."[17] It is my way of leaving evidence that we existed.[18]

My mom is *una cabeza dura*[19] for sure. She is a fighter, always wanting her way. So when she was officially labeled "blind" and given black wraparound sunglasses to wear over her regular glasses, she was in complete denial about her disability. "*Yo no soy ciega!*"[20] she would angrily state. She would refuse to wear the sunglasses, conveniently forgetting them at home or burying them deep in her purse. We would get yelled at if we tried to help her verbally or physically with where she was walking. "I know where I am going!" she would reprimand, her arms outstretched in search of a wall or obstruction. I remember being in constant fear of her falling over the banisters of our two-story Victorian home. That fear subsided when my parents moved to a one-floor ranch house years later.

My sisters and I encouraged my mother to attend training for those who are newly blind. We wanted her to learn how to use a white cane, navigate the world independently, and feel more confident in herself and her abilities. True to form, my mom refused. The training would have taken one to three months, and she would have been essentially on her own with no family members. She claimed that our father would not want her gone for so long, but I believe she was scared to be independent. She would have been on her own for the first time in her entire life. I wish she had not let her fear stop her.

My mom never wanted to be disabled. For a long time, she was in complete denial that she could not see and do things the same way as she used to. I recall how she would adamantly argue that she could still see whenever one of us would explain the location of something she was searching for or describe a photo or video in front of her. I am still hesitant to talk to her about her eyesight for fear of making her angry or more depressed than she already is.

My mother's experience as a newly blind woman introduced me to the stigma of disability in the Latino/a/x community. I was well aware of the pride we Latino/a/xs take in caring for our family members—to the point of arranging our entire lives to help loved ones—but I began to see the fear, disgust, shame, and pity we have for those with disabilities.[21] It is common for telenovelas, talk shows, and news stories to share "inspiration porn"[22] or medical stories that perpetuate ableism by pitying "*los pobrecitos*" with incurable conditions. Pilgrimages to Catholic shrines where family members of the "infirmed" pray for a "cure" or "fix" are televised. With tears in their eyes, they share stories of "*ay bendito*" to the newscaster, talking about the financial and emotional toll placed on the family as the disabled person is present but silent or ignored. My mom refused to be viewed as a burden.

I learned from my mother that you cannot let your impairment, coddling family members, or fear of the unknown stop you from what you want to do. Paradoxically, I also learned how the "multifaceted configuration of coloniality translates at the micro level into internalized racism [and ableism] combined with deficit thinking and learned helplessness."[23] Though my mother fights deficit-oriented stereotypes of people with disabilities, it is not because she has a proud disability identity. It is because she does not want to be "like them." Her refusal to acknowledge her impairment and new social identity as well as determination to be viewed as "normal" feed into her feelings of helplessness.

As a Latina with an acquired disability, I understand my mom's sadness underneath her tough exterior. It is difficult for her to let go of the memory of her ability to see, of her "healthier self," because "with each new symptom, each new impairment, [she] grieve[s] again for the lost time, the lost years that are now not yet to come."[24] In times when she is particularly vulnerable, she shares her grief with me, lamenting the things she can no longer do (e.g., drive) and the things she will never get to do (e.g., see the faces of her grandchildren). She becomes stuck in sadness, hiding from the world rather than learning to be empowered by her disability identity. It reminds me that internalized ableism requires that the "corporeality of the disabled body [be] constantly in a state of deferral, in a holding pattern, waiting for the day it will be not just repaired but made anew (cured)."[25]

During my mother's slow loss of vision, I noticed as a teenager that dishes and utensils were not always completely clean. My mom, who washed the dishes by hand, was beginning to miss remnants of food on plates, cups, forks . . . God forbid if any of us mentioned it to her! I started washing my own dishes (and the household dishes, when she let me) because of my own paranoia of finding or accidentally using a dirty plate. As an adult, I still wash my dishes, pots, and pans by hand, methodically feeling and inspecting them to make sure they are clean. I do not know if this habit started as a compulsion developed from the stress of watching my mom struggle with her transitioning eyesight or as a trauma response, but it is something I do.

I have learned to embrace washing dishes this way; I see it as a mindfulness practice. It is a way for me to relish in crip time, "a breaking of time that opens in its place slowness and consideration so that our disabled bodyminds can exist as they are and as they need to."[26] It is my chance to be, to feel the sensation of the warm water gliding over my palms, to focus on the smooth ceramic plates and cold metal pots. My fear and obsession have transformed into a way for me to ground myself and allow my bodymind to exist in the present moment.

Walking around with my mom in public can be a test of patience—not because of her slow movements but because of ableist society constantly reminding us of who the built environment is truly for. I remember one particular family outing to Animal Kingdom in Florida. As I had learned to do, I had wrapped my mom's arm around my own to guide her through the crowds of people. My mother also has a heart condition; so, our pace was slow and steady. We were perceived as barriers by the able-bodied people walking behind us, who let out a loud huff as they zoomed by, almost knocking my mother down in the process. I felt my blood pressure rising, my face flushing, and an urge to punch someone's face in. "This is why I don't like to go out," my mom said matter-of-factly. My soul mourned for her.

Most of my mom's life now consists of sitting in the same corner of the living room couch and listening to my father rant and rave about the latest thing he heard on the news, broken up by visits to various doctors and specialists. When she goes to see medical professionals, she is forced to deal with racist and ableist staff who make assumptions about her abilities. They assume that because she is blind she must also be Deaf; so, they raise their voices. Or they assume that she cannot speak English because she is Latina; so, they speak slowly (and loudly). The worst is when they do not speak directly to her at all, addressing the family member accompanying her rather than acknowledging her presence and dignity. Some nurses even go so far as to not touch her to guide her around the doctor's office. She has never told me how all of this makes her feel, but knowing my mother likes to put up a front, I am sure these are recurrent, traumatic, marginalizing experiences that reinforce the internalized ableism she already feels.

Bearing witness to how my mother is treated by others while also having the privilege of "passing" as able-bodied myself has shaped my activism and advocacy. Rather than allow anger to fester and destroy me, I put my energy toward cofounding an organization called the National Coalition for Latinxs with Disabilities / *la Coalición Nacional para Latinxs con Discapacidades* (CNLD), a burgeoning nonprofit dedicated to affirming, celebrating, and collectively uplifting Latino/a/xs with disabilities through community building, advocacy, protection of rights, resources, and education.[27]

We at CNLD want to confront ableism, especially within the Latino/a/x community, where disability is highly stigmatized. Given that our organizational leadership all identify as disabled Latino/a/xs, we understand the importance of family involvement and language in educating our community about disability, disability identity, disability rights, and disability justice. We know that large numbers of families fear or are ashamed to ask for assistance due to pride, lack of health insurance, or terror of outing themselves or a family member as undocumented. They may hide, ignore, pity, or patronize their disabled family member, perhaps going so far as to ask God to "cure" or "fix" their loved one's impairment. The Latino/a/x community is not familiar with the medical model of disability, which views a person's impairment as a problem to be treated by medical professionals to make the person's bodymind as close to "normal" as possible. The medical model is a social construct not commonly known in the Latino/a/x community. Typically, based on the perceived gravity of the disability and the belief that one should respect the advice of those who are more educated, Latino/a/xs will defer to doctors as experts and minimize the disabled person's internal desire and ability to live as they choose.

Unfortunately, Latino/a/x families, particularly those with limited English proficiency, encounter frequent communication barriers when dealing with medical professionals, even when provided an interpreter. Lack of communication can result in decreased understanding of medical instructions, unnecessarily complicated diagnoses and interventions, inadequate or excessive testing, and increased morbidity or death.[28] For example, in in-depth interviews with fourteen mothers or grandmothers of children and youth with special health care needs (the majority of whom were Puerto Rican), mothers shared worries related to having to wait for interpreters to become available as well as health care providers not listening to their observations or concerns.[29] Latino/a/x patients who do not speak English also tend to have poor self-rated health and high psychological distress[30] as a result of decreased access to care; health care professionals may "make damaging assumptions about unrelated attributes such as their intelligence, religion, culture, or attitudes towards health and illness,"[31] access to care, and marginalization.

Even language in reference to disability in the Latino/a/x community can be negative and steeped in the medical model. Similar to the perpetuation of ableism through the English language, Spanish terms like "*loco*," "*estupido*," and "*retardado*" are commonly used in the Latino/a/x community. We are socialized to view disability through a deficit lens, pitying those with impairments (e.g., "*pobrecito*," "*ay bendito*"). Jokes about disability abound, and it is difficult to translate disability rights and justice terms from English to Spanish.

In the process of learning about disability, I have learned that there is tension between the self-advocacy promoted by the independent living and disability rights movements and the emphasis on family in Latino/a/x communities. Though we value independence to a certain extent (so we are not perceived as a burden), we aim to build relationships with one another and take care of each other. There is an interdependence within and among families that the current disability rights movement does not fully understand or promote.[32] Therefore, CNLD is committed to working with and for disabled Latino/a/xs and their families. We believe that there is a need for intersectional, culturally appropriate interventions and programming to remove stigma and enhance individual agency while welcoming the active participation of Latino/a/x parents in the movement. We need to educate Latino/a/x families on how to be allies and empower their disabled loved ones. To this end, we participate in webinars and panel presentations, curate a website, organize convenings, and have one-on-one conversations with community members and activists. We emphasize the importance of interdependence and the need to balance parental roles with the identity development and independence of disabled family members.

That said, I know that our disabled Latino/a/x community needs more *testimonios*, more eyewitness accounts and stories about people who look, speak, and act like us. Just as Shayda Kafai reminds us, "We need to know the experiences and stories of our disabled ancestors of color if we are to create a space where we can celebrate our multiple identities and progress Disability Justice forward."[33] We must theorize, write, and curate the lived experiences of disabled Latino/a/xs because "they carry so much more than our forced, ableist narratives of shame"[34] and *sacrificio*.[35]

My mom got her condition from her father, who became blind with age due to a brain tumor behind his eyes. I do not remember much of him because my mom gave birth to me when she was thirty-eight years old, and he passed away when I was not more than three or four. I wish I could speak about how my grandfather's experience influenced my mother and, in turn, me, but my mother does not speak of her parents or other family members because of unhealed, unspoken trauma. I remember visiting him in a "hospital," which my young mind at the time did not know was a nursing home. It had a mixed smell of urine and medicine and brought stories of institutional abuse and family neglect, one of which was a tale of how he was left alone with no food and felt around to wind up finding and consuming cat food. My sisters and I were repeatedly told by my mother, as far back as I can remember, to never put her in a home. We understood and promised we would never do such a thing.

The fear of institutionalization is very real for the disability community; we are vulnerable to being isolated, mistreated, and quickly invisibilized. I have learned from my mother that we need "recognition, validation, and healing."[36] Despite my overbooked schedule, I try to call my mother once a week, as I live halfway across the country from her. I listen to her stories, even if I have heard them before. I validate her concerns, feelings, and experiences . . . and I write. I write about how the academy and society disable us. I bear witness to inequity, fight where I can, help where I can, rest when I can. I try to model a life of radical honesty.[37]

Some people may find it strange that I do not speak of my activism and advocacy with my mother. I am not even sure anyone has mentioned it to her. One would think that having a conversation about disability and disability justice would be reciprocally beneficial and bring us closer together given our embodied experiences as disabled Latinas. The truth is that I come from a very conservative household, and my mother is from a generation of women taught to obey and take on the opinions of their husbands—including a misinformed understanding of activism and social justice.

Now that I have children of my own, I have vowed to teach them about disability and respecting, valuing, advocating for, and standing in solidarity with every bodymind. I encourage them to ask questions, and I try to be as transparent as I can about my own disability identity development. I intend to encourage them to read disability literature; for example, I have already introduced them to disability through the children's book *My Mom Rocks; Her Chair Rolls* by disabled Latina author Pascuala Herrera[38] and the coloring book *Black Deaf Lives Matter* by my friend and Deaf studies scholar Dr. Lissa D. Ramirez-Stapleton.[39] I, along with other motherscholars, have begun to theorize what we are calling DisCrit mothering, a framework and pedagogy informed by our experiences as mothers, academics, and educators at the intersection of race and disability.

I hope that other Latino/a/x parents of disabled children and disabled Latino/a/x parents learn from my intersectional experiences. I would advise them to embrace disability as a cultural identity, to use an asset-based view when talking about disability, and to find ways to learn about and from the disability community. I would urge them to avoid labeling and forcing their children to conform to what white able-bodied society considers "normal" or acceptable for their station. Latino/a/x parents should aim for interdependence and access intimacy.[40] They should allow their children to make decisions and experience the world to the full extent possible while making it clear that they are there to support them because *nada sobre nosotros sin nosotros*.[41]

NOTES

1. Alexis Padilla, "LatDisCrit: Exploring Latinx Global South DisCrit Reverberations as Spaces toward Emancipatory Learning and Radical Solidarity," in *DisCrit Expanded: Inquiries, Reverberations and Ruptures*, ed. Subini A. Annamma, Beth A. Ferri, and David J. Connor (New York: Teachers College Press, 2021), 147–62.

2. Kimberlé Crenshaw, "Demarginalizing the Intersection of Race and Sex: A Black Feminist Critique of Antidiscrimination Doctrine, Feminist Theory and Antiracist Politics," *University of Chicago Legal Forum* 1989, no. 1 (1989): 139–67, https://chicagoun bound.uchicago.edu/uclf/vol1989/iss1/8.

3. Lisette E. Torres and Leonor Vanik, "¡PRESENTE! The National Coalition for Latinxs with Disabilities," Intervenxions, Latinx Project, November 24, 2020, https://www.latinx project.nyu.edu/intervenxions/national-coalition-for-latinxs-with-disabilities.

4. Lisette E. Torres, "*Sobreviviendo Sin Sacrificando* (Surviving without Sacrificing): An Intersectional DisCrit *Testimonio* from a Tired Mother-Scholar of Color," *Race Ethnicity and Education* 24, no. 5 (2021): 623–36, https://doi.org/10.1080/13613324.2021.1918402.

5. Jessica E. Peña, Ricardo Henrique Lowe Jr., and Merarys Ríos-Vargas, "Colombian and Honduran Populations Surpassed a Million for First Time; Venezuelan Population Grew the Fastest of all Hispanic Groups Since 2010," United States Census Bureau, September 26, 2023, https://www.census.gov/library/stories/2023/09/2020-census-dhc-a -hispanic-population.html.

6. Torres and Vanik, "¡PRESENTE!"

7. Shayda Kafai, *Crip Kinship: The Disability Justice and Art Activism of Sins Invalid* (Vancouver: Arsenal Pulp Press, 2021), 71.

8. National Eye Institute, "Retinitis Pigmentosa," NEI, last modified March 30, 2022, https://www.nei.nih.gov/learn-about-eye-health/eye-conditions-and-diseases/retinitis -pigmentosa.

9. A concept coined in 2017 by crip ancestor and disability rights activist Stacey Park Milbern and shared on episode six of the *Disability Visibility Podcast* with host Alice Wong. The episode is titled "Ep 6: Labor, Care Work, and Disabled Queer Femmes."

10. Torres and Vanik, "¡PRESENTE!"

11. Crenshaw, "Demarginalizing the Intersection of Race and Sex."

12. Padilla, "LatDisCrit"; Alexis Padilla, *Disability, Intersectional Agency and Latinx Identity: Theorizing LatDisCrit Counterstories* (Abingdon: Routledge, 2022).

13. Dolores Delgado Bernal, "Critical Race Theory, LatCrit Theory, and Critical Race-Gendered Epistemologies: Recognizing Students of Color as Holders and Creators of Knowledge," *Qualitative Inquiry* 8, no. 1 (2002): 105–26, https://doi.org/10.1177/1077800 40200800107; Erica R. Dávila and Ann Aviles de Bradley, "Examining Education for Latinas/os in Chicago: A CRT/LatCrit Approach," *Educational Foundations* 24, no. 1

(2010): 39–58; Daniel Solórzano and Dolores Delgado Bernal, "Examining Transformational Resistance through a Critical Race and LatCrit Theory Framework: Chicana and Chicano Students in an Urban Context," *Urban Education* 36, no. 3 (2001): 308–42, https://doi.org/10.1177/0042085901363002; Francisco Valdés, "Theorizing 'OutCrit' Theories: Coalitional Method and Comparative Jurisprudential Experience—RaceCrits, QueerCrits and LatCrits," *University of Miami Law Review* 53 no. 4 (1999): 1265–306, https://repository.law.miami.edu/umlr/vol53/iss4/39; Francisco Valdés, "Race, Ethnicity, and Hispanismo in a Triangular Perspective: The 'Essential Latina/o' and LatCrit Theory," *UCLA Law Review* 48 (2000): 1–41; Tara J. Yosso, *Critical Race Counterstories along the Chicana/Chicano Educational Pipeline* (New York: Routledge, 2006).

14. Subini A. Annamma, David J. Connor, and Beth A. Ferri, "Introduction: A Truncated Genealogy of DisCrit," in *DisCrit: Disability Studies and Critical Race Theory in Education,* ed. David J. Connor, Beth A. Ferri, and Subini A. Annamma (New York: Teachers College Press, 2016), 1–9.

15. Angela Calabrese Barton and Edna Tan, "Beyond Equity as Inclusion: A Framework of 'Rightful Presence' for Guiding Justice-Oriented Studies in Teaching and Learning," *Educational Researcher* 49, no. 6 (2020): 433–40, https://doi.org/10.3102/0013189X 20927363.

16. Padilla, *Disability, Intersectional Agency and Latinx Identity.*

17. Kafai, *Crip Kinship,* 25.

18. Mia Mingus, *Leaving Evidence* (blog), n.d., accessed December 17, 2023, https://leavingevidence.wordpress.com/.

19. "Una cabeza dura" means "a hard head" in Spanish.

20. "Yo no soy ciega" means "I am not blind" in Spanish.

21. Andrea Lausell, "For Years I Refused to Speak Spanish Because of How It Patronized My Disability," *Fierce,* September 11, 2018, https://fierce.wearemitu.com/identities/i-can-say-im-disabled-in-english-but-not-in-spanish/.

22. A term coined in 2012 by crip ancestor and disability rights activist Stella Young in an editorial in the Australian Broadcasting Corporation's webzine *Ramp Up*; Stella Young, "We're Not Here for Your Inspiration," *ABC News,* July 2, 2012, https://www.abc.net.au/news/2012-07-03/young-inspiration-porn/4107006.

23. Alexis Padilla, "LatDisCrit as Intersectional Agency in Decolonial Subalternity and Disability Justice," in *Crip Authorship,* ed. Mara Mills and Rebecca Sanchez (New York: NYU Press, 2023), 85–86.

24. Ellen Samuels, "Six Ways of Looking at Crip Time," *Disability Studies Quarterly (DSQ)* 37, no. 3 (2017): para. 11, https://doi.org/10.18061/dsq.v37i3.5824.

25. Fiona A. K. Campbell, "Exploring Internalized Ableism Using Critical Race Theory," *Disability & Society* 23, no. 2 (2008): 157, https://doi.org/10.1080/09687590701841190.

26. Kafai, *Crip Kinship,* 90.

27. Torres and Vanik, "¡PRESENTE!"

28. Jason Espinoza and Sabrina Derrington, "How Should Clinicians Respond to Language Barriers That Exacerbate Health Inequity?" *AMA Journal of Ethics* 23, no. 2 (2021): E109–16, https://doi.org/10.1001/amajethics.2021.109.

29. Nicola Brodie, Bruce Bernstein, Francis McNesby, and Renee Turchi, "The Experience of Latina Mothers of Children and Youth with Special Health Care Needs: A Qualitative Study," *Global Pediatric Health* 6 (2019): 1–7, https://doi.org/10.1177/2333794 X19851390.

30. Giyeon Kim, Courtney B. Worley, Rebecca S. Allen, Latrice Vinson, Martha R. Crowther, Patricia Parmelee, and David A. Chiriboga, "Vulnerability of Older Latino and

Asian Immigrants with Limited English Proficiency," *Journal of the American Geriatrics Society* 59, no. 7 (2011): 1246–52, https://doi.org/10.1111/j.1532-5415.2011.03483.x.

31. Espinoza and Derrington, "How Should Clinicians Respond," 111.

32. Allison C. Carey, Pamela Block, and Richard K. Scotch, "Sometimes Allies: Parent-Led Disability Organizations and Social Movements," *Disability Studies Quarterly* 39, no. 1 (2019), https://doi.org/10.18061/dsq.v39i1.

33. Kafai, *Crip Kinship*, 48.

34. Ibid., 73.

35. Torres, "*Sobreviviendo Sin Sacrificando* (Surviving without Sacrificing)."

36. Kafai, *Crip Kinship*, 51.

37. Bianca C. Williams, "Radical Honesty: Truth-Telling as Pedagogy for Working through Shame in Academic Spaces," in *Race, Equity and the Learning Environment: The Global Relevance of Critical and Inclusive Pedagogies in Higher Education*, ed. Frank Tuitt, Chayla Haynes, and Saran Stewart (Sterling, VA: Stylus, 2016), 71–82.

38. Pascuala Herrera, *My Mom Rocks; Her Chair Rolls* (self-published, 2021), https://sites.google.com/view/pascualaherreralibrary/my-booksmis-libros/my-mom-rocks-mi-mamá-es-la-mejor.

39. Lissa D. Ramirez-Stapleton, *Black Deaf Lives Matter* (self-published, 2021), https://www.drlissad.com/black-deaf-lives-matter-activity-bo.

40. Mia Mingus, "Access Intimacy: The Missing Link," *Leaving Evidence* (blog), May 5, 2011, https://leavingevidence.wordpress.com/2011/05/05/access-intimacy-the-missing-link/.

41. "Nada sobre nosotros sin nosotros" means "nothing about us without us" in Spanish.

3

TÀCHARAN

An "Autie"-Ethnographic Examination of
the Biopolitics of Changelings and Cyborgs

JACLYN ELLIS

Artist's Statement

I am a mixed-race, Autistic artist as well as an interracial adoptee. My spirit name is Manidoo Makwa Kwe, and I am from the Wolf clan. I was born and raised in London, Ontario. I work primarily in acrylic and ink, and I design jewelry using beadwork techniques and porcupine quill embroidery. My paintings explore themes of identity, boundaries, and human interaction with landscape. I am also the website coordinator at London Autistics Standing Together (LAST), a peer support and mutual aid group for Autistic adults in London, Ontario.

Tàcharan examines the intersection between autistic and Indigenous identities in the Canadian colonial context. I draw on changeling motifs from traditional Scottish Gaelic and British folklore[1] and Donna Haraway's evocative "Cyborg Manifesto"[2] to depict the dehumanization of othered bodies.[3] In doing so, I draw the viewer's attention to the ways in which normalcy is constructed.[4] I consider points of friction between hegemonic discourses of normalcy and counterhegemonic discourses emerging from the revitalization of Anishinaabe child-rearing practices[5] and from the feminist, disability rights, Autistic rights, and neurodiversity movements.[6]

I see painting as a political act. Through the practice of creating physical art, I reposition myself as an Autistic and Indigenous artist, out of the medical and colonial gaze and into the position of creator. The painting *Tàcharan* is intended to confront the viewer with a tangible manifestation of my inner thoughts and creative processes and to resist attempts to interpret its meanings within reductive dichotomies. In addition to the physical painting, I documented the readings,[7] theoretical considerations, and creative process that went into creating *Tàcharan* in a series of blog posts on my personal website, jackyskye.art/blog.[8]

How do the Anishinaabe think about disability, specifically infant/child disability?

I am by no means an expert in Anishinaabek conceptions of disability or traditional child-rearing practices, particularly given my adoption by a white family. I want to start by acknowledging that position. I am still very much learning and attempting to repair that loss of connection to my birth culture(s). When I write and paint, it is from the perspective of a light-skinned, mixed-race adoptee with a particular experience of Anishinaabe identity in the context of colonization, not as an authority on Anishinaabek perspectives.

Traditional Anishinaabek worldviews, speaking very generally, tend to have a more relational view of identity than settler worldviews. Anishinaabemowin is very verb based compared to English, which is very noun based. As a result, traditional worldviews tend to center identity on how people act in relation to others rather than on an assumed independent essence.[9]

The medicine wheel is a key concept in many Indigenous cultures, including Anishinaabek communities. The medicine wheel is a symbol of balance between the four directions. It also maps to other areas of creation such as the stages of life; mental, physical, spiritual, and emotional aspects of being; four sacred medicines; four seasons; and so on. As a model, it can be mapped at different scales: to individuals, to families and communities, and to where communities fit within the land and natural world. Carly Beth Christensen argues that the most analogous concept to disability within traditional worldviews is imbalance in the medicine wheel.[10] From this perspective, traditional views of disability are compatible with the biopsychosocial model of disability. Both perspectives emphasize context and community in creating and remediating imbalances or impairments.

Other authors, like Mehl-Madrona and Pennycook, are more skeptical about the applicability of settler-derived concepts to Indigenous ways of thinking.[11] In *Disability as a Colonial Construct*, Ineese-Nash emphasizes the importance of seeing children as gifts in traditional child-rearing practices. The focus on what a child brings to the community and how the community should best support them in finding *Mino Bimaadiziwin*, "the Good Path," often means that the child's impairments are not focused on.[12]

I do not see a conflict between the biopsychosocial model and what I understand of traditional teachings. They are two lenses I believe can be used effectively in concert.[13] However, I would stress that care should be taken not to elide differences between the two. While they may prompt us toward similar conclusions and a more relational view of disability than presented by the medical model, they emerge out of distinct intellectual traditions, with significant differences in understanding the role of the individual and the relationships between mind, body, and spirit.[14]

You speak about hegemonic discourses of normalcy and counterhegemonic discourses emerging from Anishinaabe child-rearing practices. Can you speak about what you see as the hegemonic discourse of child rearing and how Anishinaabe practices are different or present a challenge?

What I describe as hegemonic discourses of child rearing are the ways in which children are stereotyped, demeaned, and deployed as a metaphor within the dominant settler culture. Children are demeaned when they are stereotyped as not contributing to family or society, as lacking agency, intelligence, and ability to understand and voice their own perspectives. This construction is used to justify paternalistic and controlling stances toward children in the name of discipline and guidance.[15] Through the metaphor of childlikeness, interventions into the lives of marginalized others, including violence, are framed as acts of benevolence, with the state or other institutional actors acting *in loco parentis* over people assumed to lack the agency and competence to govern their own lives.[16]

In Anishinaabe understanding, children are central to society. They may be at a different life stage, with different levels of experience and skill, but they are still full people with agency and gifts to contribute to society.[17] Only by suppressing Indigenous understandings of childhood can the assumption that children lack competence and agency remain unchallenged. By extension, the agentive understanding of childhood represented in traditional teachings has the potential to disrupt assumptions that disabled and colonized others represent wrongly developed or underdeveloped versions of able-bodied, European personhood.[18]

As part of reconnecting with my birth cultures, I sat in ceremony to receive my name and be repatriated to my clan. Prior to the ceremony, I had the opportunity to talk with Joanne Jackson, an elder from my paternal grandmother's home community. She related to me that children choose their parents prior to being born, a belief that is in alignment with values of consent and permission. In some sense, I would have known about my mother's disabilities and the intergenerational trauma my father carried. I would have known that I would likely be placed for adoption with a white family. This sense that children, even infants, are full people with some measure of agency is deeply connected to the perception that children fulfill important roles in community.

By contrast, the dominant narrative of neoliberalism applies the values of a liberal economic system to all areas of life. Children are viewed through the narrow lens of productivity. They become sites of investment rather than full persons. Parents struggle to optimize their children's potential within the narrow parameters available in a neoliberal framework for "successful" independent adulthood.[19]

Are the Anishinaabe able to raise their children according to their beliefs? How have colonialism, disempowerment, poverty, etcetera shaped the experience of raising children?

Our family structures and child-rearing practices have been disrupted, particularly through the removal of our children through residential schools, the sixties scoop, and ongoing child welfare policies.[20] Kathleen Absolon writes:

> Severing, dismembering, separating, fragmenting, dividing and isolating are all colonial tactics that Indigenous Peoples have been combating. Colonization has been, and always will be, about the severing of people from the land and each other for the sole purpose of land, mineral and resources extraction for market trade.[21]

Settler colonialism depends on disarticulation. Through state policies like the Indian Act,[22] Indigenous people are separated from land and familial relationships. What was once a complex web of relationships and kinship between human people, place, and nonhuman persons is reduced to a conglomeration of individuals and inanimate resources ready for market exploitation.[23]

In my own family, this practice has led to separation and fragmentation. Many of my family members struggle with substance abuse and intergenerational trauma. Even after the Mount Elgin residential school shut down in 1946,[24] children weren't always able to be kept in the community. I know my grandmother placed my eldest uncle for adoption around 1960. I don't know all the circumstances that factored into her decision. There are many power imbalances in the adoption industry, and I can't rule out elements of coercion or influences of broader injustices.[25] When I was born, in the late 1980s, my father and his remaining siblings were struggling with substance abuse. Two of his brothers died in police custody in 1994; that is the last public record of my family I have been able to trace. I haven't been able to find where my aunt and my grandmother are now.

In *Tàcharan*, I grapple with this process of dismembering and fragmentation. It is hinted at in the repeating motif of wildflowers, particularly geraniums. The viewer is presented with examples of flowers that have in various ways been severed from their context. A thumbnail painting of the potted geranium featured in the infamous propaganda photographs *Thomas Moore before and after Tuition at Regina Indian Industrial School*[26] is depicted on the wall above the changeling baby. Beside it, a thumbnail version of a painting by my adoptive great-aunt Kay,[27] herself a notable disabled artist, depicts wildflowers in a vase. It is less stark and more beautiful but no less disconnected. In the next thumbnail, a framed botanical print, the theme of disarticulation reaches its height.

Disarticulation is pervasive in *Tàcharan*, but importantly it is not an end point. The birds, who have taken the place of fairies in the painting, have upset the living potted geranium on the windowsill. A canary points to the beaded *tiginaagan*. The flowers beaded on the cradleboard are not uprooted or disconnected but part of an interconnected design. Another fact about perennial geraniums is that even a fragment of root, once broken off the rhizome, can sprout a new plant. They are resilient.

In "Colonialism, Disability, and Possible Lives," Chapman describes tethered processes that exalt white able-bodied care workers and denigrate disabled Indigenous youths stemming from the dual legacies of residential schools and eugenic incarceration of disabled people.

> The idea that we were eradicating the Indian in the child through our interventions would undoubtedly have been abhorrent to every single staff person I worked with. But the idea that we were eradicating oppositional defiance disorder, attention deficit disorder or attachment disorder through our institutional practices would have seemed great to most of us. So I would like to suggest that the erasure of any trace of colonialism was facilitated through the diagnoses that justified the children's intakes. . . . It was ADHD, LD, ODD, FAS—all of the diagnostics—that made it okay, even seemingly normal, for some Aboriginal children to be removed from their families and communities and raised predominantly by white professionals, without suggesting that the legacy of the Residential Schools in any way lived on.[28]

Through the work of authors like Chapman, there has begun to be some focus on the ways in which adultism, colonialism, and ableism are coconstitutive.[29] In painting *Tàcharan*, I wanted to reflect on this cocreation that has played out in my personal experience with adoption.

Do the Anishinaabe recognize medical interpretations of disability, like the autism diagnosis? Can you / how can you / why would you draw on Western labels while drawing on Anishinaabe traditions and worldviews? Do the Anishinaabe traditions get transformed, then? Similarly, rights models are a Western construction. They are individualistic and conflict driven. How do disability rights and Autistic rights movements shape your beliefs and work and, vice versa, how does Indigenous culture shape your view of rights and of autistic identity?

I think the ways in which disability is conceptualized and the extent to which drawing on Western labels and diagnostic categories transforms the meaning of traditional worldviews, varies quite a bit between individuals and communities. Certainly, there was a very different understanding of the types of traits we call "autism" prior to colonization.[30] There is also the issue of autism being underdiagnosed in Indigenous communities due largely to lack of access to specialist assessment as well as stereotyping on the part of professionals. There is a corresponding disproportionate rate of diagnosis of Fetal Alcohol Spectrum Disorder, for example, while fewer Indigenous people are diagnosed with autism than their white counterparts.[31]

I was fortunate to be assessed for autism and diagnosed at the age of twenty-four. The only reason I was assessed at all is because my adoptive parents could afford to support me in seeking private assessment financially and by providing old school records. I imagine that I may have received a different diagnosis if there hadn't been documentation that my First Mom didn't drink or smoke during pregnancy.

There are certainly some Indigenous people who identify as Autistic in Autistic advocacy spaces. Personally, I've drawn a lot of strength from reading the work of J. Meunier, like their essay "We Autistics, We Villages, We Humanoids."[32] Knowing I'm not alone, especially in largely white disability activism spaces, has been important in allowing me to find my own voice as a mixed-race Autistic adoptee.

A teaching that has been strongly impressed on me by several elders is the idea that we are a permission people—content and permission are core values in our culture. This idea is reflected in everything from laying tobacco before gathering medicine to etiquette around learning from other communities. For example, if you learn to smudge a certain way or learn a song a certain way, then that is the way that teaching was given to you. If you go to another community and they do things differently, it isn't right to tell them to change how they do things. The important thing is to practice the knowledge you are given accurately to how you were taught and to be respectful of other ways of doing things when you encounter people who were given a different understanding.[33]

There is no single "correct" set of teachings for all Anishinaabe people. Our cultures have never been static. There has been a history of portraying the Anishinaabe perspective and other Indigenous perspectives as diametrically opposed to Western thought. At its worst, this tendency has resulted in portrayals of Indigenous worldviews as frozen in time.[34] I wanted to be careful to avoid this damaging tendency in painting *Tàcharan*. Anishinaabe worldviews have always been heterogeneous and open to change, adaptation, and dialogue with other perspectives.

I do think that in Indigenous spaces, there is currently more of a focus on addressing disability in terms of colonization, which is understandable given the scale of the impact of intergenerational trauma and ongoing socioeconomic inequalities. There isn't a lot of room in those discussions for disabilities like autism. Before colonization, many of what we now consider autistic traits would have been understood differently, even positively,[35] but we don't live in a precolonial world. There is a need to grapple with how to best negotiate the colonial medical system and support Indigenous children with autistic traits. I think this discussion is still very much unresolved. I have written more fully in "Imagining Neurodivergent Futures from the Belly of the Identity Machine" about the need to engage strategically and consciously with dominant discourses such as rights frameworks.[36] In this article, I draw heavily on work that has already been done within Indigenous rights spaces.

The ways in which I personally have made sense of my autistic traits through the lenses of my identities as an adoptee, an Anishinaabe person, and an Autistic person have always been fluid. It is empowering to see some of my autistic traits not as part of a disability in the medical sense but as an expression of "blood memory."[37] In interpreting myself this way, I emphasize that while I have been separated from my family, my assimilation into settler culture has never been complete. I embody a physical rejection of the assimilationist project. I am uncomfortable with eye contact, prefer to wear my hair long, and struggle with language not because I am in some way pathological but because my spirit remembers that I am Anishinaabe, and a colonizer's language sits heavily on my tongue.

At the same time, my First Mom bounces on their toes and shares my difficulty with eye contact and language and my sensory differences—and is not Anishinaabe. They have come to realize, after a lifetime of diagnostic limbo, that they might just be Autistic. Autism ties our experiences together and gives us a name for forms of ableism that have shaped our lives. In claiming an Autistic identity, I reclaim and re-lineate[38] myself as the child of a Disabled mother. Both perspectives are important and, in their own ways, true. My experience as a mixed-race adopted person requires an ability to code switch. I paint and write from the position of someone with ties to multiple cultures and perspectives whose position within any community is always precarious. My intention with *Tàcharan* is to explore the space of tension between those perspectives.

Like in the stories of changelings, adoption tends to create doubles of adoptees. We are haunted by questions of *what if*?[39] Perhaps in a world where colonization hadn't happened, or had happened differently, there is another Manidoo Makwa. This Manidoo Makwa prefers to speak in an Indigenous sign language still widely used in this other world. They are not a changeling, not a perennial outsider, moving between speaking Gaelic with their mother and Ojibway with their father, their fingers picking up where their voice stumbles. Autism has never been invented as a category for them to fit themself into. (Do they still feel a need for a word that describes how they are different from those around them?) Almost certainly, they know the name of their gender. This is an overly romanticized fantasy, perhaps. It says little about my identities within the constraints of colonized Turtle Island or what labels I use to bind myself to communities of shared struggle. It does open spaces in the strictures of reality, making it possible to know that things need not always be as they are now.

Allies and Obstacles **looks at parent activism. Are your parents activists? In terms of Indigenous cultures? In terms of disability?**

My non-Autistic, adoptive parents never really had the opportunity to connect with other parents of Autistic people when I was a child. Prior to reuniting with my First Mom, my differences with both my peers and my adoptive parents were viewed through the lens of adoption. My sensory and motor difficulties were attributed to my premature birth, and my social difficulties and periods of mutism were attributed to attachment problems. I think my adoptive parents often did not feel empowered to advocate for me because they didn't have a framework to understand why I was struggling. If I could go back and change one thing about my childhood, it would be to push my parents to connect with other parents of transracial adoptees and of disabled kids despite the tensions adult activists have with those communities. I would also encourage them to connect more with Anishinaabe families who have stayed connected with traditional culture. My parents have always been supportive and loving, but they haven't always had the tools and knowledge to take on the challenges of parenting a mixed-race, queer, Disabled, adopted child. They never gave up in spite of being underprepared, and that much, I can say, is real love.

Currently, my adoptive parents are supportive of my activism. They sometimes help my Autistic friends with things like navigating the medical system or even just having transportation to events. They are part of the community we are building in London. I know my friends see them as examples of how parents can be good allies, but I don't think *they* see what they do as activism per se.

My First Mom is Scottish by ancestry. They have told me that they feel a responsibility to be more politically active as an ally to Indigenous people because my father couldn't be that for me. They are the one who went with me to round dances with Idle No More. They marched beside me each year they were physically able at walks honoring missing and murdered Indigenous women and girls. They have also been involved in election reform and queer community spaces at various times in their life. They are the one who taught me to think strategically and use what tools are available even when they don't line up perfectly with my theoretical standpoint. They've always been equal parts unconditionally supportive and willing to challenge my assumptions. I've learned so much from them when it comes to navigating the world as a multiply disabled and multiply marginalized person. They have been an important role model for me—both at the level of building community and advocating for change and on a more day-to-day level of existing as a disabled person. I can honestly say that I wouldn't be here if I hadn't been successful in reuniting with them.

Allies and Obstacles **looks at the tensions between parent activists and the activism of disabled people. Do you see this in your communities? How so? Do you see alliances?**

I certainly see tension between parent activism and Autistic activists. I'm the social media coordinator for a local Autistic organization called London Autistics Standing Together, and there is distrust of mainstream parent groups among many in that community. However, as our organization is aimed at Autistic adults, the boundaries between parent activists and Autistic activists are sometimes blurred. Some of our members are parents themselves, often of neurodivergent children. My First Mom and their current partner are some of those neurodivergent parents of neurodivergent children.

I've heard from Autistic parents that they often feel alienated from groups led by non-Autistic parents. I think the racial and class makeup of parent-led organizations in our area plays into that. I've repeatedly heard critiques that mainstream parent-led organizations are made up predominantly of white, middle-class parents and lack an intersectional framework. Their approach to disability tends to be highly individual and does not take into account systemic ableism and other social contexts. Several of our support group members, including myself, have been vocal in critiquing this approach, which I think has caused some of the parent-led groups in our area to view us as troublemakers.

I see similar dynamics in the intercultural adoptee community. There is a feeling that our voices, the perspectives of the people most impacted, are ignored in favor of the voices of (often white, wealthy, and middle class) potential adoptive parents and adoption professionals. Adoptees are frequently infantilized, discounted as mad, or dismissed as unable to represent the majority of adoptees due to the diversity of adoption stories. We are simultaneously pushed into a position of hypervisibility and invisibility, where intimate details of our lives become fodder for public discussion around reproductive rights and what defines a family, but we are not considered potential sources of expertise in those same discussions. We are too often discounted as having a right to belong to our first cultures and denied the space to tell our own narratives of identity. This contradiction produces an understandable but deep sense of outrage.[40]

I think sometimes it's easy to focus our critiques and outrage at parents. After all, they have more access to power on a structural level than we do. Space is made for them in broader discourse on adoption and disability, even if it is allocated unevenly along class lines. Parents are the ones who are congratulated and exalted for taking us on as children.[41] We see the power differences between their position and our position firsthand because we live with them or have lived with them for at least part of our lives. It's harder to pick out, for example, the ways in which the adoption industry prioritizes state, nationalist, and religious agendas above even the needs of prospective adoptive parents.[42]

Despite many of my Autistic peers voicing a distrust with parent groups, I still hear from members of LAST that openness to alliances with non-Autistic parents remains important to them. There is a general agreement that we have important insights to offer non-Autistic parents. Some LAST members have also pointed out that our advocacy would benefit from the resources and social capital some non-Autistic parents have access to. There is a basis for building alliances here, but more non-Autistic parents will need to take a close look at the ways in which ableism intersects with other forms of oppression before the trust and mutual understanding necessary for those alliances can be strengthened.

NOTES

1. Henry Fuseli, *Der Wechselbalg*, 1781, black chalk and watercolor on paper, Kunsthaus Zürich, Zürich, https://gd.wikipedia.org/wiki/Faidhle:Füssli_-_Der_Wechselbalg_-_1780.jpeg; Sir Walter Scott, "On the Fairies of Popular Superstition: Introduction to 'The Tale of Tamlane,'" in Minstrelsy of the Scottish Border, ed. Robert Cadell (Edin-

burgh: Ballantyne, 1849), 254–336; Robert Hunt, "The Piskies' Changeling," in *Popular Romances of the West of England: The Drolls, Traditions, and Superstitions of Old Cornwall*, ed. Robert Hunt (London: John Camden Hotten, 1871), 95–96; Walter Y. Evans-Wentz, "A Changeling Musician," in *The Fairy Faith in Celtic Countries*, ed. Henry Frowde (Oxford: Oxford University Press, 1911), 128–29; Kirsty McRoberts, "Shape Shifting, Metamorphosis and the Cycle of Life and Death in Early Modern Scottish Poetry" (master's thesis, University of Glasgow, 2004), 86, ProQuest Dissertations & Theses Global.

2. Donna J. Haraway, "A Cyborg Manifesto: Science, Technology, and Socialist-Feminism in the Late Twentieth Century," in *Manifestly Haraway* Donna J. Haraway (Minneapolis: University of Minnesota Press, 2016), 3–90.

3. Teunie van der Palen, "A Cyborg Autobiography: Autism & the Posthuman" (master's thesis, Utrecht University, 2014), 126, https://studenttheses.uu.nl/handle/20.500.12932 /17487.

4. Mary Douglas, *Purity and Danger: An Analysis of the Concepts of Pollution and Taboo* (London: Routledge, 1966); Michel Foucault, *The Birth of the Clinic: An Archaeology of Medical Perception* (New York: Random House, 1973); Shelley L. Tremain, *Foucault and Feminist Philosophy of Disability* (Ann Arbor: University of Michigan Press, 2017); Anna N. de Hooge, "Binary Boys: Autism, Aspie Supremacy and Post/Humanist Normativity," *Disability Studies Quarterly* 39, no. 1 (winter 2019), https://doi.org/10.18061/dsq.v39i1.6461.

5. Alexandra Kahsenniio Nahwegahbow, "Springtime in n'Daki Menan, the Homeland of the Teme-Augama Anishnabai: Babies, Cradleboards and Community Wrapping" (master's thesis, Carleton University, 2013), 160, https://doi.org/10.22215/etd/2013 -10668.

6. Anne McGuire, *War on Autism: On the Cultural Logic of Normative Violence* (Ann Arbor: University of Michigan Press, 2016); Jen (Gzhibaeassigaekwe) Meunier, "We Autistics, We Villages, We Humanoids," in *All the Weight of Our Dreams: On Living Racialized Autism*, eds. E. Ashkenazy, Lydia X. Z. Brown, and Morénike G. Onaiwu (Lincoln, NE: DragonBee Press, 2017), 425–34; Tremain, *Foucault and Feminist Philosophy of Disability*; Melanie Yergeau, *Authoring Autism* (Durham, NC: Duke University Press, 2018).

7. Janet C. Berlo and Ruth B. Phillips, *Native North American Art* (Oxford: Oxford University Press, 1998); Sara Lige, "Adults with Intellectual Disabilities and the Visual Arts: 'It's NOT Art Therapy!'" (master's thesis, University of British Columbia, 2000), 223, https://dx.doi.org/10.14288/1.0072346; Joyce Green, "Canaries in the Mines of Citizenship: Indian Women in Canada," *Canadian Journal of Political Science / Revue canadienne de science politique* 34, no. 4 (December 2001): 715–38, https://doi.org/10.1017 /s0008423901778067; Bonita Lawrence, "Gender, Race, and the Regulation of Native Identity in Canada and the United States: An Overview," *Hypatia* 18, no. 2 (spring 2003): 3–31, https://doi.org/10.1353/hyp.2003.0031; Whitney Chadwick, *Women, Art, and Society* (New York: Thames & Hudson World of Art, 2007); Alan Sears and James Cairns, *A Good Book, In Theory* (Toronto: University of Toronto Press, 2013); Marion Quirici, "Geniuses without Imagination: Discourses of Autism, Ability, and Achievement," *Journal of Literary & Cultural Disability Studies* 9, no. 1 (January 2015): 71–88, https://doi.org/10.3828/jlcds .2015.5; Monique Mojica, "Verbing Art," in *Me Artsy*, ed. Drew Hayden Taylor (Madeira Park, BC: D & M, 2015), 15–28; Rabia Belt, "Contemporary Voting Rights Controversies through the Lens of Disability," *SSRN Journal* 68, no. 6 (2016): 1491–550, https://doi.org /10.2139/ssrn.2780693; Meunier, "We Autistics," 425–34; Stephan Lindner, Ruth Rowland, Margaret Spurlock, Stan Dorn, and Melinda Davis, "'Canaries in the Mine . . . ' the Impact of Affordable Care Act Implementation on People with Disabilities: Evidence from

Interviews with Disability Advocates," *Disability and Health Journal* 11, no. 1 (2018): 86–92, https://doi.org/10.1016/j.dhjo.2017.04.003; de Hooge, "Binary Boys."

8. Jacky Skye, 2020. I paint under the name Jacky Skye, which is a combination of my adoptive first name and the middle name my birth mom gave me. I present my work under this name because it feels more representative of who I am and because I paint about personal themes such as transracial adoption and intergenerational trauma. Painting under a different name provides a buffer between my artwork and my personal life and allows me to comment on my experiences of adoption without revealing confidential information that might be traceable if I painted under my legal last name.

9. Carly Beth Christensen, "Exploring Conceptions of Disability Held by Anishinaabe Secondary School Students" (PhD diss., University of Cambridge, 2019), https://doi.org/10.17863/CAM.51837, 144–46; Nicole Ineese-Nash, "Disability as a Colonial Construct: The Missing Discourse of Culture in Conceptualizations of Disabled Indigenous Children," *Canadian Journal of Disability Studies* 9, no. 3 (2020): 29–30, https://doi.org/10.15353/cjds.v9i3.645; Kathleen E. (Minogiishigokwe) Absolon, *Kaandossiwin: How We Come to Know Indigenous re-Search Methodologies* (Black Point, Nova Scotia: Fernwood, 2022), 89–94.

10. Christensen, "Exploring Conceptions of Disability," 147–68.

11. Lewis Mehl-Madrona and Gordon Pennycook, "Construction of an Aboriginal Theory of Mind and Mental Health," *Anthropology of Consciousness* 20, no. 2 (fall 2009): 91–93, https://doi.org/10.1111/j.1556-3537.2009.01017.x.

12. Nahwegahbow, "Springtime in n'Daki Menan," 3–4; Ineese-Nash, "Disability as a Colonial Construct," 28–30.

13. Christensen, "Exploring Conceptions of Disability," 367.

14. Mehl-Madrona and Pennycook, "Construction of an Aboriginal Theory," 94–95.

15. China Mills and Brenda A. Lefrançois, "Child as Metaphor: Colonialism, Psy-Governance, and Epistemicide," *World Futures* 74, no. 7–8 (2018): 504, https://doi.org/10.1080/02604027.2018.1485438.

16. Chris Chapman, "Colonialism, Disability, and Possible Lives: The Residential Treatment of Children Whose Parents Survived Indian Residential Schools," *Journal of Progressive Human Services* 23, no. 2 (2012): 150–53, https://doi.org/10.1080/10428232.2012.666727; Mills and Lefrançois, "Child as Metaphor," 504–6, 517.

17. Nahwegahbow, "Springtime in n'Daki Menan," 160; Mills and Lefrançois, "Child as Metaphor," 518–19; Ineese-Nash, "Disability as a Colonial Construct," 30.

18. Mills and Lefrançois, "Child as Metaphor," 518–19; Ineese-Nash, "Disability as a Colonial Construct," 29–30.

19. Rebecca Mallett and Katherine Runswick-Cole, "Commodifying Autism: The Cultural Contexts of 'Disability' in the Academy," in *Disability and Social Theory*, ed. Dan Goodley (Houndmills: Palgrave Macmillan, 2012), 33–51; McGuire, *War on Autism*, 126; Allison C. Carey, Pamela Block, and Richard K. Scotch, "Sometimes Allies: Parent-Led Disability Organizations and Social Movements," *Disability Studies Quarterly* 39, no. 1 (winter 2019), https://doi.org/10.18061/dsq.v39i1.6281; Ahoo Tabatabai, "Mother of a Person: Neoliberalism and Narratives of Parenting Children with Disabilities," *Disability and Society* 35, no. 1 (2020): 111–31, https://doi.org/10.1080/09687599.2019.1621739.

20. Elisabeth Graham, *The Mush Hole: Life at Two Indian Residential Schools* (Waterloo, Ontario: Heffle, 1997); Anthony J. Hall, "A National or International Crime? Canada's Indian Residential Schools and the Genocide Convention," *Genocide Studies International* 12, no. 1 (Spring 2018): 72–91, https://doi.org/10.3138/gsi.12.1.05; Mills and Lefrançois, "Child as Metaphor," 516–19; Christensen, "Exploring Conceptions of Disability,"

367; Allyson D. Stevenson, *Intimate Integration: A History of the Sixties Scoop and the Colonization of Indigenous Kinship* (Toronto: University of Toronto Press, 2020).

21. Absolon, *Kaandossiwin*, 89–90.

22. Indian Act, Revised Statutes of Canada 1985, c I-5, https://www.sac-isc.gc.ca/eng/1100100010252/1618940680392.

23. Hall, "A National or International Crime?" 72–91; Mills and Lefrançois, "Child as Metaphor," 518; Ineese-Nash, "Disability as a Colonial Construct," 32–35.

24. Graham, *The Mush Hole*.

25. Madeline H. Engel, Norma Kolko Phillips, and Frances A. DellaCava, "Indigenous Children's Rights: A Sociological Perspective on Boarding Schools and Transracial Adoption," *International Journal of Children's Rights* 20 (2012): 287–93, https://doi.org/10.1163/157181811X612873; Angela Tucker and Emily N. Bartz, "An Interview with Angela Tucker," *Adoption & Culture* 9, no. 1 (2021): 79, 81, https://doi.org/10.1353/ado.2021.0007; Grace Newton, "The Trauma and Healing of Consciousness," *Child Abuse & Neglect* 130, no. 2 (August 2022): 105563, https://doi.org/10.1016/j.chiabu.2022.105563.

26. Department of Indian Affairs, *Thomas Moore before and after Admission to Regina Indian Industrial School*, 1987, Saskatchewan Archives Board, Regina, https://www.researchgate.net/figure/Thomas-Moore-Before-Picture-Thomas-Moore-before-and-after-admission-to-Regina-Indian_fig1_347811217.

27. Kathleen Heart-Ellis, *Wildflowers from Byron*, n.d., London, Ontario.

28. Chapman, "Colonialism, Disability, and Possible Lives," 140.

29. Chapman, "Colonialism, Disability, and Possible Lives," 140–42; Meunier, "We Autistics," 425–34; Mills and Lefrançois, "Child as Metaphor," 503–24; de Hooge, "Binary Boys"; Caleigh E. Inman, "Absence and Epidemic: Autism and Fetal Alcohol Spectrum Disorder in Indigenous Populations in Canada," *Canadian Journal of Disability Studies* 8, no. 4 (2019): 227–61, https://doi.org/10.15353/cjds.v8i4.531; Ineese-Nash, "Disability as a Colonial Construct," 29–51.

30. Ineese-Nash, "Disability as a Colonial Construct," 29–30.

31. Inman, "Absence and Epidemic," 227–61.

32. Meunier, "We Autistics," 425–34.

33. Basil Johnston, *Th!nk Indian: Languages Are beyond Price* (Wiarton, Ontario: Kegedonce Press, 2011), 24–33, 46–53, 168–76.

34. Suzanne Crawford, "(Re)Constructing Bodies: Semiotic Sovereignty and the Debate over Kennewik Man," in *Repatriation Reader: Who Owns American Indian Remains?*, ed. Devon Abbott Mihesuah (Lincoln: University of Nebraska Press, 2000), 211–30; Lawrence, "Gender, Race, and the Regulation of Native Identity in Canada and the United States," 22.

35. Ineese-Nash, "Disability as a Colonial Construct," 29–31.

36. Jaclyn (Manidoomakwakwe) Ellis, "Imagining Neurodivergent Futures from the Belly of the Identity Machine: Neurodiversity, Biosociality, and Strategic Essentialism," *Autism in Adulthood* 5, no. 3 (September 2023): 225–35, https://doi.org/10.1089/aut.2021.0075.

37. Joanna Ziarkowska, "From Blood Memory to Genetic Memory, and the Emergence of Native American DNA: A Story of Biocolonialism at the Turn of the Millennium," in *Indigenous Bodies, Cells, and Genes* (London: Routledge, 2020), 133–55.

38. Jennifer Natalya Fink, *All Our Families: Disability Lineage and the Future of Kinship* (Boston: Beacon Press, 2022).

39. Shannon Gibney and Kimberly D. McKee, "An Interview with Shannon Gibney and Kimberly D. McKee," *Adoption & Culture* 9, no. 1 (2021): 24–33, https://doi.org/10.1353/ado.2021.0002.

40. Tucker and Bartz, "An Interview with Angela Tucker," 74–83; Gibney and McKee, "An Interview," 24–33; Newton, "The Trauma and Healing of Consciousness," 105563.

41. Chapman, "Colonialism, Disability, and Possible Lives," 132–34.

42. Tucker and Bartz, "An Interview with Angela Tucker," 74–83; Gina E. Miranda Samuels, "Epistemic Trauma and Transracial Adoption: Author(iz)ing Folkways of Knowledge and Healing," *Child Abuse & Neglect* 130, no. 2 (August 2022): 105588, https://doi .org/10.1016/j.chiabu.2022.105588; Newton, "The Trauma and Healing of Consciousness," 105563.

4

EMPATHY DEFICITS AMONG
NEUROTYPICALS

BRIDGET LIANG

Many neurotypical people have a problem feeling empathy toward autistic people. If they experienced empathy toward autistic people, they'd believe autistic people's experiences and respect autistic people's bodily autonomy.

Bodily autonomy is a fundamental human right. As human beings, we should be allowed to choose what happens to our bodies and make choices for our lives as long as we don't infringe on the lives of other people.

Writing from the position of an autistic, trans, disabled, mixed-race, queer person, I use bell hooks's framework of the Oppositional Gaze.[1] Through satire, a self-narrating zoo exhibit,[2] and argumentation, I scrutinize how neurotypical people lack empathy. Neurotypical empathy deficits aren't recognized because neurotypicals are the ones who defined what counts as an empathy deficit in the first place.

To begin the process of healing from some of the harms neurotypicals have inflicted on autistic people, I advocate for bodily autonomy and informed consent. Basic human rights should be respected; the fact that they aren't demonstrates a lack of understanding of other people's worth and desires. So many issues would be resolved if more people respected basic human rights and had empathy for those different from themselves.

Do neurotypicals have an empathy deficit?

(A satire . . . or not?)

Introduction

Whenever I read or watch the news, whenever I read about events in history, whenever I interface with people online or in person, I'm struck by the pain and suffering going on all over the world. When I was a teenager, I felt like I could hear the cries of suffering of countless people, and it nearly overwhelmed me. Despite waves of apathy, fear, and avarice produced by late-stage capitalism, I've somehow held onto my heart. It's a heart that hurts because poverty, bigotry, climate change denial, and other human-made ills exist. When I glance into someone's eyes while they step over a homeless person and see blankness, I feel a chill pooling in my belly. How can they not acknowledge another's humanity? How can people double down when presented with evidence that their actions are causing harm to others? How do people eat the flesh of an animal without revulsion? How am I the one with an empathy deficit because I'm autistic?

In order to explore whether neurotypicals have an empathy deficit, we need to define some terms. "Neurotypical"[3] refers to people whose minds fit the societal norm. Neurotypicals make up a socially privileged category. An "empathy deficit"[4] is a trait often associated with autistic people among others. It refers to a clinically significant deficit in relating to the experiences and needs of others. If this is the definition of an empathy deficit, the number of neurotypical people who display abysmal levels of empathy is astronomical. Why aren't neurotypicals with empathy deficits taken seriously and put through the same gold-standard treatments as autistic people?

There are countless examples of people with severe deficits in empathy throughout time and the world—for example, all sovereigns, politicians, and world leaders who use war to take land and resources away from *Other* people through murder and call it "collateral damage," "holy war," or "glory." War inevitably results in the deaths of thousands of poor people who are drafted or trying to escape poverty caused by scarcity, which is manufactured through leaders hoarding resources without ever getting their hands dirty fighting on the front lines. What reason is there for murder, pillaging, poverty, blatant greed, slavery, and sexual violence? Leaders lack the empathy to fathom that their soldiers and neighbors are fully fledged human beings deserving of a good life. The thought that another person is undeserving of the same rights and responsibilities as another—isn't that a significant impairment to one's ability to relate to another person? Perhaps the people who define "empathy deficit," in fact, have empathy deficits themselves and need to be treated. The world would be a much kinder place if people didn't have a deficit in empathy.

We can see examples of empathy deficits holding innocent people captive in a box in their minds. We have the technology to easily feed the world multiple times over and give every person a comfortable lifestyle, but much of neurotypical humanity lacks the empathy to care enough to respect everyone's personhood. If unborn fetuses matter so much to some people, why aren't uterus owners or born children just as worthy of life and liberty? Will the world end if Disney casts a Black woman as Ariel in *The Little Mermaid* and it brings Black kids joy to see someone with their complexion as a princess for once? Can clinical autism experts with decades-long careers built on the backs of poor, racialized clients fathom that their theories are wrong and have harmed autistic people and their families? How can billionaires value money over the survival of the planet? With so many people suffering from disordered empathy, it should be labeled an uncontrollable pandemic.

To address a criticism of this perspective, not everyone has an empathy deficit as severe as a warmonger. We can look at empathy deficits as a spectrum from mild to clinically severe. This spectrum is ranked from levels one through three, with one being the mildest and three the most severe.

Even when we consider the mildest of empathy deficits, this disease has brought suffering to countless people and is a danger beyond pandemic proportions. It needs to be treated with intensive, forty-hour-a-week therapies to bring people out of the prison of their mind!

While I use some tongue in cheek in this introduction to satirize the ableism experienced by autistic people, there's a hint of truth. Many neurotypical people have frighteningly low empathy, and levels of empathy are dropping.[5] Despite autistics being the ones labeled as having an empathy deficit, neurotypical people need to take a hard look at themselves and think about how their actions harm others. We should apply empathy to all people instead of having this unspoken notion that only certain people count as human beings[6] and deserve to be given rights and dignity.

One way people can begin to address this alarming empathy deficit is by listening to and respecting autistic people's fundamental human rights to self-determination and bodily autonomy. Listen to what autistic people say they do and don't want, and act accordingly. While we're at it, we can all, collectively—including autistics—learn to respect fundamental human rights.

Autistic people aren't robots without feelings. But neither are we saints or pinnacles of empathy—me included. Milton's concept of the Double Empathy Problem[7] is defined as "a breach in the 'natural attitude' that occurs between people of different dispositional outlooks and personal conceptual understandings when attempts are made to communicate meaning." Autistic and neurotypical people are from different social locations and may have trouble bridging the divide between their experiences. We see this disconnect in the polarized differences between autistic and autism parent communities.

I don't want this essay to be an autistic people versus autism parents fight. I want good allies. Parents of queer and trans folks with open hearts and minds have been some of their children's staunchest allies. What makes them different from autism parents is that they listen to and take direction from queer and trans folks. With organizations like PFLAG (Parents and Friends of Lesbians and Gays), queer/trans folks mentor parents to support other parents of queer/trans people. In my own research on autism parent blogs,[8] I found that parents of autistic people with more pathologizing and negative views of autism didn't cite or talk about autistic adults in their lives. In contrast, parents who did have autistic people in their lives and/or were autistic themselves spoke about the need for autistic human rights and understanding from parents. There needs to be something like PFLAG for parents of autistics to accept and support their children and fight for autistic human rights. It's win-win because autistic people would get to grow up supported and their parents would have access to community members who may have gone through some of the same things as their children.

To begin this process of bridging the gap, more neurotypical people need to be willing to admit that decisions they've made on behalf of autistic people have been harmful. Then they need to help fix the harms they've caused through their decisions. Isn't saying sorry and trying to fix your mistakes something many people were taught to do as small children?

To take these first steps to heal the divide between autistics and neurotypicals, I discuss how autism is defined differently among autistic people and in the official diagnosis, then the history of how autism discourse has been harmful. I curate some history of parent and autistic activism to demonstrate how the autism movement arrived where it's at. I advocate for bodily autonomy and informed consent as two issues for people to start working on because these issues are fundamental to healing and fixing how autistic people have been harmed. I end this paper with recommendations on how to treat autistic people better and how we can all develop skills in empathy. I don't deny that there are autistic people who lack empathy. There are autistic people who use generational wealth to buy social media platforms to promote hate and intolerance. But zeroing in on autistic people for having empathy deficits fails to shine a light on the empathy deficits of those who never imagined asking autistic people how they felt about the hypotheses about what autistic people need or experience.

Definitions of Autism

It is interesting how autism is defined differently by the experts who designed the clinical diagnosis and by autistic people themselves. Paraphrased, the *Diagnostic and Statistical Manual of Mental Disorders*, fifth edition (DSM-5),[9] says that "autism spectrum disorder (ASD) is a neurological disorder. Individuals who are affected have social interaction and communication difficulties, narrow interests, and repetitive behaviours."[10]

The Autistic Self Advocacy Network (ASAN), a nonprofit organization based out of the United States and made up of autistic people lobbying for human rights for autistic people, defines autism as "a developmental disability that affects how we experience the world around us. Autistic people are an important part of the world. Autism is a normal part of life, and makes us who we are."[11]

The DSM defines autism by the ways autistic people function less effectively than neurotypical people. While I agree with the traits named in the definition, it frames autistic people as disordered, as having something wrong that needs reordering for them to be able to function in society.

ASAN, in contrast, refers to autism as a disability over a disorder and frames autism as a difference instead of a problem. It values autism as an integral part of someone's life and a normal experience in the world.

The contrast between how experts and self-advocates define autism demonstrates fundamental differences between what each group believes to be an autistic person's position and value in society, impacting how each believes services and support should look for autistic people. ASAN came into existence because the needs of autistic people weren't being met by the establishment designed to support them. How could caring, empathetic people working in a helping profession not pause and reflect when the people they serve organize a nonprofit to call them out? How do they not reach out, consult with the group, and work together to readjust practices to do a better job? It's as if autistic people don't count as people and are excluded from the conversation about what kind of support they need to thrive.

The History of Autism as Deficit

Autism as a classification didn't exist until Dr. Eugen Bleuler, a Swiss psychiatrist, coined the term in 1911.[12] Autism is a social construction; a label people have given meaning. While we can't say definitively who throughout history counts as autistic, children thought to have been replaced with changelings[13] or aliens[14] or possessed by demons[15] in stories demonstrate autistic traits.

Bleuler's understanding of autism was drastically different from today's. He also coined the term "schizophrenia" and viewed autism as a symptom of the most severe cases of schizophrenia in children.[16] He described autism as the infantile wish to avoid reality through hallucinations and fantasies. Bleuler's work was in conversation with the work of colleagues, such as Sigmund Freud's autoeroticism, for its focus on self, and Pierre Janet's perte de la fonction du réel. All three psychology theorists hypothesized around the experience of those who seem to be *not there*—people they couldn't understand, who may act differently or engage in different forms of communication, who they defined as having a psychosis.

Discussion on children's mental health and development blossomed as a field. Austrian American psychiatrist Leo Kanner[17] was notable for defining autism not as a subtype of schizophrenia but as a disorder that impacts communication and social skills, with repetitive habits that come with dislike of change. He is also credited with being an early proponent of the biological basis of autism; he perpetuated the notion that lack of maternal warmth is to blame for autism. Some of Kanner's work was refined by psychoanalyst Bruno Bettelheim[18] and his concept of "refrigerator mothers," which built on hypotheses that autism is caused by absent mothers who do not care enough for their children. This theory has, thankfully, been debunked, but it has had negative effects on autism communities that persist to this day.[19] The theory defines autism as a problem and blames mothers for it.

This paper responds most to British clinical psychologist Simon Baron-Cohen's theorization that autistic people have an empathy deficit.[20] His concept of mind-blindness, in his own words, is meant "to describe the circumscribed nature of the cognitive deficit in autism, and to emphasize the gulf that I imagine must exist between these children and the access people without autism naturally have to other people's minds."[21]

This definition, while an interesting view into Baron-Cohen's thought process, doesn't encapsulate the whole definition of mind-blindness. I turned to the American Psychological Association's dictionary of psychology for a more succinct definition: "a deficit in theory of mind that is characteristic of people with autism. A person with mindblindness cannot 'read the minds' of others—that is, understand their behavior in terms of belief–desire reasoning. This definition builds on the theory that autistic people are so focused on their own inner world that they have trouble imagining another person's experiences as different from their own."[22]

The ability to imagine how someone else might think or believe differently from oneself forms the basis of empathy (the ability to relate to what another person is feeling). If someone can't fathom that another person could feel differently from themselves, they experience a deficit in empathy.

This definition of empathy and its association with autism is at the crux of a disagreement between autistic people and those who have the empathy to fathom and act on autistic experiences.[23] If Baron-Cohen can't fathom asking autistic people to confirm whether what he imagines about them is true, and if he can't fathom that autistic people may disagree with the career he's built on imagining what it's like to be autistic, perhaps he suffers from an empathy deficit.

As a result of this genealogy of autism experts, autism is constructed as a thing that kidnaps or traps children and locks them away in their minds.[24] This notion was popularized in Bettelheim's famous book *The Empty Fortress: Infantile Autism and the Birth of Self.*[25] Autism is framed as a tragedy that brings suffering to families, and an epidemic with alarmingly high rates.[26] The exact number of autistic people in existence changes depending on the study, but one study says one in sixty-eight in America.[27] This terrifying picture of autism has led to funding for research to find better treatment, prevention, or a cure.[28]

The tragic construction of autism has also led to pseudoscientific claims that autism can be caused by mercury in vaccines, contaminated water, gluten, and many other things. Autism cures with no scientific support that may cause significant harm or death to a child are peddled to misinformed parents.[29] These alleged cures remain unregulated and allowed in countries like Canada despite lack of peer-reviewed scientific support.

From the narrative of autism trapping a child in their mind to defining people as children lacking empathy and social skills, blaming mothers for giving birth to autistic children, and associating autism with suffering and epidemics to misinformation campaigns and profiting off of misinformed families without consequences, the discourse surrounding autism is grim. It is understandable that people believe autism needs to be fought and defeated; that there is a war with autism.[30] All of this points, once again, to lack of understanding and empathy toward autistic people.

A Brief History of Parent-Led Autism Advocacy

McGuire[31] discusses that autism advocacy was first observed in 1962 in the United Kingdom. Parents formed a group called the Autistic Children's Aid Society of North London, later renamed the National Autistic Society. Cold mothers as the cause of autism was a popular discourse at the time. Kanner's works throughout the forties and fifties built on cold mothers causing autism five years before Bettelheim coined the term "refrigerator mothers." Thus, activism by mothers of autistic children carried an undercurrent of having to be "good mothers" or else the specter of autism would take their child as if it were a changeling. These activist mothers raised awareness of autism as a disorder and demanded support from the British government. While fathers and other allies were part of the activist work, Bettelheim's work specifically targeted mothers, which may have motivated more mothers to campaign and rally for autism services.[32]

These activists chose to symbolize autism with a puzzle piece. Hellen Allison, the founder of National Autistic Society, said, "Our children are handicapped by a puzzling condition; this isolates them from normal human contact and therefore they do not 'fit in.' The suggestion of a weeping child [emblazoned on their puzzle piece logo] is a reminder that autistic people do indeed suffer from their handicap."[33]

Through decades of activism, parents, especially mother activists across the Global North, have fought for better conditions for their children. They have advocated for inclusion in schools, access to services and treatments, policy and legal rights, and the breaking down of institutionalization and stigma.[34] In the tireless work of parent activists, therapies such as Floor Time, Sensory Integration Therapy, TEACCH, and Applied Behavior Analysis (ABA) have been tried and evaluated.

Out of these therapies, ABA has become the most popular; the self-proclaimed "gold standard" of autism treatment. ABA was developed by Ole Ivar Lovaas using behaviorist methods to change an autistic child's behavior to better conform to normative social expectations. ABA was popularlized by Bernard Rimland, a research psychologist, autism parent, and cofounder of the Autism Society of America (ASA) in 1965. It was Rimland's tireless work introducing Lovaas to other autism parents that made Lovaas' controversial treatments wildly popular. This method requires twenty to forty hours a week of intensive training for years for results to be seen and stick.[35] With the amount of resources needed to use this therapy, cost is very high for children who undergo it, families that need to integrate ABA appointments into their lives, and governments and families who pay for services.

Despite the high cost of ABA for everyone except practitioners, its marketing as the gold standard has made it the go-to service many parents lobby governments for more access to.[36] This activism comes into conflict with the experiences of autistic activists and is a central conflict between autistic, parent, and service provider interest groups. If more neurotypical parents internalized how and why ABA has historically harmed autistic people who might be their children, if neurotypicals in charge of autism communities and services valued feedback from the people they claim to serve, perhaps we could have a conversation about what actually helps autistic people thrive. Very recent, unpublished work I had the privy to read demonstrates that there are some ABA practitioners who are reflexive and making changes from within institutions to address the harms and ineffectiveness of ABA as designed by Lovaas. I cannot comment on if the changes are effective at this time, but I'm willing to be in community with service providers that respond to feedback from autistic people, from other social minority needs, value consent and bodily autonomy, and see themselves as a tool to address specific needs.

Autistic Activism and Self-Advocacy

Alongside the growing culture of autism[37] were autistic people themselves. Despite the best efforts of parents and professionals to fight and eradicate autism, autistic children grew into autistic adults. In the 1990s, autistics who had grown up with diagnoses of autism in the 1970s and 1980s came of age. Joining their ranks were parents and adults who had discovered they too were autistic, often after their child's diagnosis.[38] As adults, they talked about autism and made community to discuss their experiences of treatment, sometimes in conversation with parents, service providers, and each other. These discussions led to a greater understanding and acceptance of autism as a part of someone and not a disease to be eradicated.

Some autistic communities joined up with the greater disability rights movement, as had some autism communities. The fight for self-determination, self-advocacy, acceptance, disability pride, and the social model of disability over the medical model became part of autistic thought.[39] Concepts such as neurodiversity[40] and neurodivergence[41] sprang up within autistic communities.

Neurodivergence and neurodiversity normalize all the different ways minds exist in the world instead of pathologizing them or associating their existence with suffering. Common autistic behaviors such as stimming, limited diets, sensory needs, specialized interests, eye contact aversion, direct conversations with different social cues, and echolalia were normalized and understood as coping mechanisms instead of undesirable traits to be trained out of autistic people.[42]

The narrative of autism as a disease, an epidemic, was incompatible with autistic people who accepted themselves as autistic. Decades of activism for services and support by parents were suddenly being questioned by the very people parents had been advocating on behalf of.[43]

Since ABA is the primary service funded for autistic people in Canada and America, much conflict surrounds its services. The goals of ABA still are in conflict with the neurodiversity and neurodivergence movements. Teaching compliance, even without electroshock[44] and other forms of negative reinforcement, doesn't teach life skills like independence, emotional and sensory self-regulation, or consent.[45] Furthermore, under the pretext of early intervention, autism services are only geared to young children, as invoked by the Ontario Autism Coalition's (OAC) 2018 campaign, "Autism Doesn't End at Five."[46] Lack of support for autistic people outside of a narrow band of "intervention" demonstrates how limited the scope of support is.

Another growing criticism of ABA is its association with the conversion therapy inflicted on queer and trans people. Ivor Lovaas, the man who designed ABA, was principal investigator for the Feminine Boy Project, the method that formed the basis of conversion therapy. The methods of ABA are based on Lovaas's methods for conversion therapy.[47] In Canada, conversion therapy has been a criminal act since December 8, 2021.[48] Yet the bill criminalizing conversion therapy for queer and trans people doesn't extend to autistic people, despite Lovaas having designed both methods.[49]

A number of studies by external researchers have evaluated the efficacy of ABA and brought up possible issues of evidence-based effectiveness and conflicts of interest in research done by ABA researchers, including failure to report adverse reactions, detection bias, lack of random control trials, and bioethical concerns.[50] Multiple books by autistics have disclosed negative and abusive experiences with ABA.[51] Despite evidence that questions ABA's efficacy and documentation of abuse, there is pushback from parents of autistic people when it comes to ABA.[52] It is still funded in Canada over other services and hasn't been criminalized.

The sheer mental gymnastics and intentional ignorance needed to turn away from mounting evidence is mind-boggling. If autistic adults were listened to as integral parts of designing autism services, research, and parenting, how would the landscape of autism change?

The issue is much more complex than what I've presented. In a non–peer reviewed quantitative study done by an autistic advocate and blogger, 5.19 percent of autistic respondents (N = 3,431) agreed or strongly agreed that they support ABA for autistic children.[53] Granted, the study was small and lacked random control trials, but it does demonstrate that there are diverse opinions in autistic communities. Experiences with services also vary for neurotypical parents and family members who work with autistic activists and parents who want what's best for their children. ABA service providers may use other modalities in their work in order to be intelligible to funding bodies until recently, only paid for ABA. The point is, enough parents, service providers, and researchers have demonstrated that they're not affected by autistic people's actual suffering and that they are a barrier to making support for autistic children and adults possible.

Regardless of perspective on autism, both neurotypical parents and autistic people (including those who are parents themselves) desire autistic and family services, inclusion in education, destigmatization, and a good quality of life. I ask and advocate for more mutual understanding and empathy so autistic people and their families can have basic human rights to self-determination and bodily autonomy and, hopefully, thrive. I want everyone to have good health, full bellies, and contentment with their lives.

The Case for Bodily Autonomy and Informed Consent

The first issue I'm advocating is for people to respect other's fundamental human right to bodily autonomy. This means that anyone, including a child, disabled person, or elder, is allowed to make decisions about what happens to their body, including how their body is touched and interacted with and where their body goes. Bjorn Andersson, the UNFPA Asia-Pacific Regional director, defines bodily autonomy as "the power to make our own choices about our own bodies."[54]

Everyone should have the right to make decisions about their body, including autistic people and autistic children. Of course, children can't legally give consent, but adults have the responsibility to not traumatize children. When a child says no, we should respect that. Even if we think it is in their best interests, we need to respect another person's no. But a no doesn't have to be the end of the discussion.

In order to get to a place where we can ask for consent, we need to give people, including children, information about possible consequences and choices—including ones we may not like—in language and methods they can comprehend. We need to offer informed consent or at least informed assent.

The Belmont Report defines informed consent as follows: "respect for persons requires that subjects, to the degree that they are capable, be given the opportunity to choose what shall or shall not happen to them."[55] While this definition is used for research, I argue that informed consent should be offered whenever an interpersonal decision that directly impacts another's bodily autonomy and self-determination is being made, from asking children if they want to give relatives a kiss to including elderly people in nursing homes in discussions about their health.

There are challenges to this broad argument. Many people can't give consent under law, but we should always offer in good faith to at least get assent. Many people—children, people with certain kinds of disabilities, those in institutions, those whose mental capacities are reduced either permanently or temporarily—are considered vulnerable, and care needs to be taken to ensure we don't coerce or exploit them. At the same time, we shouldn't infantilize them. We should make reasonable efforts to ensure informed consent is negotiated in matters involving another person.

Instead of blanket dismissal of vulnerable peoples' ability to consent, Patterson and Block advocate for focusing on capacity to consent and power to resist manipulation.[56] Even after they are assessed for capacity to consent and resist manipulation, some people will be unable to consent or even assent. In those cases, avoid the thing that requires informed consent, or if it's unavoidable, be mindful of possible harm, pay attention to nonverbal cues for no, and try to do the least harm.

We must be aware and grapple with the role of those who make decisions on behalf of people who can't legally give consent. Parents have the ability to gatekeep or override a child's wishes. At the same time, parents are well-positioned to be their child's best advocate.[57]

As described in a 2016 news story, a mother named Jennifer reported child abuse from an in-home ABA service provider. She noticed that something was off with her son: "Usually, Adam would greet Jennifer excitedly at the door when she arrived home from work. That September day, he stood with his head bowed, clutching his stomach."[58] It alerted her that something was not quite right. She installed a hidden camera and through it found out that the service provider was abusing her son. Through multiple instances of sudden behavior changes, Jennifer was able to successfully identify that something was wrong and get her son out of the situation and with another provider where he was reportedly happy.

The UN Convention on Rights of a Child[59] makes no explicit mention about giving children the right to informed consent and/or bodily autonomy. It asserts the right for children to be alive, to not be sex trafficked, to not become child soldiers, and many more; however, the way these rights are framed does not offer children the right to knowledge to make decisions about their body and life.

The fact that we need a document detailing the rights of a child in the first place indicates that there is a problem with adults exploiting children. For good or ill, parents and caregivers are the ones expected to make decisions on behalf of children. If a parent refuses to support a child's choices, such as if they want to get vaccinated and the parent is antivax, the child has little recourse because such actions aren't considered abuse. The child can either choose to endure their parent's decisions until they're the age of majority or try and do as they wish covertly. Either way, the parent's decision on behalf of their child is seen as more legally valid. Sharing knowledge, reasoning, wisdom, and power to develop consent capacity is not an inherent right for children or responsibility for parents; it is a luxury. How children and vulnerable people are treated demonstrates lack of empathy and understanding that they are individuals with their own needs and desires.

My Experiences with Bodily Autonomy and Informed Consent

I may not have gone through ABA or grown up in autism communities, but I was born with a minor physical disability and had my bodily autonomy steamrolled. My problems began when I was born—not because my disability brought me suffering but because of how adults in my life decided to treat me. My mother's first words to me weren't of love but that she wished she'd listened to her mother and never married my dad. Apparently, it was my dad's fault that I was born with an uncommon condition called microtia, which meant my right ear and outer ear canal hadn't formed fully. The doctors advised that I get plastic surgery so my physical disability wouldn't be noticeable and I could live like a "normal" child. In the first few years of my life, I went under the knife and had a skin graft taken from a thigh and rib cartilage, leaving scars on my body before I was even cognizant of the world.

The first important crossroads in my life happened when my dad asked me if I wanted to have more surgeries at the age of four. Before he could say what would happen and why, I began screaming and attacking anything in sight because my body remembered the trauma of surgery even if my conscious mind didn't. To this day, I don't know why I developed medical trauma. I'm still working it out of my system. The difference now is that I can interrupt and catch my reactions before I reach panic. No further surgeries happened, and my dad argued with everyone that it was my choice when and whether that surgery would happen.

I'm forever grateful I was given that choice. I only found out a few years ago that the doctor who performed my surgery performed it incorrectly and too early. Standard practice would have been to wait until I was six, grown enough to understand what was happening and be physically big enough for surgery results to look "normal." He also didn't make an earhole during the first surgery, as is standard procedure. By not having another surgery, I was spared further medical misconduct.

I don't blame my parents for the decisions they made. The information they were presented with did not allow them to make an informed choice. They weren't presented with more than one surgeon, and the surgery was couched in terms as if it would help prevent me from being bullied. I wish my parents had understood, like Jennifer did, that a child who is fearful, who screams and attacks, is not okay and needs support.

If everyone had waited a few years and I had been given the *gift* of informed choice, if the doctors had given me information about why they were recommending surgery, what it would entail, and what would happen afterward, maybe I wouldn't have ended up needing ten years of therapy to work through what happened.

Maybe I'd have decided I didn't want rib cartilage and a skin graft taken to have a fairly cosmetic surgery. I am grateful my dad actually thought to ask me if I wanted surgery, but I wish he had found a way to delay when the surgery would be done. My disability didn't put me at risk for dying, but surgery did. With the risks of surgery weighed against my quality of life as a healthy disabled child, my parents could have decided to leave my body alone until I was ready to choose what I wanted to do with it. I grieve for the child I could have been. Did the doctors anticipate that children would pick on me anyway because I had Frankensteinish scars?

I grew up hating my body because I was told there was something wrong with it that needed to be fixed by the adults in my life. I hated my body more because of the scars made by a doctor who had the caucacity[60] to believe that plastic surgery was preferable to a physical disability. I don't have any memory of the surgeries themselves, but they left scars deep on my subconscious. I'd panic at the mention of seeing a doctor and meltdown if I had to see one. No one named my experience as medical trauma or addressed *why* I had it. It was not until I began seeing a therapist as a teen that I began healing. I only saw a therapist because a teacher finally recognized my cries for help and sent me to guidance instead of to the principal.

I blame the cultural belief that disabled people aren't worthy of the basic human right of making informed decisions about their own body. There was nothing wrong with my body. Sure, I didn't have as much hearing as other children, but there was nothing wrong with me. I could have been given the choice of whether I wanted better hearing or a more normative body. I could have been encouraged to use the hearing aid that lived in my mother's closet.

Due to the unrecognized trauma, I didn't have access to much health care. I was treated for colds and flus by my laolao, my maternal grandma who had been a doctor in China. But I couldn't get vaccines or see a dentist, and I was very lucky to have had a stellar emergency doctor who managed to deescalate me enough to set my broken wrist.

No one noticed I was autistic for my entire childhood because much of my autism was explained away by my being a kid who had survived a major car crash and reacted badly to doctors; living in a single mother plus grandparents immigrant household where adults were busy trying to juggle poverty, racism, and cultural/language barriers; experiencing abuse because my mother and grandparents didn't have good coping mechanisms; and, despite all of this, being a bright, chatty, obedient child who loved reading and learning new things.

All of my traumas probably could have been avoided if adults had had more empathy for someone with a different body from their own and if I had been given the support I needed to make my own choice about my body. Even more of the issues in my life could have been avoided if my mother and grandparents had had better access to community and resources and had not faced discrimination.

The Importance and Complexity of Communities

Communities are important spaces for people to develop interdependent relationships with others with shared identities and experiences. Queer and trans communities have played an integral role in shaping who I am today. Without the support they provided me, especially when I was younger, I doubt I'd be alive or have reached a spot where my autism could be recognized. They continued to be my central communities even after I went looking for autistic communities because of the lack of support I found with autism communities.

My autism was recognized by a psychiatrist when I was twenty-three. For that reason, some neurotypical parents say that my perspective on autism is invalid because I'm "not like their child."[61] Having to respond defensively to people who should be part of my community, who could have been my mentors, demonstrates how negative my experiences have been. Regardless, I won't deny that I'm unlike their child because I'm not their child.

Their point is used to try and invalidate my arguments and feelings because of the assumption that I have what they call "higher functioning" autism. Other people have already laid out this argument here in this endnote.[62] I'm verbose and intelligent, and they see me act in ways they consider normal. In contrast, their child may be nonverbal, seem behind in childhood milestones, and behave in ways that are more destructive.

I agree that I'm not like their child. I don't have the same desires, the same lived experiences or dreams as their child. But I am still an autistic person, or else I wouldn't have received a formal diagnosis. There is a reason I received a formal diagnosis. My life experiences may differ from their child's, but that doesn't mean that my views are inherently invalid.

Instead of having my autism recognized as a child, I was labeled "gifted" and streamed into that program. I remember my mother once saying that she had had to fight the school about putting me in special ed, and she reminded me that I was lucky to be in the gifted class instead. I was in a strange limbo place of "You're special ed, but not THAT special ed. You're the smart kind."

The gifted program put me in a complex spot. On the one hand, I was getting age-appropriate schoolwork and, sometimes, more advanced work. On the other hand, my education was very hands off and didn't identify deficits or strengths or support me in becoming the best learner I could be. So yes, I may not have the same experiences as an autistic child, but I could still pass on valuable lessons that aren't being listened to.

My most important educators were my therapist and the queer social workers my therapist referred me to. My therapist unraveled considerable trauma and gave me language to talk about my experiences. She challenged my unhealthy behaviors and gave me space to be weird without judgment because she was an outcast when she was younger. I had a safe space to name myself as queer and leave the door open to being trans. She was transparent about what she was doing with me and had good boundaries around what she could and couldn't do.

Queer social workers created safer spaces in the form of youth groups, and they believed in me and who I could be. They introduced me to healthy relationships and consent, histories of queer and trans activism, comprehensive sexual health education, and queer and trans histories of our city. They brought me to learn new skills, like public speaking, research, activism, event planning, group facilitation, organizational management, networking, solidarity building, intersectional thought, and so much more. They cheered me on when I got into university and introduced me to people in the city I was moving to. They took on the role of parents and mentors I had never had because my family wasn't shaping me for the better.

Thanks to the spaces my queer social worker mentors created, I had friends for the first time in my life. I had a network of people to care for and support me; space to learn, grow, and make mistakes; and people who believed in what I could bring to the table and what I could bring to the table in the future with more guidance. As a teen in the queer community surrounded by friends, mentors, peers, and allies, I felt valued and safe for the first time in my life.

In contrast, as a twenty-three-year-old queer and trans adult with shiny, new autism recognition, I found an autism community devoid of transparency, care, and support. While I had been given refuge, space to grow, and mentorship in queer and trans communities, there was nothing at the time to support an autistic adult outside of private therapists. I lacked the generational wealth to afford support. I met a few autistics in my classes, but they didn't have the social justice, community care–oriented perspective I had developed in queer and trans communities. All I learned from them can be summed up as "ABA bad, Temple Grandin good." A centralized community was missing, and it meant that I lacked ways to manage the systemic barriers I faced due to this new label of autism. All I had were the queer and trans communities I had made for myself.

The leaders of the community (if you can call it a community) I met were parents of autistic people, which I found very strange. In queer and trans communities, leaders were queer and trans, and they imparted wisdom of their experiences on how to cope with a world not designed for us to thrive in. The autism parents I met felt like there was something "off" about them. They didn't talk about intersectionality, human rights, or justice; have any understanding of antioppressive values; or think communally. They were all middle-class, white, cisgender, heterosexual people without named disabilities. Even with some parents more critical of autism discourse, they never thought to draw me into their circle, yet they were willing to draw in many nonautistic white people. It was like interacting with parents of queer and trans folks who don't support their children or want to associate with any queer/trans folks. Later, I met a few of their kids, who were now adults who had experienced homelessness just to get away from their parents.

It wasn't until I found autistic communities online that I found a sense of belonging. There was such a difference between communities of all autistic people versus the parents of autistic people. It felt like the difference between talking with queer and trans folks and the parents of queer and trans folks. Having autistic space meant that there were people with similar experiences to mine and strategies to manage the issues in my life. There was an *understanding* of what it meant to be different even if there were major conflicts within communities. People just got it if someone was having a bad brain day, didn't engage in small talk, communicated in memes, or had intolerances for certain smells, textures, tastes, or sounds. There was also a vein of critical consciousness raising that looked at our collective issues and saw systemic problems, like the cultural association of autism with a lack of qualities that make someone human. It turned out that many autistics are also queer/trans[63] and had gained some of the same knowledge and support I was given as a teen.

I was lucky enough to find a huge group of BIPOC (Black, Indigenous, people of color) autistics who also talked about what it was like being both nonwhite and autistic. All these autistic communities I found felt familiar with their interest in changing the world so people like us can live better lives.

The only thing my autistic communities lacked were community elders who could speak to how things were in their day. There were few people to pass on histories and wisdom to us, and there were no centralized community spaces where newly recognized people could get oriented. Autistic communities are a lot younger than queer and trans communities. While doing research for my PhD, I read that autistic communities only began surfacing in the 80s and 90s,[64] while queer and trans communities have been around for much longer. Community elders pass on wisdom and insight on how far things have come to the new generation. With the lack of autistic elders at this time, I have to look to other communities, make guesses based on parallels, and triangulate what the future may look like in the fight for body autonomy and better understanding of consent.

As I've emphasized repeatedly, I want people to have good lives, thrive, and be heard. I want empathy to be a valued trait in humans so people don't need to keep talking about fundamental human rights to such simple things as your own body. I found empathetic people through queer and trans communities and not autism parent communities. Good support begins with believing in people's experiences and skills as always in progress. Good support looks like passing on and sharing knowledge and wisdom and helping each other become better people.

A Modest Proposal

While I could try and satirize eating autistic babies, I'm done playing around. To emphasize my seriousness, I'm leaning into my autisticness and speaking plainly.

Can we please value empathy as a species and raise children to care about how they interface with other beings? Can we please respect basic human rights like bodily autonomy and informed consent? Can we please make good faith efforts to actually have a world where people don't starve to death, where we aren't under threat of nuclear winter (again) or global warming (again)? Can we please put an end to greed, lying, oppression, murder, neglect, bad faith actions?

We need rights and laws to protect people BECAUSE there are people who cause harm and we have to try and deter/prevent more harm. We have words like "consent" and "bodily autonomy" BECAUSE sexual violence, coercion, manifest destiny, and autocratic decision makers exist and need to be curtailed. If we lived in a world where people had the empathy to understand and respect basic human rights, we wouldn't need to protect them in the first place.

Throughout this paper, I've focused on how neurotypical people demonstrate a lack of empathy toward autistic people. Yet it is autistic people who are labeled as having clinically significant deficits in empathy. I argue that neurotypical people need to reflect a lot more on who they consider unworthy of human rights and the ways they dehumanize Others like autistics. When schools are built without wheelchairs in mind in this day and age, school designers demonstrate that they can't relate to the needs of a wheelchair user. When a white autistic guy thinks his interest in trains is universally autistic culture and same-food staples are chicken nuggets and pop, he hasn't considered how other populations of autistics may have different interests and like different foods.

I don't deny that many autistics have gaps or had empathy trained out of them through compliance methods. But empathy can be taught, and empathy deficits aren't just something autistic people experience. When neurotypicals and autistic people interface (as with any populations who have different social locations), there likely is a communication gap, a double empathy problem. Autistic and neurotypical people may have trouble understanding each other's perspectives and feelings. Neither autistic nor neurotypical people can claim to intrinsically have empathy or an empathy deficit. There are autistic people who have as much empathy as a Wall Street corporate lawyer and neurotypical people with the heart of Guan Yin. It is harmful to characterize only autistic people as having an empathy deficit.

I propose framing the solution using the Platinum Rule—treat others how they want to be treated. It should be common practice to ask people how and whether they want to be touched, how they want to be interacted with, and to respect when they say no. Everyone, especially decision makers, should practice this value, this framework. When we ask people what they want or need, when we ask for permission, when we integrate all relevant parties in our actions, we offer them the dignity, respect, and care they deserve as human beings. This is a gross oversimplification, but it is at least a start.

I'm not asking for anything radical. Don't kill. Don't force people to do things. Talk it out. Don't touch people without consent—and that includes kisses and hugs from relatives. Explain things so people can understand the world better and make their own conclusions.

This is beyond the scope of this paper, but when it comes to power structures that deprioritize empathy for Others, I wonder who benefits from not giving power and knowledge to children and marginalized folks. What would happen if children and other marginalized folks were given the forbidden fruits of critical thinking, capacity building, institutional knowledge, and leadership skills?

If any of these suggestions raise hackles in you, perhaps you're the one with an empathy deficit after all, dear reader.

NOTES

1. bell hooks, *Black Looks: Race and Representation* (New York: Routledge, 2015).

2. Jim Sinclair, "Self-Narrating Zoo Exhibit," Everything2, December 20, 2002, https://www.everything2.com/index.pl?node_id=1404508.

3. In this paper, I use "nonautistic" and "neurotypical" intentionally. I choose to emphasize neurotype or lack of autism.

4. Simon Baron-Cohen, "Autism: The Empathizing–Systemizing (E-S) Theory," *Annals of the New York Academy of Sciences* 1156, no. 1 (March 2009): 68–80, https://doi.org/10.1111/j.1749-6632.2009.04467.x.

5. Sara H. Konrath, Edward H. O'Brien, and Courtney Hsing, "Changes in Dispositional Empathy in American College Students over Time: A Meta-analysis," *Personality and Social Psychology Review* 15, no. 2 (May 2011): 180–98, https://doi.org/10.1177/1088868310377395.

6. Alexander G. Weheliye, *Habeas Viscus: Racializing Assemblages, Biopolitics, and Black Feminist Theories of the Human* (Durham, NC: Duke University Press, 2014).

7. Damian E. M. Milton, "On the Ontological Status of Autism: The 'Double Empathy Problem,'" *Disability & Society* 27, no. 6 (October 2012): 883–87, https://doi.org/10.1080/09687599.2012.710008.

8. Bridget Liang, "Divided Communities and Absent Voices: The Search for Autistic BIPOC Parent Blogs," *Studies in Social Justice* 16, no. 2 (March 11, 2022): 447–69, https://doi.org/10.26522/ssj.v16i2.3407.

9. American Psychiatric Association, *Diagnostic and Statistical Manual of Mental Disorders 5th edition* (Arlington: American Psychiatric Association, 2013).

10. Thin Nguyen, Thi Duong, Svetha Venkatesh, and Dinh Phung, "Autism Blogs: Expressed Emotion, Language Styles and Concerns in Personal and Community Settings," *IEEE Transactions on Affective Computing* 6, no. 3 (July–September 2015): 312–23, https://doi.org/10.1109/TAFFC.2015.2400912.

11. "About Autism," Autistic Self Advocacy Network, accessed December 12, 2023, https://autisticadvocacy.org/about-asan/about-autism/.

12. Allison C. Carey, Pamela Block, and Richard K. Scotch, *Allies and Obstacles: Disability Activism and Parents of Children with Disabilities* (Philadelphia: Temple University Press, 2020).

13. Julie Leask, A. Leask, and Natalie Silove, "Evidence for Autism in Folklore?" *Archives of Disease in Childhood* 90, no. 3 (March 2005): 271, https://doi.org/10.1136/adc.2003.044958.

14. Ian Hacking, "Humans, Aliens & Qutism," *Daedalus* 138, no. 3 (Summer 2009): 44–59, https://doi.org/10.1162/daed.2009.138.3.44.

15. Patricia Ranft, "Ruminations on Hildegard of Bingen (1098–1179) and Autism," *Journal of Medical Biography* 22, no. 2 (May 2014): 107–15, https://doi.org/10.1177/0967772013479283.

16. Bonnie Evans, "How Autism Became Autism: The Radical Transformation of a Central Concept of Child Development in Britain," *History of Human Sciences* 26, no. 3 (July 2013): 3–31, https://doi.org/10.1177/0952695113484320.

17. Marina Heifetz, "Autism Spectrum Disorder (ASD) in Canada," Canadian Encyclopedia, June 4, 2018, https://www.thecanadianencyclopedia.ca/en/article/autism-spectrum-disorder-asd-in-canada.

18. Bruno Bettelheim, *Empty Fortress: Infantile Autism and the Birth of the Self* (Glencoe: Free Press, 1967).

19. Carey, Block, and Scotch, *Allies and Obstacles*; Steven K. Kapp, ed., *Autistic Community and the Neurodiversity Movement Stories from the Frontline* (London: Palgrave Macmillan, 2020); Anne McGuire, *War on Autism: On the Cultural Logic of Normative Violence* (Ann Arbor: University of Michigan Press, 2016).

20. Simon Baron-Cohen, *Mind-Blindness: An Essay on Autism and Theory of Mind* (Cambridge: MIT Press, 1995). In the first chapter of his book, he writes in depth about mind-blindness and how he cannot fathom what it is like to be mind-blind. But he does not follow this point up by asking if/how autistic people experience mind-blindness.

21. Simon Baron-Cohen, "Autism: A Specific Cognitive Disorder of 'Mind-Blindness,'" *International Review of Psychiatry* 2, no. 1 (1990): 81–90, https://doi.org/10.3109/09540269009028274. This is the definition Baron-Cohen refers to in his book on mind-blindness. Since his definition is not very clear, I had to resort to the APA dictionary to get a more accurate definition of his own word.

22. "Mindblindness," APA Dictionary of Psychology, American Psychological Association, n.d., accessed December 16, 2023, https://dictionary.apa.org/mindblindness.

23. McGuire, *War on Autism*; Milton "On the Ontological Status of Autism," 883–87; Christie Welch, Deb Cameron, Margaret Fitch, and Helene Polatajko, "From 'Since' to 'If': Using Blogs to Explore an Insider-Informed Framing of Autism," *Disability & Society* 37, no. 4 (2022): 638–61, https://doi.org/10.1080/09687599.2020.1836479; Melanie Remi Yergeau, *Authoring Autism: On Rhetoric and Neurological Queerness* (Durham, NC: Duke University Press, 2017).

24. Beth A. Haller, *Representing Disability in an Ableist World: Essays on Mass Media* (Haller: Avocado Press, 2010); McGuire, *War on Autism*.

25. Bettelheim, *Empty Fortress*; Ellen Herman, "The Autism History Project," Autism History Project, 2019, https://blogs.uoregon.edu/autismhistoryproject/.

26. McGuire, *War on Autism*.

27. Amit Saha and Nitin Agarwal, "Modeling Social Support in Autism Community on Social Media," *Network Modeling Analysis in Health Informatics and Bioinformatics* 5, no. 8 (2016), https://doi.org/10.1007/s13721-016-0115-8.

28. Carey, Block, and Scotch, *Allies and Obstacles*.

29. Anne B. King, "Submission to the CAHS Autism Assessment Panel," Autistics4Autistics Ontario, May 20, 2021, https://a4aontario.com/wp-content/uploads/2021/05/2021_CAHS_Campaign_Against-Phony_Autism_Cures.pdf; "Treatments That Are Not

Recommended for Autism," National Health Service, accessed December 16, 2023, https:// www.nhs.uk/conditions/autism/autism-and-everyday-life/treatments-that-are-not-rec ommended-for-autism/; McGuire, *War on Autism*.

30. McGuire, *War on Autism*.

31. Ibid.

32. Carey, Block, and Scotch, *Allies and Obstacles*; Eric Garcia, "I'm Not Broken: What This Washington Reporter with Autism Wants You to Understand," *The Atlantic*, December 4, 2015, https://www.theatlantic.com/politics/archive/2015/12/im-not-broken/44 6550/; McGuire, *War on Autism*.

33. "1963. First NAS Logo Developed," National Autistic Society, n.d., accessed December 16, 2023, http://www.tiki-toki.com/timeline/entry/21729/Our-story-so-far/#vars !panel=193670.

34. Carey, Block, and Scotch, *Allies and Obstacles*.

35. Ibid.

36. McGuire, *War on Autism*.

37. Kapp, *Autistic Community*; McGuire, *War on Autism*.

38. Carey, Block, and Scotch, *Allies and Obstacles*; Kapp, *Autistic Community*; McGuire, *War on Autism*.

39. Carey, Block, and Scotch, *Allies and Obstacles*; Kapp, *Autistic Community*; McGuire, *War on Autism*.

40. Cara *Liebowitz,* "Here's What Neurodiversity Is—And What It Means for Feminism," Everyday Feminism, March 4, 2016, https://everydayfeminism.com/2016/03/neu rodiversity-101/.

41. Kassiane Asasumasu, "Radical Neurodivergence Speaking," *Radical Neurodivergence Speaking* (blog), https://timetolisten.blogspot.com/.

42. Kapp, *Autistic Community*.

43. Susan Abel, Tanya Machin, and Charlotte Brownlow, "Support, Socialise and Advocate: An Exploration of the Stated Purposes of Facebook Autism Groups," *Research in Autism Spectrum Disorders* 61 (May 2019): 10–21; Carey, Block, and Scotch, *Allies and Obstacles*; Kapp, *Autistic Community*; McGuire, *War on Autism*; Welch, Cameron, Fitch, and Polatajko, "From 'Since' to 'If,'" 638–61.

44. "#StoptheShock," Autistic Self Advocacy Network, 2023, https://autisticadvocacy .org/stoptheshock/.

45. Aileen Herlinda Sandoval-Norton, Gary Shkedy, and Dalia Shkedy, "How Much Compliance Is Too Much Compliance: Is Long-Term ABA Therapy Abuse?" *Cogent Psychology* 6, no. 1 (2019): 1–8, https://doi.org/10.1080/23311908.2019.1641258; Owen McGill and Anna Robinson, "'Recalling Hidden Harms': Autistic Experiences of Childhood Applied Behavioural Analysis (ABA)," *Advances in Autism* 7, no. 4 (October 2021): 269–82, https://doi.org/10.1108/AIA-04-2020-0025.

46. Canadian Press, "Parents of Children with Autism Skeptical of Ford Funding Promise," *CTV News*, June 6, 208, https://www.ctvnews.ca/canada/parents-of-children-with -autism-skeptical-of-ford-funding-promise-1.3961832.

47. Julia Gruson-Wood, "'I'm a Juggling Robot': An Ethnography of the Organization and Culture of Autism-Based Applied Behaviour Therapies in Ontario, Canada" (PhD diss., York University, 2018), 220, https://yorkspace.library.yorku.ca/xmlui/bitstream/handle /10315/35587/Gruson-Wood_Julia_F_2018_PhD.pdf; McGuire, *War on Autism*; Jake Pyne, "'Building a Person': Legal and Clinical Personhood for Autistic and Trans Children in Ontario," *Canadian Journal of Law and Society / Revue Canadienne Droit Et Société* 35, no. 2 (August 2020): 341–65, https://doi.org/10.1017/cls.2020.8; Yergeau, *Authoring Autism*.

48. Bill C-4, An Act to Amend the Criminal Code (Conversion Therapy), 1st session, 44th Parliament (2021), https://www.parl.ca/DocumentViewer/en/44-1/bill/C-4/royal-assent.

49. Pyne, "Building a Person," 341–65.

50. King, "Submission to the CAHS Autism Assessment Panel."

51. Julia Bascom, *Loud Hands: Autistic People, Speaking* (Washington: Autistic Press, 2012); John Elder Robinson, *Look Me in the Eye: My Life with Asperger's* (New York: Random House, 2017).

52. Carey, Block, and Scotch, *Allies and Obstacles*; McGuire, *War on Autism*; Welch, Cameron, Fitch, and Polatajko, "From 'Since' to 'If,'" 638–61; Yergeau, *Authoring Autism*.

53. Chris Bonello, "11,521 People Answered This Autism Survey. Warning: The Results May Challenge You," Autistic Not Weird, October 1, 2018, https://autisticnotweird.com/2018survey/.

54. UN Women, "Bodily Autonomy, a Fundamental Right, Remains Elusive for Millions of Women and Girls in Asia-Pacific and Globally," UN Women Asia and the Pacific, May 20, 2021, https://asiapacific.unwomen.org/en/news-and-events/stories/2021/05/bodily-autonomy.

55. Office for Human Research Protections, *The Belmont Report: Ethical Principles and Guidelines for the Protection of Human Subjects of Research* (Washington, DC: U.S. Government Printing Office, 1979).

56. Stephanie Patterson and Pamela Block, "Disability Vulnerability and Capacity to Consent," in *Research Involving Participants with Impaired Cognition: Ethics, Autonomy, Inclusion, and Innovation*, ed. Ariel Cascio and Eric Racine (Oxford: Oxford University Press, 2019), 67–76.

57. Melinda McCormick, "Feminist Research Ethics, Informed Consent, and Potential Harms," *Hilltop Review* 6, no. 1 (2012): 23–33, https://scholarworks.wmich.edu/hilltopreview/vol6/iss1/5.

58. Leah Hendry, "Hidden Camera Reveals ABA Therapist Interacting 'Roughly' with Autistic 4-Year-Old Boy," *CBC News*, May 25, 2016, https://www.cbc.ca/news/canada/montreal/aba-therapy-hidden-camera-1.3597575.

59. United Nations, "Convention on the Rights of the Child," OHCHR, November 20, 1989, https://www.ohchr.org/en/instruments-mechanisms/instruments/convention-rights-child.

60. "It's the Straight-Up Caucacity for Us," ON Canada Project, n.d., accessed December 16, 2023, https://oncanadaproject.ca/blog/2qx21ira2iy79cxigc2bc1rfid9rvs.

61. Amy Sequenzia, "Parenting and Advocating with Autistic Children," Autistic Women and Nonbinary Network, November 20, 2017, https://awnnetwork.org/parenting-advocating-autistic-children/.

62. "Functioning Labels Harm Autistic People," Autistic Self Advocacy Network, December 9, 2021, https://autisticadvocacy.org/2021/12/functioning-labels-harm-autistic-people/.

63. Annelou L. C. de Vries et al., "Autism Spectrum Disorders in Gender Dysphoric Children and Adolescents," *Journal of Autism and Developmental Disorders* 40, no. 8 (January 22, 2010): 930–36, https://doi.org/10.1007/s10803-010-0935-9.

64. Sarah Pripas-Kapit, "Historicizing Jim Sinclair's 'Don't Mourn for Us': A Cultural and Intellectual History of Neurodiversity's First Manifesto," in *Autistic Community and the Neurodiversity Movement*, ed. Steven K. Kapp (Singapore: Palgrave Macmillan, 2020), 23–39.

5

BLACK DEAF ORDINARY WHO
DELIBERATELY SIGNS

JENELLE ROUSE

I am a cis woman of Caribbean and European-African descent living in Ontario, Canada. I was born in the afternoon on a sunny yet cold day. It was the twelfth day between fall and winter seasons. I am the youngest (last) child of my large, predominantly hearing blended family—a third daughter to my mother, Melba, and seventh to my father, Ambrose. My skin is dark, not as light as Melba but not as dark as Ambrose.

Melba was a teacher and registered nurse before her retirement, and she was familiar with Canadian medical, educational, and societal systems. Ambrose was a business owner, an independent constructor with a supervisory position before his retirement. He has worked with people of all kinds.

Both my parents were born in Barbados. They moved to Ontario, Canada, at different times and for different reasons. Ambrose moved to Canada on a visa permit in his early twenties for his studies. He decided to become a Canadian citizen to build his career in Canada. Melba studied in Barbados to become a teacher. After a few years of teaching in Barbados, she decided to change careers by moving to England and studying a new field of working with people: nursing. After obtaining a three-year diploma as a registered nurse, Melba was sought out by the Canadian government for her experience and knowledge. The government invested in her by hiring and moving her to work at one of the three top hospitals in Ontario, Canada. There, she became a Canadian citizen. My parents met for the first time in Canada (Greater Toronto area), not Barbados. That makes sense because during their childhood and early adulthood, there were approximately 200,000–250,000 people living in Barbados.[1] My parents' lives were different in Barbados until their careers led them to meet in Canada.

Years after the adventures and career explorations, I was born to my parents. They named me Jenelle, which is spelled out J-E-N-E-L-L-E, not J-A-N-E-L-L-E. My name can be phonetically pronounced "j eh n eh l."

Within my culturally and linguistically signing community, I have three different name signs, each with a characteristic story. My first name sign has the letter "J." It places at the corner of my lips and moves upward representing a sheepish smile. It fit my personality as a small child. When I was successfully certified as a teacher, the letter of my last name, "R," was added, and my name sign evolved into "J-R" in the same area. The third name sign was a gift for the completion of my education studies in the applied linguistics doctorate program. It was during the difficult year of 2020. At that time, a small group of Black Deaf Canadians and I celebrated my hard-earned milestone. A person from that group name-signed me "D(J)-R." It has a special symbolic meaning where the letter "D" starts in the air to emphasize that I have a doctorate and then morphs into an "R" while moving in a curve as if writing "J" before reaching to the corner of the lips with the letter "R." This name sign is used at special occasions. For many in the community, I am still known as "J-R."

These name signs match my personality, outlook, and endeavors. I have been observant since the moment of my birth, including the moment I began to walk and inquire. I was attentive to details and hyperaware of individual behavior and action to make sense of the world. I have two languages: American Sign Language (ASL) and English. I navigate between two different worlds (cultures): Deaf and hearing. My parents, as primary advocates, instilled in their children the message that being educated would lead to success if we worked hard.

Although I navigate my life through two languages, ASL and English, not all my family members communicate with me in ASL. Out of my seven siblings, one sister knows ASL and another knows basic manual alphabet while the rest of my siblings speak and/or write in English. Both my parents speak while my father at times opts to use an artificial sign system called "total communication."

Total communication is a manual sign system produced simultaneously with speech.[2] It was a popular system in late 1980s and early 1990s before ASL and other natural sign languages were legitimately accepted. I am fortunate to have had such languages as my foundation to live life from then to now.

My family members make sure I have access to information any way they know how. For example, if they choose to speak, they know that they have to face me or make sure I see them before they start to speak. They are willing to write or type notes when I get tired or when my brain is at its capacity from continued speech reading. I comfortably switch between both languages and have from the start because of my initial access. My family made sure I was included in everything, surrounding me with books, reading to me, and retelling information through imaginary plays and performances. We would play games and make up stories through storytelling, sketching, and/or writing.

In short, reading, blasting music, playing, singing, running, dancing, scribbling, painting, playing predictability games and board games, doing mathematics, teasing, writing, and participating in activities of all kinds contributed to my natural love for literature and arts.

I was deliberately navigated through the Ontarian educational and societal systems, where my race, gender, language, and disability are typically underrepresented, marginalized, and/or underestimated. I went to several types of schools, including an inner-city school designed in a sign language environment for day students (where the instructions were taught in both languages—ASL and English), a mainstream English-speaking school (formerly known to the community as an oral or auditory-oral school, sometimes with sign language interpreters), a self-contained day program for the deaf in a public school (often with some staff who know ASL, including sign language educational assistants, interpreters, and volunteers), and a bilingual-bicultural school (ASL and English). This last school is fully immersed in two cultures and two languages basically twenty-four hours/seven days a week when its immediate (Deaf; sign language) community is involved.

Decision Making: Cochlear Implants and Sign Languages

This chapter reveals my narrative account of my parents' choices: the decisions they made and their timing of letting me self-advocate for my right to exist and be seen as a human. Throughout the story, some historical background and information explain rationales behind my parents' choices and my responsive actions.

The choices all started with Melba, who gave birth to me, her third and last daughter, the last and seventh daughter of Ambrose, in Ontario, Canada. By the time I moved to Barbados with my family, I was quite lusty. I was alert. According to my parents, I had the highest degrees of hearing; I heard everything and was ready for anything. At eleven months, I was doing all the activities my sister would get me to do. She would get into my playpen and show me different things like books and toys. She would make sure I was included in everything she did. Because of that, I was advancing in everything offered to me.

There was nothing for my parents to be concerned about. I was very healthy—no colds, no fever, nothing. But something happened when I turned eighteen months.

When my parents called my name, Melba explained to me, "Most of the time, I pointed and I more or less commented to your dad, *Jenelle is not listening, she is not paying attention and you call her and be stood up.*" My parents also noticed that I was oblivious when people called my name. Even though I was still active, more active and alert than usual while doing everything my sister used to do, I was not responsive to their calling.

My parents took me to see a doctor in Barbados, who referred me to an audiologist. Once I was identified as deaf, Melba was devastated while Ambrose was relieved. *Two different reactions. Two different perspectives. Two different reasons.*

Ambrose, being a father, was relieved to know that I was physically and mentally okay. Melba, being a mother, was worried about how my being deaf would be affected by her profession as a nurse. The medical model perceives the need to fix "missing" sensorium in any individual, observing people whose ability, experience, and/or physical form are different as victims, abnormal, diseased, and/or having defects—something to fix, something to modify and assimilate.

Instead of falling into the trap of the medical perspective, Melba stepped up to become my full-time advocate. She began by traveling back to Canada and looking for resources for me to maintain my development, language, and keen interest in learning.

At that time in Barbados, the population in the island was about 257,000 people, and out of about 14,000 people with a disability, only 1,400 people were deaf.[3] Resources and treatments were not available enough in Barbados to recognize and promote deaf individuals. The majority of education was either practicing life skills or providing technical training, and vocational/collegiate training was not always an optimal option for deaf people.[4] My parents knew my potential before I even stepped into the schooling world.

The Cabinet of Barbados finally recognized the right of people with disabilities to have a better life by establishing an advisory committee in June 2022. To think, that was barely a year from the date I write this, and decades after my parents learned of my being deaf! Melba knew this. With all of her experience and professional background as well as being a teacher herself, she flew back to Canada and searched for better resources.

In Barbados, Ambrose made sure I was not treated any different from my siblings. During my toddler years, there was no delay in my developmental stages; according to my parents, I accelerated as quickly as my sister (the one who involved me in everything).

Once Melba found a team of audiologists, otolaryngologists, and speech therapists in Ontario, Canada, she brought me from Barbados. Around at that time, the culturally Deaf and linguistically signing community had become a strong-willed collective fighting to get appropriate education in preferred sign languages.[5] In 1990, the government passed the Ontario Education Act to ensure that sign languages are used as instruction in classes.[6]

An otolaryngologist observed me and mentioned to my parents that I was a good candidate for cochlear implants. My parents and otolaryngologist consulted with me, explaining how cochlear implants would benefit me. At around two and a half years old, I understood what "cochlear" meant and how ears worked. I understood that the cochlear has hair cells, sound waves, eardrums, and so on. I understood what was going on. I was empowered to inform my mother that I did not want cochlear implants. I explained that I was fine with wearing hearing aids, which I could take off at any time. I added that I was quite content using sign language. I used my voice all the time with my family and close circles of friends.

I was fortunate that I was not rushed or pushed into getting cochlear implants. Not many children experience that respect. Parents at that time often were told that deaf children are not *normal*. They were forced to choose between a cochlear implant with auditory-speech therapy sessions and natural development of sign language. They were made to believe that sign language is difficult to learn and that there are no sign language resources available to support learning.[7] Despite sign languages being viewed as a less desirable choice, my parents treated me as a human being with the ability to make conscious choices. They also made sure that languages (basically everything) were available and part of my development growing up.

Times have changed as I have grown older. Especially now, I get glares of great dismay from medical professionals and some, if not most, non-medical people when they learn about my cochlear implant declination.

How could I not want to hear just like everyone else? Why get temporary hearing aids when permanent cochlear implants are possible?

When asked these questions during my early teenage years, I would reply: "I do not want to be a machine where I possibly risk glitches, repeated surgeries and missing out on the life I could have had if I were left at home for months to recover and practice listening and speaking in a rigid manner when I should learn it naturally."

Currently, my straightforward response is, "How could they not let me *be*?"

Access to information is critical and considered *just* when given independent choices to determine what works best equally for self *and* family. At any age and any degree of hearing, decision making requires consistent support and commitment to working together to achieve desired goals. This observation is based off of life experience and my dissertation work. My work has detailed accounts of parents' choices for their deaf children's well-being that lean toward implantation and how medical (and societal) pressures are at play in their decisions.[8]

As a highly independent, multitalented, Black, Deaf, Canadian education specialist, I want to explain that *any degree or ability to hear is irrelevant. I have everything you have. I was taught and raised to be aware of my surroundings. The only difference between us is language.*

Sign language as a language foundation is possible, especially with proper support and resources. By maintaining a sign language, I am skilled at broadening my horizon and perceiving big pictures with details ahead of time. Anyone who has a preconceived notion that incorporating sign language early in life impedes one's ability to comprehend and navigate the audio-centric world is erroneous. I am proof that the notion is not true. I know because I am an adult who lives and breathes as a Black and culturally Deaf person. I never, not once, have had any self-pity for being Black and Deaf. I am a Black Deaf woman who uses sign language. I am a Black Deaf woman who consciously and intentionally chose not to speak—my choice, my decision.

I am aware that I live in an ableist and audist world, where living as such is unimaginable. I am aware that Black and/or Deaf people are perceived as less, a disease, something to be pitied. There are names for these discriminatory words. *Racism* against *Blackness* and *audism*. The latter is a theoretical form of systemic oppression regarding hearing and the ability to access and use spoken languages. Dr. Tom Humphries coined the term; he describes it as an irrational conviction that "one is superior based on one's ability to hear or behave in the manner of one who hears."[9] I explored that notion as one of the themes of my dissertation, in which educators and parents offer accounts about how audism exists in a systematic attitude toward degrees of hearing and languages.[10] At this time of writing, community-based accounts of experiencing and living in Canada as Black and Deaf in the face of racism and audism are being discussed in a special issue called "Reconstruct(ing) Hidden History: Black Deaf Canadian Relat(ing) Identity."[11] Experiential knowledge and understanding of ASL and Black American/Sign Language (BASL or BSL) as well as critical race and critical disability theories are included in the article.

Let me move back to the point where motivation, constant and holistic support, barrier-free access, and familial, school, and communal involvement are put into service in the midst of audist society. I encourage the reader to mull over the rest of the chapter to learn and identify strategies people of interest used throughout my life.

With the Harris Cut in the middle of the 1990s, $50 million were cut from social, community, and education services and programs.[12] The consequences were dire. Many barriers and obstacles were formed to intentionally (or unintentionally) prevent parents from finding resources or services. My parents pivoted by telling me what was going on in conversations, shows, and so on. They made sure I understood what was said. They also fully backed my decision; my mother would say, "You wear hearing aids just like people wear glasses."

Strategies at Play: Internalize Sign Language

As far as my education was concerned, I went to Metropolitan Toronto School for the Deaf (MTSD, now permanently closed) at three and half years old. This school had a division of the public school sharing a building with a division called Davisville Junior Public School. It had day programs with ASL and spoken English, serving deaf students from kindergarten to grade eight. During my years there, I had rich barrier-free resources where my school, community, educators, and families intermingled. Courses in literature, arts, physical education, health, numeracy, and more were available. Recesses were filled with interest-based clubs (dances, sports), performances, games, chit-chat, gossip, and boundary testing. Sign language interpreters were available. Every staff member was capable of using sign language. There, sign languages were not seen as a tool, a thing to accommodate, a burden, a modality. They were seen as a human language and a culture, just like other languages such as Haitian, Mandarin, or Italian. Because of this perception, I was able to explore my literate capability in both languages at ease with letters, research, stories, performances, and so on to learn as the years went by. I could work with sign language interpreters and with people who did not share a similar language. I could turn to books, papers, and news to make sense of events.

I remember experiencing my very first research project where I had to interview and present my findings when I was eight or nine years old. I interviewed my parents and siblings, asking them about Barbados. I had to research the island's flag, learn about its symbol and colors, and understand their history and meanings. I had to craft and write a simple report prior to giving a presentation to my class. For a Black Deaf student, I was proud to own my learning.

Because my parents were active advocates, they regularly went to parent-teacher meetings and school-community events. As my father told me with confidence, "We were not worried about you at all, and no one could come to us with foolishness where you were concerned, you know your dad, and you know no one could come to him with foolishness." True, there could be no foolishness. If there were any concerns, my parents would follow up with people and stand firmly while asking, "Why did you . . . ? Why . . . ? How . . . ?" My parents even involved me in some of the meetings. Sign language interpreters were there. My parents made sure my educators knew my ability and potential. They made sure no one kept me down. They would ask the "why."

All my educators were actively aware of my potential. They would eagerly inform my parents that I always finished my work ahead of time and helped others in my class. This experience probably was a significant hint that directed me to pursue a teaching career! I was involved in making decisions about my education, language preferences, and needs. At such a young age, I was already developing self-advocacy skills. That was how, after a month at the oral school, I demanded my right to return to MTSD when my needs were not being met.

In grade nine, I went to a bilingual-bicultural secondary school, and I was placed in a basic (life-skills) class because of my race, educational, and familial background. The school administration assumed I had had a poor education. Thanks to MTSD, I had a healthy sense of who and what I was: a Black Deaf Canadian who signs. I surpassed that school's expectations with my quality of work and work ethic. Within a few weeks, I was promoted to the top of the advanced level, so high that I broke a preconceived notion of what a Black Deaf Canadian newcomer should be. My dark skin helped me to see true color in people perceiving me, responding to me. At thirteen years old, I witnessed and experienced a breaking point in the midst of changes, especially with an overflow of microaggression (i.e., being placed in basic/life-skill classes), dismissal, misassumption (i.e., inner-city school equals poorer quality of education), discrimination, and prejudice—for being who and what I am. I had to be at my best by being that Black Deaf Canadian who signs.

For grade ten, I transferred to a mainstream secondary school where I had all my needs met. The last four years of secondary school, I was in an old curriculum. The old curriculum had three levels of courses—basic (life skills), general (applied), and advanced (academic)—in the vocational and collegiate training programs. A resource teacher who barely knew me suggested to my parents that I be placed in the general level. Once again, my race, educational, and familial background were the factors the resource teacher looked at. I stood firm and took various advanced courses such as geometry, chemistry, biology, business, history, and some less stressful courses such as physical education, health, visual arts, and drama. I hosted dance and sign language clubs. I even participated in homeroom student councils as a union representative. I was active and invested in my own pathway. Although I did not recognize my privileges living in Canada at that time, I believed freely in my own capabilities.

Through my experience of being involved in various dynamics, I became independent as a fast learner and found a group of people with a similar niche. On honor roll thrice in a row, I graduated with a scholarship to attend a postsecondary school in Toronto. I left at the right time, when the Harris government formally established the Education Quality and Accountability Office (EQAO) for grades three, six, nine, and eleven, including the grade ten literacy test.[13]

At university, my family and I met a sign language interpreter who happened to be a Black Canadian female. We immediately loved her and wanted to work with her. As an undergraduate student, I was able to work with her and her chosen interpreting team. Throughout my four years of study, I learned about myself as an adult while transitioning from being a teenager who often turned to family for support to a young adult who had to be self-reliant, live on my own, and face challenges head on. I was involved in a mentorship program as a mentor and worked in signing environments as a program director, counselor, and day-camp counselor. After I graduated, I went on to study at two different universities to complete my lifelong goal of becoming a teacher.

Once I became a teacher, I did not stop there. I went after my dancing career, although secretly at the time. I kept studying until I finally completed my graduate studies in 2020. In 2021, I applied all my skills, knowledge, and interests to the thing I have been dreaming of—being a resourceful combination of leader, scholar, researcher, consultant, facilitator, presenter, workshop provider, external reviewer, and artist. At my pace, I make sure that sign linguistically, community, home, school, and networks are interconnected. I do this in the same country of 38.5 million people where I was born, grew up, and acquired languages and skills,[14] the same country that perceives 6.2 million Canadians with disabilities as different.[15] While embracing being different as a Black Deaf female who uses sign language, I am aware that I self-advocate; I fight for the right to live, educate, and celebrate so current and next generations can have a better life such as I have had with a great investment by my family, education, and life. Family. Identity. Race. Deaf. Sign Language. Education.

Consequential Choices as Black Deaf Canadian Who Signs

Now I step back to consider my experiences in the broader context of Deaf Black Canadians. Not all Black Deaf individuals experience the same things. Not all experience the same struggles and accomplishments. Black Deaf individuals are typically coerced into assimilating into society and isolated from each other. I am one of many individuals who intentionally dissimilated from norms (audio-centric standard or expectation). I first self-advocated for my rights at two or three years old, and I did so again at eleven years old when it came to my education.

I choose to stay in the province where I was born, grew up, and acquired milestones. I want to be contented with who and what I am without unnecessarily repairs: a Black Deaf Woman with all-round environments where I am able to access information via languages at my disposal because of the reality of the society. I choose to either sign, speak while sign, or write the same way people choose to sign, gesture, speak, or write/text around me. That is the reality. It is up to people to determine whether to enter that reality and embrace transparency and differences with mutual respect. Although my choices might be similar and relatable, one example is Black Deaf American actress Lauren Ridloff, who chose to stop using her voice altogether at thirteen and maintained sign language. Like her, I have learned that every time the voice is used, real-time connection with people is lost because they immediately fixate on unrealistic expectations between sounds, linguistics, and cognition, assuming that if one sound or tone is off, my language and cognition must be delayed or I must be uneducated. Oh, how wrong they are!

Being the one Deaf member in a large circle of family does not prevent me from having authentic relationships with my family. My siblings have never treated me differently, accepting me as their deep-thinking and mischievous sister. Experiences have shaped who and what I am. I do not let society measure or direct how I should look, behave, or express myself. I am fortunate that my parents were my advocates from the moment they learned about my being deaf to the moment I independently navigated and self-advocated at a young age, knowing I could always turn to them for guidance. My parents (my family) embraced me by pushing me to know my worth and suppress erroneous or run-down expectations. I value social justice, in particular sign language accessibility. I feel that while we each have extensive knowledge and experience based on our activities, we should connect and learn more about each other.

This push is a main reason I turn to the desire to make transformative changes in educational and societal contexts with a focus on sign language accessibility. I engage in various projects of local and international nontraditional academic and ethical community-based literacy learning, dialoguing, researching, and teaching. I independently initiated a groundbreaking long-term community-based research project with a great community team to support an increased network among Black Deaf Canadians. This project enables members to seek information that in turn influences how they live, teach, converse, study, write, or even play. I am participating in another first-ever sign language Canadian research-led team for a three-year project for which I am conducting an independent study of racialized Deaf Canadian employability using alternative methodology. In the study, I work with a group of racialized participants in a participatory strategy where we actively contribute to changes by, for example, brainstorming resources/solutions to identified issues related to race and underrepresentation and creating employability pathways. I work with different individuals with similar interests (e.g., artists, researchers, educators, directors, activists, parents/guardians, advocates for sign language/accessibility). We get together to artfully and educationally recognize that everyone, regardless of ethnic background, especially Deaf, is human. Everyone, including people who choose sign language, is human.

Basically, resources, knowledge, skills, understanding with compassion, experience, and acceptance are fluid keys to unlock all aspects of a successful, contented life with a strong support system. To be a working activist (Black Deaf who uses sign language), it is important to stand for what we believe in—to fight for justice—and put ourselves into a forethought rather than afterthought.

NOTES

1. "Historical Population Data. Barbados Population 1950–2923," Macrotrends, n.d., accessed December 17, 2023, https://www.macrotrends.net/countries/BRB/barbados/population.

2. Sue Schwartz, *Choices in Deafness: A Parent's Guide to Communication Options* (Bethesda, MD: Woodbine House, 1996).

3. "Deaf in Barbados," Joshua Project, 2023, https://joshuaproject.net/people_groups/19007/BB.

4. "Media Centre," Barbados Council for the Disabled, 2023, http://barbadosdisabled.org.bb/media-centre/.

5. Clifton F. Carbin, *Deaf Heritage in Canada: A Distinctive, Diverse, and Enduring Culture* (Toronto: McGraw-Hill Ryerson, 1996).

6. Ontario Education Act, 1990, § 298: Operation of schools—general.

7. Jenelle Rouse, "Exploring the Acquisition of American Sign Language by Deaf Kindergarten Children: Early Language Access and the Use of Appropriate Resource" (PhD dissertation, University of Western Ontario, 2020), 172, https://ir.lib.uwo.ca/etd/7184.

8. Ibid.

9. Tom Humphries, "Communicating Across Cultures (Deaf/Hearing) and Language Learning" (PhD dissertation, Union Graduate School, 1977), 108, ProQuest Dissertations & Theses Global.

10. Rouse, "Exploring the Acquisition," 172.

11. Jenelle Rouse, Amelia Palmer, and Amy Parsons, "Reconstruct(ing) a Hidden History: Black Deaf Canadian Relat(ing) Identity," *Social Sciences* 12, no. 5, (May 17, 2023): 305, https://doi.org/10.3390/socsci12050305.

12. "Ontarians with Disabilities Legislation," ODA Committee, November 23, 1999, http://www.odacommittee.net/hansard39.html.

13. Stephen E. Anderson and Ben J. Sonia, "Policy Trends in Ontario Education 1990–2003," ICEC Working Paper, University of Toronto, September 2003, http://fcis.oise.uto ronto.ca/~icec/policytrends.pdf.

14. Statistics Canada, "Population Estimates, Quarterly," Government of Canada, accessed December 17, 2023, https://doi.org/10.25318/1710000901-ENG.

15. Statistics Canada, "Measuring Disability in Canada," Government of Canada, December 2, 2022, https://www150.statcan.gc.ca/n1/pub/11-627-m/11-627-m2022062-eng .htm.

6

INTERSECTIONS OF DEAFNESS, BLINDNESS, DEAFBLINDNESS, AND GENDER

The Deaf Community, Blindness, and Deafblind Activism in Families

CHERYL NAJARIAN SOUZA

Introduction

The concept of what it means to be disabled has changed with historical shifts including the rise of the scientific method and institutionalization, the founding of the Americans with Disabilities Act (ADA) of 1990, deinstitutionalization, and the notion of inclusion in schools and colleges across the United States. Historically, scholars have looked specifically at those with intellectual and physical disabilities in terms of these events and contemporary scholarship views "disability" as a contested term. Families operate as a key site of socialization for individuals who are labeled "disabled," and how a family as a unit thinks of the term "disability" impacts how a child grows up to think of their own identity.[1] Although there is significant diversity among the Deaf, the Deaf community rejects the medicalization of deafness as a disability and considers itself part of a larger linguistic minority in a hearing society.

In this chapter, I examine the intersection of family and Deafblindness, attending to complex dynamics of activism that play out in Deaf activism, blind activism, and Deafblind activism. To do so, I analyze three organizations and their websites to see how families operate when raising a family member who is Deaf, blind, or Deafblind. These organizations include the National Association of the Deaf (NAD), the National Federation of the Blind (NFB), and the American Association of the Deaf Blind (AADB). After looking at tensions on a more macro level through the three websites, I take the firsthand accounts of two Deafblind women, Helen Keller and Haben Girma, and use their memoirs to analyze historical shifts in how Deafblind women think of themselves in their own words. I use a more micro level analysis to show how gender and race are also part of this meaning-making process and intersect with the term "Deafblind." I illustrate moments that highlight tensions between these women and their able-bodied parents.

Literature Review

The Concepts of Disability and Ability

Many scholars have written about the concept of disability as a social construct.[2] Linton[3] argues for claiming the term "disability" and putting disability studies at the center of our analyses because, as she states, it adds "a critical dimension to thinking about issues such as autonomy, competence, wholeness, independence/dependence, health, physical appearance, aesthetics community, and notions of progress and perfection—issues that pervade every aspect of the civic and pedagogic culture." Some scholars argue that a constructionist view risks missing important connections between disability, bodily pain, suffering, and materiality.[4] These scholars tend to agree, though, that the term "disability" is culturally associated with a stigma and narrative created by individuals in society and then reinforced by social interactions within social institutions such as schools, the media, families, and workplaces.

Deaf Studies

In the United States, the lowercase "deaf" describes the audiological condition of not hearing, whereas the uppercase "Deaf" refers to a group of deaf people who share a common language—American Sign Language (ASL)—culture, and history.[5] Instead of viewing itself as disabled, the Deaf community defines being Deaf as a culture and part of a linguistic minority whose primary language is ASL.[6] By claiming their identity as a civil rights issue, the Deaf are in an uncomfortable margin, relying on disability benefits and laws but drawing on a different framework to fight for human rights. People who are deaf are often, although not always, older Americans who lose their hearing and become deaf later in life; they usually do not consider themselves part of the Deaf community since they did not attend a school for the Deaf or become immersed in Deaf culture in their early years. Deaf studies scholars contest the distinction between the terms "deaf" and "Deaf." In their study of deaf and hard of hearing youth and welfare policies of the disabled, Haualand, Grønningsæter, and Hansen[7] discuss how it becomes problematic to place individuals into such categories because doing so risks reducing people's complex identities to one particular status. Instead of using either "deaf" or "Deaf," they adopt a "minority approach" and a "disability approach." Breivik[8] adopts a similar perspective regarding how individuals navigate being deaf/Deaf.

Regardless of political or theoretical orientation, D/deaf people and their families must navigate a complex environment that imposes the stigma of disability on them. My own analysis of life history narratives of college-educated Deaf women in paid work and mothering experiences reveals that they face oppression and resist being stereotyped as disabled and unable to do paid or unpaid work.[9] Mauldin[10] analyzes the experiences of mothers who navigate getting a cochlear implant for their deaf child and reveals that the culture of what is normal affects whether deafness is understood as a disability and how it is responded to.

Mauldin's research provides a framework to think through tensions that arise with hearing parents and the NAD. The NAD's stance is to advise parents to teach their Deaf children ASL and raise their children to be part of the Deaf community in identity and political orientation. Parents may receive this advice but also get advice from medical professionals centered on fixing or erasing deafness. NAD contests the dominance of the medicalization discourse and its influence on parents raising children who are deaf. Mauldin[11] develops the concept of "ambivalent medicalization" to discuss how parents weigh pros and cons of medicalized approaches. In this way, scholars link the concepts of narrative, voice, and how stories are told to social constructions of disability, ability, and the spaces in between.[12] Scholars like Talila Lewis, a Black scholar and activist who works to abolish deaf incarceration and addresses the intersection of racism and ableism, have recently redefined ableism to be specifically intersectional.[13] Communities of color may have far less access to either effective health care or vibrant linguistic signing communities and education, fundamentally altering the strategies and goals of families raising a deaf child. This scholarship shows why it is important to use an intersectional lens when looking at the concept of ableism.

The issue of intersectionality has long been discussed in sociological and feminist literature,[14] but the term has not been used as widely by disability studies scholars. Frederick and Shifrer[15] highlight how the intersection of race and disability remains a particularly neglected area in sociology. They argue that research has marginalized the experiences of disabled people of color and masked processes by which whiteness and able-bodiedness have been privileged in discussions of activism. They emphasize that there needs to be a centering of the positionality of disabled people of color so that an intersectional analysis can show how racism and ableism intertwine to develop unique forms of inequality and resistance.[16]

Blind Studies

Some scholars have studied family challenges and the blind in terms of how family attitudes affect "successful rehabilitation" for blind family members.[17] These kinds of studies are interesting but accept a medical model of disability where the family seeks to "cure" and normalize their child to function in the family. Other scholars have written about the meaning of blindness itself and challenged the existing binary system of those who are sighted and those who are not.[18] Although these ideas about blindness do not speak to tension in families, they do, in fact, affect family groups, especially sighted parents of blind children who are educated by medical professionals about how to "cure" or "fix" their blind children. In his research, Rod Michalko,[19] drawing from his own understanding of blindness and narratives of people with disabilities, connects lived experiences with social theory to show how sightedness is assumed within ideas of normalcy. As a youth going blind, Michalko struggled to pass to maintain membership in his "sighted homeland." Only once he reached adulthood and built relationships with the blind community did he discover the value of blind ways and perspectives.[20] Frederick's[21] work on mothers who are blind and have sighted children illustrates that medicalized perspectives are oppressive and deny blind people rights, especially the right to parent. These scholars highlight that the primary issue for parents with blind children is navigating the medical approach to blindness versus embracing an approach rooted in human rights and disability culture.

Finally, scholars have looked at the issue of internal hierarchies and whether they exist between blind and Deafblind people. For example, Fannon[22] explores hierarchies in her study about gender and blindness and how blind women navigate gender norms despite not seeing bodies. She finds that blindness actually seems to amplify gender expectations regarding body image,[23] suggesting the importance of studying visual aspects of identity and how people navigate them in the social environment.

Deafblind Studies, Intersectionality, and Helen Keller

Literature on the Deafblind has not, as a whole, highlighted family tensions. Goode[24] investigates the lives of two children who are deaf, blind, and have an intellectual disability to illustrate that although they may seem to communicate "in a world without words," they are not in a world without communication. He finds that the children and families in his study were able to develop communication in an alternative way so that they could share each other's life experiences.

Stoffel,[25] a Deafblind individual, analyzes the narratives of twelve Deafblind people to illustrate the challenges this lived experience presents in family and school environments. These narratives are important because they show another dimension to the experience of being Deafblind and situate Deafblind individuals as experts in their own personal stories of oppression.

Another area of research examines the issue of sensory connection and the importance of touch, such that touch deprivation acts as a form of social and communication deprivation for Deafblind people. Emadi[26] finds that Deafblind people were especially marginalized during the COVID-19 lockdown when they were denied using their sense of touch to communicate and had to practice social distancing. She also illustrates how "favouring vision over other senses means we risk missing out on a host of rich experiences and connections."[27] This concept can be connected to communication challenges faced in families with someone who is Deafblind, but it also highlights how we could potentially communicate in new and enlightening ways.

Hersh[28] also supports Deafblind individuals as active participants of care instead of mere recipients of support. Using interview data of twenty-eight Deafblind people in six different countries, she showed how without proper supports in place, individuals experience isolation and depression. The individuals in the study want to be involved and contribute to society, especially with regards to organizations of blind and Deafblind people.[29] Activism, then, is a key component in the lives of Deafblind people and necessary for their families to incorporate.

Interesting research has been done on race with regards to Deafblind individuals. Garcia-Fernandez,[30] using autoethnography, discusses her first-generation DeafChicana identity as a college student and her experiences navigating structural inequity in educational institutions. Much like Girma, a Deafblind woman of color who went to Harvard, Garcia-Fernandez, through her experience and identity, illustrates the need to look at Deafblind individuals as experts while also analyzing gender and race to show how Deafblindness, gender, and race intersect in a variety of social institutions and spaces. Once scholars can see how oppression fully operates in complex ways, social change can occur as people dismantle the systems that establish and reinforce ableism, racism, and sexism.

Helen Keller is arguably the most famous and most studied Deafblind person in the world, so an examination of her life is important to the analysis in this chapter. Crow[31] describes Helen Keller as a "problematic icon." Although Keller was a writer, radical activist, and socialist, she is framed in the public imagination as an "eternal child" who "overcame" her disability.[32] In *Beyond the Miracle Worker: The Remarkable Life of Anne Sullivan Macy and Her Extraordinary Friendship with Helen Keller*,[33] Kim Nielsen tells the story of Anne Sullivan Macy, who grew up from troubled beginnings, and her complex relationship with Helen Keller.[34] Nielsen traces how Keller financially supported Sullivan toward the end of Sullivan's life. Sullivan, who became progressively disabled herself through loss of vision and the emotional stress of her childhood (having been institutionalized in an asylum and abandoned by her father), was also emotionally dependent on Keller. As Nielsen argues, "Annie's emotional, financial, and physical dependence on Helen thus raises questions about the meanings of disability. In some ways, Macy lived a life far more vulnerable than that of Keller."[35] Despite this enriching analysis of Keller's life as a Deafblind woman, it is important to note that Keller was a white woman who came from a privileged family in the southern part of the United States. Therefore, to fully understand the experiences of Deafblind individuals and view them as experts, it is important to consider intersecting dimensions of race, ethnicity, and class.

In thinking about all these literatures, some central questions connect with this volume: how do families and people who might be labeled Deaf, blind, or Deafblind navigate their relationships? Specifically, how do families navigate issues of disability identification, medicalization, and/or cultural connections in their daily lives? What are the obstacles these families and individuals face in family situations? How do they resist these obstacles, and how might they build alliances? Specifically, since families with a member who is Deafblind are at the intersection of Deafness and blindness, do they share commonalities with these families in their struggles, or do they seem more unrelated and to stand alone? Finally, how might intersectional analysis aid scholars in understanding these groups more fully?

Methodology

Through content analysis of three websites in 2023, I looked at how identities of disability, ability, and the spaces in between were articulated and related to family dynamics. These websites were the National Association of the Deaf (NAD), the National Federation of the Blind (NFB), and the American Association of the Deaf Blind (AADB). I chose these websites because they belong to the major organizations associated with each of these three communities. While viewing the websites, I sought to answer the following research questions: How do organizations define being Deaf, blind, and Deafblind? How do they navigate doing "family"? What advice, if any, do they give to parents? How might they incorporate able-bodied parents into their activism? How do they define and navigate the concept of disability? How might they resist stereotypes? How may the messages of the NAD and the NFB connect or disconnect with the visions that parents of Deafblind children contend with? Why do the Deafblind need their own organization if these other two organizations exist?

In this investigation, I also wanted to see how Deafblind people themselves articulate needs and identities in their organization and to see the spaces where they may clash with their families about decisions regarding health and well-being. To this end, I used memoirs as a site of analysis. Scholars have used memoirs as an important site of analysis to highlight the experiences of marginalized groups. For instance, Carey[36] uses memoirs of parents who have children with intellectual disabilities to analyze how these memoirs "shape the public discourse related to disability, the family, and the community". Memoirs offer invaluable data and make stories of marginalized groups visible.

I chose to focus on the Deafblind community and used these memoirs for the micro part of the analysis because, of the three websites, knowledge of the family experience seemed to be missing the most from the Deafblind. I wanted to know: how do individuals who are Deafblind describe their family experiences and the struggles they face within their families? How do individuals who are Deafblind resist these challenges? I also wanted to look at intersecting concepts of Deafness, blindness, gender, and race to gain a richer understanding of the intersections of these elements of one's identity. To date, there are five memoirs by Deafblind women. Table 6.1 highlights these books and their authors. For the purposes of this paper, I focus on comparing the experience of Helen Keller as the first known Deafblind woman to have written a memoir alongside the story of Haben Girma as one of the most recently published examples. I juxtapose Keller and Girma as Haben Girma is the first woman of color who is also Deafblind to write and publish such a memoir.

I analyze Helen Keller's *The Story of My Life* to show a firsthand account of the most famous Deafblind woman in American history (and the world). I analyze Haben Girma's *Haben: The Deafblind Woman Who Conquered Har-*

TABLE 6.1 MEMOIRS		
Title	Author	Year of Publication
The Story of My Life	Helen Keller	1902
Invisible: My Journey through Vision and Hearing Loss	Ruth Silver	2012
Not Fade Away: A Memoir of Senses Lost and Found	Rebecca Alexander	2014
Haben: The DeafBlind Woman Who Conquered Harvard Law	Haben Girma	2019
Being Seen: One DeafBlind Woman's Fight to End Ableism	Elsa Sjunneson	2021

vard Law to include a more micro analysis that looks at the intersections of Deafblindess, gender, and race. I read these memoirs and coded them for main themes that I saw arising in terms of struggles with families. I also looked to see how these women defined their families and support systems throughout their lives.

Through the use of grounded theory method, I sought to have themes arise from the various stories, position statements, narratives, and articles on families on these three websites and in the memoirs.[37] Using open coding, I coded each website and memoir for overlapping themes and made notes of themes that stood alone on each individual website. In the tradition of feminist methodologies, along with my qualitative analysis, I reflexively analyzed my data and situated myself within my findings.[38] To this end, I think it is important to briefly reflect on my own recollections and experiences with the concept of disability and, in my case, deafness. As a white, hearing woman who grew up with hearing parents and a brother who is deaf, I recall learning about Helen Keller in my elementary school years. I remember learning that Keller was brought out of her "dark" state of not being able to communicate and causing disruptions by her teacher, Anne Sullivan, who taught her sign language. I also remember learning Sign Exact English (SEE) instead of ASL because schools were telling hearing parents and their families to learn SEE to help their deaf children and siblings learn oral English. Due to learning SEE as a child and despite viewing the Deaf community as a linguistic minority, I have, in some ways, been part of the system that serves to uphold stereotypes; I have spent a great deal of my career contesting them in my research and teaching.

Findings

The Websites: Tensions and Language Choice in Families

National Association of the Deaf—NAD

The National Association of the Deaf (NAD) website opens with the goal of the organization. On the homepage is the statement: "The mission of the National Association of the Deaf is to preserve, protect and promote the civil, human and linguistic rights of Deaf, DeafBlind, DeafDisabled, Hard of Hearing, and Late-Deafened people in the United States of America."[39] The website provides links to four articles and videos in ASL, which include president updates for each month, a summary of a case seeking communication access for Deaf people on parole and probation in Georgia, and a story detailing the rejection of a Deaf couple seeking a marriage license and their announcement of a lawsuit to protect their rights. The website further provides links to topics such as "deaf kids" (encompassing younger children, teens, and college students), "seniors," and "resources," which includes a comprehensive list of advocacy areas such as education and fair housing. The NAD's top priorities list for 2022–2024 includes deaf youth well-being, equity in deaf education, ASL resources for deaf babies, deaf senior issues, and racism in the Deaf community.[40]

These resources socialize parents to the potential dangers of the medical approach and the value of ASL and Deaf culture. For example, under the category of ASL resources for deaf babies, the NAD states that the problem to be addressed is the following:

> More than 90% of Deaf, DeafBlind, DeafDisabled, and Hard of Hearing babies are born to hearing parents and are often the first person the parents meet from the community. Parents often look to medical professionals for guidance and often get recommendations to "fix" the child. These recommendations can be and often are harmful to the child. Parents leave the hospital without meeting a Deaf, Deaf-Blind, DeafDisabled, or Hard of Hearing adult and without getting appropriate resources and often have to wait until after their follow up appointment in 30 days to get any information. We believe that all parents should receive information on programs, services, and ASL resources upon getting screening results. ASL classes should be available to families as early as possible.[41]

This statement shows tension between medicalization, the medical advice hearing parents get about their deaf child, and the NAD's position on deafness as a valued linguistic minority. The website focuses on the civil rights of Deaf Americans and provides advice to parents who are hearing and have a deaf child regarding protecting these rights and knowing how to advocate for them. A major focus is access to things hearing individuals have, seen in topics such as marriage, education, and health care. This focus is juxtaposed with discussions of topics needed specifically by this population like access to ASL and interpretation.

Since members of the Deaf community consider themselves a linguistic minority in a larger hearing society, the website consistently stresses the importance of ASL as the native language of Deafness. The position statement on ASL in the home and at school includes the following advice to parents of deaf children:

> Preparing deaf children to achieve optimal linguistic fluency in both ASL and English enables them to later engage in meaningful adult discourse as fully participating, contributing, and productive members of American society.

The NAD urges parents of deaf infants and children to learn about the benefits of the dual language approach (ASL and English) and the rich heritage of the American deaf community. The NAD also urges its affiliates and individual members to welcome deaf children and their families into the deaf community, to work with these families in becoming familiar with the lives and successes of deaf persons, to assist them in learning ASL, and to serve as a resource and source of support. . . . The NAD reiterates its position that acquisition of language from birth is a human right for every person, and that deaf infants and children should be given the opportunity to acquire and develop proficiency in American Sign Language (ASL) as early as possible.

This statement provides insight into how hearing parents especially might educate and raise their children who are born deaf. It highlights tension that often exists between parents and children. Solomon[42] shows that parents of deaf children who are hearing and their deaf children often experience a gap created by language difference, an obstacle in terms of communication. We see from the language in this position statement that the NAD views learning ASL as a human right and therefore a priority when raising a child who is deaf.

National Federation of the Blind—NFB

The National Federation of the Blind (NFB) website promises that "you can live the life you want; blindness is not what holds you back."[43] The opening words on the website state that members are "welcome to the movement." Under the topic "featured programs," the organization highlights surveys that have been done and states that the NFB "works to advance disability rights." In contrast to the NAD, the NFB, in some ways, accepts and uses the framework of disability and disability rights. It does not, however, accept the medical model, instead accepting a social model of blindness. This point is illustrated in an article on the website titled "A Definition of Blindness" that originally appeared in the *Blind American* in 1962, in which Kenneth Jernigan discusses how "blindness can best be defined not physically or medically but functionally or sociologically." In this article and its main argument, one can see how the NFB's position on disabilities is in many ways similar to the NAD's— both resist medical definitions of what it means to be deaf or blind. The NFB, however, accepts a social model view of disability and therefore sees blindness as a disability to the degree that people face discrimination and lack of access. NAD does not use this model; it rejects the term "disability" and its application to being deaf. Instead, it fights for rights as a linguistic minority.

Another relevant and overlapping difference between the two organizations is the role of language and culture in group identity. Simply put, unlike the Deaf community, which uses ASL as a native language, there is no native language of blind individuals, and there is no discussion of language and the role it plays in the lives of blind Americans on the NFB website. The website also states that there is "no such thing as blind culture."[44] Therefore, unlike the Deaf community, the NFB places far less stress on language and culture and instead focuses on rights, access, and inclusion. The NFB states in the center of the home page of its website that "blindness is not the characteristic that defines you or your future. Every day we raise the expectations of blind people, because low expectations create obstacles between blind people and our dreams."[45] This is perhaps why the NFB focuses more on inclusion in schools than the NAD seems to. On its website is a comprehensive list of programs, services, and resources to help blind people navigate their lives. With regards to families, the NFB seems more interested in helping to "provide information and support to blind children and adults . . . [to] build a community that creates a future full of opportunities."[46] A key takeaway for parents of blind children is that as long as children have family support, access, and rights, they can succeed in the community.

NAD and NFB both respect the expertise of deaf and blind adults as leading voices of their respective communities rather than nondisabled parents or medical professionals. Regarding families under the topic "Our Community," there is a link to the National Organization of Parents of Blind Children (NOPBC). The NOPBC is part of the NFB and is considered one of the best models for parents working with and explicitly under disabled activists.[47] There is also a link to a section dedicated to blind parents. There is a blind parent connection podcast where parents who are blind can be mentored by other blind parents on how to do the work of parenting.

American Association of the Deaf Blind—AADB
Interestingly, there is little mention of families on the AADB's homepage. The major issue and most recent update on the homepage is an open letter in response to the rise of the COVID-19 pandemic to help Deafblind and health care professionals be more prepared if Deafblind people are admitted into the hospital. The letter, posted in April 2020, states:

> Hospitals are now upping their restrictions by allowing patients only at the hospital. Their companion cannot attend the facility with the patient. This causes an underlying and dramatically impacting dilemma for the DeafBlind. The DeafBlind often requires an in-person interpreter, CDI (Certified Deaf Interpreter) and/or SSP (Support Service Provider) to facilitate. This helps the DeafBlind make well-informed medical decisions on their own. When DeafBlind is admitted in the surging pandemic may be forced to be unattended without a person

such as family member or interpreters to be by their side. This spells out what being left in the dark really means. AADB urges medical staffers to take heed of the DeafBlind Accessible tools and tactics for a much more directive approach albeit any interpreters present.[48]

The inclusion of this statement on the website and the fact that it remains there in 2023 highlights a continued struggle both the NAD and the NFB advocate for—the right to access. Access is viewed as interdependent with or broader than the individual and includes the need for other people, potentially family, to be with them. It is a civil right to have access to health care and to medical decision making with adequate supports. The theme of access, then, occurs on the websites of all three organizations.

There is less emphasis on family and family tensions on this website. Topics highlighted include a description of Deafblind camps, support service providers (SSPs), technology, and emergency preparation, to name a few. The Deafblind camps page has various links to the websites of camps in different states and countries. One example is the DeafBlind Camp of Maryland, which states on its website that its mission is

> To provide DeafBlind adult campers with an inclusive week of safe and fun-filled activities that are barrier free and exciting. It is also the mission of the camp to provide an environment that is conducive to the personal, spiritual, and educational growth of the DeafBlind individual.[49]

I would argue, then, that the AADB is at a point where it is still serving its community by helping get basic needs and rights met. It is less concerned (at least on this website) with educating parents who have a DeafBlind child or giving advice to parents who are DeafBlind about how to raise a child. Instead, it is mostly concerned with the equal access and civil rights issues of Deafblind individuals and inclusivity for members of this community.

The organization is defined as

> a national consumer organization of, by, and for deaf-blind Americans and their supporters. "Deaf-blind" includes all types and degrees of dual vision and hearing loss. Our membership consists of deaf-blind people from diverse backgrounds, as well as family members, professionals, interpreters, and other interested supporters.[50]

Despite supporting a variety of Deafblind Americans, the organization prides itself on helping people to gain access. While it does not explicitly criticize the medical model, like the NAD or the NFB websites do, the website focuses on rights and access, implicitly critiquing the medical model and supporting the social model. Members of the AADB are fighting for their basic civil rights as human beings.

The issue of being both blind and deaf for families is highlighted on the website in the section "Frequently Asked Questions about Deaf-Blindness."[51] Although it lists the Helen Keller National Center for Deaf-Blind Youth and Adults (HKNC), the National Consortium on Deaf-Blindness, and Minnesota's online resource for the topic of a "deaf-blind community," it does not seem to discuss common culture or give advice on education, as the NAD website does. Instead, it discusses how the HKNC offers "comprehensive vocational rehabilitation services for individuals who are DeafBlind,"[52] and the focus seems to be more on job and training opportunities than on explaining a community or culture linked by a common language.

To conclude the section on websites, we see that parents of Deafblind children receive little advice or direction from the national-level Deafblind activist organization. Turning to national organizations related to Deafness and blindness, parents encounter divergent conceptualizations of disability, culture, and inclusion with little explicit attention to Deafblindness. All three organizations challenge the medical model, promote access and rights, and situate Deaf, blind, and Deafblind adults as experts, but the pressing decisions faced by parents such as school choice, technology use, and language choice may be more obscured for parents of Deafblind children, who exist at the intersection of deafness and blindness.

The Memoirs—Tensions in Families Regarding "Disability" and Deafblindness

After taking a macro approach to viewing how three organizations of the Deaf, blind, and Deafblind communities view the concept of disability and tensions in families, I turn to a micro approach to look specifically at the Deafblind community for individual accounts of identity, family, and struggles. A variety of themes emerged in the websites, including the issue of language acquisition, Deaf culture, inclusion, access, and expertise. Although not all of these themes emerge in the memoirs, themes of language acquisition, inclusion, access, and expertise are represented.

Helen Keller—Her Early Family Life and "My Friends Have Made the Story of My Life"

In the early pages of her memoir, Keller describes her family's reaction to finding out she had become deaf and blind after an illness:

My parents were deeply grieved and perplexed. We lived a long way from any school for the blind or the deaf, and it seemed unlikely that anyone would come to such an out-of-the-way place as Tuscumbia to teach a child who was both deaf and blind. Indeed, my friends and relatives sometimes doubted whether I could be taught (p. 10).

The grief her parents felt, similar to the feeling after a death or great loss, was passed on to Keller's own sense of self. She did not view her Deafblindness as enabling contributions to her family, which affected how she interacted with others. Importantly, although the sense she was lacking something was imposed on Keller, her identity and sense of self opened up when she learned to communicate with her teacher, Anne Sullivan Macy. From her early childhood, her parents, particularly her mother, tried to find the best education possible. They paid Anne Sullivan to come to their home, boarded her, and hired her as Keller's teacher. This relationship continued through Keller's later educational career and college years, which involved sign language but was not delivered in a context that promoted access to the Deaf or Deafblind community or Deaf/Deafblind adults as experts.

We have come a long way from the time of Helen Keller. Society still has a long way to go, but Keller's reflection in her memoir, *The Story of My Life*, speaks to how far we have come. Keller states in the last few words of her book:

Thus it is that my friends have made the story of my life. In a thousand ways they have turned my limitations into beautiful privileges, and enabled me to walk serene and happy in the shadow cast by my deprivation (p. 77).

Despite Keller's good relationship with her family, she was still forbidden to marry and have children—a product of her social environment and time period but also a belief, it seems, of her own family. During her time period, women with disabilities were particularly oppressed; however, she was able to obtain a college degree and create a life for herself. It is worth noting that Keller does not cite her own family at the closing of her book. Instead, she states that her friends made her who she is today. They are the ones who took her "limitations" and let her "walk serene and happy" in the world. Despite Keller not discussing tensions in her book outright, this statement highlights the role of her close friends who became like family, including her teacher, Anne Sullivan Macy, and let her do advocacy work. Her reinvention of her family allowed her to be the person she was meant to be and to advocate for the rights of women, the blind, and the poor. This reinvention of family required both independence and choice. Keller, in this memoir, does not really discuss being part of a Deaf community, despite that being part of her identity. She does discuss advocating for the blind and Deafblind. Her friends seem to be, for the most part, hearing and sighted people she met in her travels, she is given access to larger society. Although she became an advocate for the blind, Keller does not really advocate for the rights of the Deaf community in this memoir.

Haben Girma—Being Deafblind and the Family Experience
As a child of refugees from Eritrea, Girma comments in the beginning of her book about her experience of being Deafblind:

> I like my Deafblind world. It's comfortable, familiar. It doesn't feel small or limited. It's all I've known; it's my normal.[53]

Girma's discussion of her identity here is interesting for two reasons. For one, like members of the Deaf community and the blind community (as seen on their organizations' websites), she resists medical definitions of her disability. To Girma, being Deafblind is her "normal," a positive aspect of her identity. Although the AADB website does not highlight such experiences, it seems there is a link and common theme between all three groups—Deaf, blind, and Deafblind—in that they all contest and resist medical definitions of their identity as disabling and stigmatizing. Girma's use of the word "world" is also important; she is part of a world that is different from her birth family, yet it carries equal weight, if not more, to her sense of self. Despite describing being Deafblind in these terms, she does not really address a community of Deafblind individuals in this memoir. Her account seems like an individual success story of navigating the world. In her epilogue, she does discuss her mission to "help increase opportunities for people with disabilities through education-based advocacy." One could argue that she sees her identity in a broader context, less in a cultural one. She is seen as disabled because of her position in society, not based on her language or culture of being Deafblind.

In her fascinating story of coming of age and growing up in California, we see the tension of this resistance play out with her hearing and sighted parents. In 2003, as a high school student, Girma wanted to go to Mali, West Africa, to help build a school with the group buildOn. When faced with asking her parents for their permission, Girma describes the following conflict, where her father asked, "What about your disability?" Girma recalls her reaction:

> I brace myself for a tricky conversation. Guiding him through his disability fears requires summoning up enough courage for all of us. My own fears need to stay hidden. Any sign of nervousness on my part will trigger their protective instincts. The production of courage for three people, my parents and I, feels draining. I've been doing it more

and more; my steps towards independence keep bringing up their fears for my safety. They raised me with stories of their long, arduous journeys to freedom, and I'm determined to reach for mine, too.[54]

Here, Girma does the work of advocating to her parents not only as a woman but also as a woman who is seen as disabled. She has to emotionally guide her father and mother through the decision and advocate for herself and her needs as an independent woman. These kinds of stories do not exist on the websites I analyzed and enrich understandings of how Deafblind women navigate independence in family environments with able-bodied parents.

Finally, Girma discusses what it was like to navigate her gender and racial identity and the complexities surrounding this lived experience when she attended Harvard Law School. She states:

> I'm in the confounding position of being both ultra visible and invisible. People will stare—it's human nature. Eyes are drawn to people who stand out, like a black woman with a dog and strange computer in the middle of a Harvard Law School reception. People will judge— that's human nature, too. A lot of people will decide to avoid me, assuming I don't have anything of value to contribute. I can't control their actions, but I can control the messages I send.[55]

The message here is about space. Keller was not allowed admittance to Harvard because of her gender. Later, Radcliffe College offered Keller admission, and she graduated in 1904. Keller was a fairly affluent white woman, so her experience is similar yet different from Girma's experience. Despite her family supporting her going to Harvard, Girma is stared at because Deafblind Black women do not typically attend Harvard Law School. In this way, just by the visual nature of her identity, she is paving a way and creating space in this arena for women of color seen as disabled. Without the overall support of her family, it is possible that Girma would not have had the conviction and self-esteem to contest this space. Lastly, Girma is an active agent of social change and activism. As she states, "I can control the messages I send." This theme connects with the AADB website, which illustrates Deafblind individuals not as recipients of assistance but as experts and active agents in creating change. Her example illustrates that there is a connection to the intersecting parts of her identity in terms of ability, gender, and race.

Lessons Learned

What do we learn from the discourses of these websites and memoirs about tensions in families of Deaf, blind, and Deafblind children? How might it influence the approach—specifically medical, social, and/or linguistic—used by families? What is the role of gender and race in the meaning-making process?

The overarching theme from the NAD, NFB, and AADB websites and the memoirs of Helen Keller and Haben Girma is one of access. In this way, families and individuals are still fighting for equal access and human rights for those who are Deaf, blind, and Deafblind. Another theme that arises in all three websites and the memoirs is that of contesting the ideas of disability and normality. As seen in the NAD's website, the Deaf do not consider deafness a disability. Rather, they see themselves as a linguistic minority in a larger hearing society, having to navigate tensions in the world and in their families. Tensions are seen in families in the memoirs especially. Girma has to convince her parents she can still do "normal" things like volunteer in another country and attend college and that her Deafblindness is not disabling. In Girma's account, being Deafblind is her "normal." She does not see being Deafblind as a disability; instead, she views it from a social model and highlights how various contexts limit her access. Keller, who was denied the right to marry and have children and perhaps access to other valued roles, resists the notion that family is limited to blood ties. Instead, she cites her friends as chosen family and the people who "made the story of my life." The tension between her family and her led her to embrace her teacher, Anne Sullivan Macy, as her chosen family and the person with whom she lived and traveled for many years. In this context, Keller was really able to thrive.

A theme unique to the Deaf community as seen on the NAD website is the issue and role of language access and rights. For hearing parents who have a deaf child, it is the NAD's position to not deny the child the human right to learn ASL and develop a sense of Deaf culture and pride. Tensions in families arise when they encounter medical "experts" who advise them to get a cochlear implant for their deaf child or to not teach them sign language at all. The effects of medical advice have been devasting to the Deaf community and viewed as a kind of cultural genocide of Deaf Americans.

Finally, Girma's memoir illustrates that an analysis of gender, race, and disability is necessary when understanding family tensions between nondisabled parents and children born with a disability. Girma's parents were refugees and had, as she describes, "long, arduous journeys to freedom." The experience of being marked different because of race made them cautious for their own daughter, who was seen as different because of race as well as being Deafblind and a woman, and heightened their "protective instincts." At first glance, their reaction may seem paternalistic, but when we unpack the layers of her identity as Black, a woman, and Deafblind, their reaction is contextualized and can be analyzed using an intersectional lens. While we may better understand the paternalism, it still presents a problem for youth in protective environments that constrain their opportunities.

Conclusion

Where do we go from here? The knowledge this data gives us about disability rights and the role of families is important. First, it is imperative to listen to and support people who are labeled Deaf, blind, and Deafblind as experts in the process of getting equal treatment and protecting their human rights. Memoirs provide insights into the lives of people with Deafblindness in a way that macro approaches alone cannot, showing the dire need to methodologically get firsthand accounts of people who identify as Deafblind. Keller and Girma resist a medical view of Deafblindness as a disability and highlight environmental factors that deny them access. Second, as the Deaf community shows us, we must consider issues of language as key identity components to human rights and protect linguistic signed culture. One of the many themes of this volume has been to look at parent-disability activist constituencies in terms of tensions that arise in these situations. This chapter adds to these efforts while including the Deafblind community and linking it to the challenges families face and how they incorporate activism in their daily lives. It adds to scholarship more broadly focused on family and parenting in sociology, disability studies, and gender studies. Finally, to achieve social justice for all, we must include more analyses in disability studies and beyond that incorporate an intersectional view of disability, race, and gender. None of us will truly be free until we do so.

ACKNOWLEDGMENTS

I would like to thank the amazing editors of this volume, Pam, Allison, and Richard, for their helpful insights, editorial comments, and support. I dedicate this chapter to my father, Aram C. Najarian, in memory of him and his love of learning and family. I also dedicate this chapter to my mother, Patricia H. Najarian, whose activist work and love of family knows no bounds.

NOTES

1. See Laura Mauldin, *Made to Hear: Cochlear Implants and Raising Deaf Children* (Minneapolis: University of Minnesota Press, 2016); Allison C. Carey, Pamela Block, and Richard K. Scotch, *Allies and Obstacles: Parents of Children with Disabilities and Disability Rights* (Philadelphia: Temple University Press, 2020); Linda M. Blum, "Mother-Blame in the Prozac Nation: Raising Kids with Invisible Disabilities," *Gender & Society* 21, no. 2 (2007): 202–26; Melanie Panitch, *Disability, Mothers, and Organization* (New York: Routledge, 2007).

2. Robert Bogdan, *Freak Show: Presenting Human Oddities for Amusement and Profit* (Chicago: University of Chicago Press, 1988); Robert Bogdan and Douglas Biklen, "Handicapism," *Social Policy* 7, no. 5 (1977): 14–19; Robert Bogdan and Steven J. Taylor, *The Social Meaning of Mental Retardation: Two Life Stories* (New York: Teachers College Press, 1994);

Simi Linton, *Claiming Disability: Knowledge and Identity* (New York: New York University Press, 1998).

3. Linton, *Claiming Disability*, 118.

4. Tobin Siebers, *Disability Theory* (Ann Arbor: University of Michigan Press, 2008); Carol Thomas, *Sociologies of Disability and Illness: Contested Ideas in Disability Studies and Medical Sociology* (London: Red Globe Press, 2007); Rosemarie Garland-Thomson, *Extraordinary Bodies: Figuring Physical Disability in American Culture and Literature* (New York: Columbia University Press, 1997); Susan Wendell, *The Rejected Body: Feminist Philosophical Reflections on Disability* (New York: Routledge, 1996).

5. Carol A. Padden and Tom Humphries, *Deaf in America: Voices from a Culture* (Cambridge: Harvard University Press, 1988).

6. Harlan Lane, *The Mask of Benevolence: Disabling the Deaf Community* (San Diego: DawnSign Press, 1999); Padden and Humphries, *Deaf in America*; Joseph P. Shapiro, "The Deaf Celebration of Separate Culture," in *No Pity: People with Disabilities Forging a New Civil Rights Movement*, ed. Joseph P. Shapiro (New York: Three Rivers Press, 1996), 74–104.

7. Hilde Haualand, Arne Grønningsæter, and Inger Lise Skog Hansen, "Uniting Divided Worlds: A Study of Deaf and Hard of Hearing Youth," *Fafo report* 412 (February 11, 2003), https://www.fafo.no/media/com_netsukii/412.pdf.

8. Jan-Kåre Breivik, *Deaf Identities in the Making: Local Lives, Transnational Connections* (Washington, DC: Gallaudet University Press, 2005).

9. Cheryl Najarian Souza, "Deaf Mothers: Communication, Activism, and the Family," *Disability Studies Quarterly* 30, no. 3/4 (2010a), https://doi.org/10.18061/dsq.v30i3/4 .1276; Cheryl Najarian Souza, "Deaf Women's Work Experiences: Negotiating Gender, Ability, and Theories of Resistance," *Research in Social Science and Disability: Disability as a Fluid State* 5 (2010b): 231–52; Cheryl Najarian, "Deaf Women: Educational Experiences and Self-Identity," *Disability & Society* 23, no. 2 (2008): 117–28; Cheryl Najarian, "Deaf Mothers, Maternal Thinking, and Intersections of Gender and Ability," *Scandinavian Journal of Disability Research* 8, no. 2–3 (2006a): 99–119; Cheryl Najarian, *"Between Worlds": Deaf Women, Work, and Intersections of Gender and Ability* (New York: Routledge, 2006b).

10. Mauldin, *Made to Hear*.

11. Ibid.

12. Laura Mauldin and Tara Fannon, "The Sociology of Deafness: A Literature Review of the Disciplinary History," in *Sociology Looking at Disability: What Did We Know and When Did We Know It, Research in Social Science and Disability*, ed. Sara E. Green and Sharon N. Barnartt (Leeds: Emerald Group, 2016), 9:193–225.

13. See A. J. Withers, Liat Ben-Moshe, Lydia X. Z. Brown, Loree Erickson, Rachel da Silva Gorman, Talila A. Lewis, Lateef McLeod, and Mia Mingus, "Radical Disability Politics," in *Routledge Handbook of Radical Politics*, ed. Ruth Kinna and Uri Gordon (New York: Routledge, 2019), 178–93.

14. See Kimberlé Crenshaw, "Mapping the Margins: Intersectionality, Identity Politics, and Violence against Women of Color," *Stanford Law Review* 43, no. 6 (1991): 1241–99.

15. Angela Frederick and Dara Shifrer, "Race and Disability: From Analogy to Intersectionality," *Sociology of Race and Ethnicity* 5, no. 2 (2018): 200–14.

16. Ibid.

17. J. Elton Moore, "Impact of Family Attitudes toward Blindness/Visual Impairment on the Rehabilitation Process," *Journal of Visual Impairment and Blindness* 78, no. 3 (1984): 100–106.

18. Georgina Kleege, "Blindness and Visual Culture: An Eyewitness Account," in *The Disability Studies Reader*, 5th ed., ed. Lennard J. Davis (New York: Routledge, 2017), 440–49.

19. Rod Michalko, *The Two in One: Walking with Smokie, Walking with Blindness* (Philadelphia: Temple University Press, 1998); Rod Michalko, *The Difference That Disability Makes* (Philadelphia: Temple University Press, 2002).

20. Michalko, *The Difference That Disability Makes.*

21. Angela Frederick, "Risky Mothers and the Normalcy Project: Women with Disabilities Negotiate Scientific Motherhood," *Gender & Society* 31, no. 1 (2017): 74–95.

22. Tara A. Fannon, "Out of Sight, Still in Mind: Visually Impaired Women's Embodied Accounts of Ideal Femininity," *Disability Studies Quarterly* 36, no. 1 (2016), https://doi.org/10.18061/dsq.v36i1.4326.

23. Ibid.

24. David Goode, *A World without Words: The Social Construction of Children Born Deaf and Blind* (Philadelphia: Temple University Press, 2010).

25. Scott M. Stoffel, ed., *Deaf-Blind Reality: Living the Life* (Washington, DC: Gallaudet University Press, 2012).

26. Azadeh Emadi, "The Magic of Touch: How Deafblind People Taught Us to 'See' the World Differently during COVID," *The Conversation*, October 10, 2022, https://theconversation.com/the-magic-of-touch-how-deafblind-people-taught-us-to-see-the-world-differently-during-covid-191698.

27. Ibid.

28. Marion Hersh, "Deafblind People, Communication, Independence, and Isolation," *Journal of Deaf Studies and Deaf Education* 18, no. 4 (October 2013): 446–63.

29. Ibid.

30. Carla Garcia-Fernandez, "Intersectionality and Autoethnography: DeafBlind, DeafDisabled, Deaf and Hard of Hearing-Latinx Children Are the Future," *Disability Justice, Race and Education* special issue 6, no. 1 (2020): 41–67.

31. Liz Crow, "Helen Keller: Rethinking the Problematic Icon," *Disability & Society* 15, no. 6 (2000): 845–59.

32. Ibid.

33. Kim Nielsen, *Beyond the Miracle Worker: The Remarkable Life of Anne Sullivan Macy and Her Extraordinary Friendship with Helen Keller* (Boston: Beacon Press, 2009).

34. See also Kim E. Nielsen, *The Radical Lives of Helen Keller* (New York: New York University Press, 2004); Kim E. Nielsen, *Helen Keller: Selected Writings* (New York: New York University Press, 2005).

35. Nielsen, *Beyond the Miracle Worker*, xiv.

36. Allison C. Carey, "Parents and Professionals: Parents' Reflections on Professionals, the Support System, and the Family in the Twentieth-Century United States," in *Disability Histories*, ed. Susan Burch and Michael Rembis (Chicago: University of Illinois Press, 2014), 58.

37. Barney G. Glaser and Anselm L. Strauss, *The Discovery of Grounded Theory: Strategies for Qualitative Research* (New York: Aldine De Gruyter, 1999).

38. Marjorie DeVault, *Liberating Method: Feminism and Social Research* (Philadelphia: Temple University Press, 1999); Shulamit Reinharz, *Feminist Methods in Social Research* (New York: Oxford University Press, 1992).

39. National Association of the Deaf, "About Us," NAD.org, 2023, https://www.nad.org/about-us/.

40. National Association of the Deaf, "About Us: Priorities," NAD.org, 2023, https://www.nad.org/about-us/priorities/.

41. Ibid.

42. Andrew Solomon, *Far from the Tree: Parents, Children and the Search for Identity* (New York: Simon and Schuster, 2012).

43. "National Federation of the Blind," NFB.org, 2023, https://nfb.org/.

44. Barbara Pierce, "No Such Thing as Blind Culture," NFB.org, November 2008, https://nfb.org/sites/default/files/images/nfb/publications/bm/bm08/bm0810/bm081007.htm.

45. "National Federation of the Blind," NFB.org, 2023, https://nfb.org/.

46. National Federation of the Blind, "Our Community," NFB.org, 2023, https://nfb.org/our-community.

47. Carey, Block, and Scotch, *Allies and Obstacles*.

48. "American Association of the Deaf Blind," aadb.org, n.d., accessed December 20, 2023, http://www.aadb.org/.

49. DeafBlind Camp of Maryland, "Mission Statement," deafblindcampofmd.org, 2022, https://www.deafblindcampofmd.org/mission-statement.

50. American Association of the Deaf Blind, "About AADB," aadb.org, n.d., accessed December 20, 2023, http://www.aadb.org/aadb/about_aadb.html.

51. American Association of the Deaf Blind, "Frequently Asked Questions about Deaf-Blindness," aadb.org, n.d., accessed December 20, 2023, http://www.aadb.org/FAQ/faq_DeafBlindness.html#resources.

52. "Helen Keller National Center," helenkeller.org, 2023, https://www.helenkeller.org/hknc/.

53. Haben Girma, *Haben: The Deafblind Woman Who Conquered Harvard Law* (New York: Twelve, 2020), 12.

54. Ibid., 67.

55. Ibid., 210.

7

Aging Out of Children's Hospitals

People with Complex Medical Conditions and Their Families in the Twentieth and Twenty-First Centuries

PAMELA BLOCK

Introduction

The lives of children and emerging adults with complex medical conditions intersect experiences of disability, health, precarity, surveillance, and incarceration.[1] The challenge for emerging adults and their families is to find pathways for more than a "bare life" and access to basic human rights like community life, education, work, and adult relationships. In a context of modern realities—such as the COVID-19 pandemic, climate change causing unpredictable power outages, shrinking social safety nets, and overextended and underpaid support workers—such paths are difficult to traverse. Additional factors include regional differences in services, campaigns against undocumented families, the realities of systematic racism and white supremacy, and the large number of families with insufficient health coverage. With these obstacles, perilous paths turn out to be more survivable for some than others, as systemic barriers and discrimination may lead to institutionalization and preventable death. Some find pathways to livable futures, at least for a while, and it is important to understand how they do so and how others might be supported to do the same.

This chapter considers the experiences of children and emerging adults with complex medical conditions and their families. It focuses on people with complex medical conditions who have high needs involving technology and 24/7 skilled nursing support to survive. This category includes polio survivors, many of whom require mechanical ventilation either temporarily or permanently. American survivors of the twentieth-century polio epidemics and their families became powerful activists central to disability rights activism and the establishment of the independent living movement. In the twenty-first century, children with complex medical needs commonly have communication or cognitive access barriers, meaning that parents remain primary advocates even when people in this group emerge into adulthood. However, this is not always the case. Some children with complex medical conditions emerge into adulthood as powerful activists, becoming parents and parent activists themselves.

Polio survivors were central to establishing community-based supports to allow themselves and others to live, work, learn, and love in community. They transformed the policy landscape in the United States with protests, court cases, and new laws and policies.[2] However, standardized legal requirements for disability access do not fit all bodies, and not everyone has been able to leave congregate care settings.

Though health systems and services for children and youth with complex medical conditions always focus on the person being able to stay home with their parents, this goal is not always possible due to the complexities of some medical conditions and the technologies needed for survival. People with a disability have elected to live in congregate care settings, feeling it is the best option for them. I worked with a cohort of individuals with spinal cord injuries who lived in such a setting in my first federally funded research project in 2001–2002. In the era before tablets and smart phones, it was difficult to connect with them, and I could not believe how long it took to get to that former tuberculosis asylum given the small New England state it was located in. Yet these individuals had the fewest struggles with transportation and human support to access the research project, which featured recreational and leisure activities all over the state. Though advocates are fighting for the most home-like settings possible, activists caution that in the current landscape, pragmatic choices sometimes mean that some form of congregate care is needed. In these contexts, people still seek the power to choose what a home might look like, with the needed technologies and human supports. They dream of a future where having a home with these technologies and supports is possible. The sections of this chapter outline twentieth-century experiences of people with complex medical conditions and activists who changed the world to enable themselves or a loved one to be part of it.

Gini Laurie: Early Advocacy for Children with Complex Medical Conditions

In the process of engaging in policy work, technology innovation, and activism and learning about the historical experiences of children and adults with complex medical conditions, I came to know Joan Headly, executive director of the International Ventilator Users Network (IVUN) and Post-Polio Health International (PPI) networks. Both organizations were started by Gini Laurie, Headly's mentor. As I learned about Laurie, I found her story, activism, and scholarship compelling, perhaps because, like me, she is a "sibling"— someone who grew up with one or more disabled sisters or brothers. The account that follows comes from a variety of archival sources including Joan Headley's six-part series of interviews available on YouTube through "It's Our Story" and documents and summaries available on Polio Place and other online sources.[3]

Laurie was born in 1913 and named Virginia Grace Wilson. Virginia and Grace were the first names of her two older sisters who died of polio before she was born. Laurie and her parents, Grace Cunningham, an artist, and Robert E. Wilson, a medical doctor at St. John's Hospital in St. Louis, Missouri, were profoundly impacted by their family's traumatic and tragic experiences with polio. Polio likely came into the family home from the father treating patients during an outbreak. Laurie's mother created artwork in memory of her lost children, including a mural on the chapel ceiling at a historical location of St. John's Hospital (no longer existing) depicting her daughters Virginia and Grace as angels. Laurie and her younger sisters grew up in the shadow of their dead older sisters and with their older siblings, Ella and Robert, who had survived polio but were disabled. Robert died at the age of twenty-two due to underventilation and the long-term impact of polio on his body.

Laurie began volunteering at polio-focused service activities, most notably with Toomey Pavilion in Cleveland Ohio, in 1949. The Toomey Pavilion started off as a ward for people with infectious diseases but became a respiratory-care center for polio survivors funded by the March of Dimes. The March of Dimes campaign to cure and treat polio was initiated by President Franklin Delano Roosevelt, himself a polio survivor.[4] In 1955, Laurie became coeditor of a newsletter called the *Toomeyville Jr. Gazette*,[5] which started as a mimeographed bulletin and evolved into newsletters for the twin organizations PPI and IVUN. The gazette included articles, poems, and artwork by hospitalized children. One of its purposes was to give children something to do, whether simply to read or to create and write for. One young journalist, Donna McGwinn, wrote in an early issue:

Here I sit in my wheelchair, stick in mouth, with a typewriter staring me in the face. I stare back. But being quite certain the typewriter, whom I shall call Blacky, is leering at me, I decide to ignore it. Seconds go by, then minutes, and then as the first hour passes, I get a brainstorm. Why not start writing on the Doctor of the Month? So out goes a scout to find Dr. Cotton. More minutes pass; scout returns; no luck. Doggone!

Maybe something in the ward would be interesting to write about. Mrs. Thomson is stretching Sue. Nope! A torture story is too morbid. Robilee is reading. Book review might be fun to do. Nope! Everybody's motor is working perfectly. Nope! Too fantastic! Oh dear! By now two hours have flown by and Blacky is getting impatient. It rattles its keys at me in disgust and shatters my nerves completely. Blacky can be so impatient at times!

About this time I decide to give up but a vision of Mrs. Randolph pops up and I change my mind. Good thing I did because ------- Hot Ziggedy!!! This time I've really got a brainstorm!!! Why not write about what I've just been thinking? It would take up space anyway. Good Idea.[6]

Through the gazette, children were able to express themselves and share joys, frustrations, accomplishments, and hopes for the future.

As children left the polio wards to reenter society, Laurie stayed in touch with them and helped them remain in contact with each other. A mutual support network for community-based living comprised of youth and young adult polio survivors was born. The gazette became a means for polio survivors to connect socially, exchange information about equipment and adaptive strategies for community living, and, ultimately, lobby and protest for structural change that would allow them to participate in social life in meaningful ways.

Independent Living Movement

The long-term consequences of the polio epidemic in the United States included not just the disability experiences of thousands of individuals but a national movement, including many key leaders who were polio survivors, to transform community-based services for disabled children and adults; this movement resulted in new laws and policies instituted between the 1970s and 1990s to protect disabled children's right to public education[7] and ensure access to higher education, work, communication, and transportation[8] and the right to live in the community. The Katie Beckett Waiver[9] was created in 1981 from the advocacy of a mother (Julie Beckett) on behalf of her daughter Katie to ensure funding on a national level to help children with complex medical conditions live at home with their families. It is likely this waiver that allowed Nick Dupree to live at home throughout his childhood. In contrast, the Olmstead v. L. C. decision mandating least restrictive environments and emphasis on community settings was not issued until 1999 and did not provide adults with complex medical conditions the same level of support as the Katie Beckett Waiver.[10] Disabled activists in the United States started the independent living movement, which transformed the sociocultural and political landscape both nationally and internationally.[11] By the twenty-first century, most disabled children lived outside of hospitals, though a subset with complex medical conditions continued to reside in hospitals periodically or permanently. Technologies have evolved to allow children with a variety of complex and rare conditions to survive into adulthood, but the community-based supports acquired in the twentieth century do not meet these children's needs.

Polio activists, notably Judy Heumann, Ed Roberts, and Justin Dart, were centrally involved in the independent living movement in the United States.[12] This movement was led by disabled people and pushed for policy and legislative change to allow disabled people access to education, transportation, communication, and employment.[13] The newly formed independent living movement collaborated with older groups such as the networks and supports Laurie facilitated. Family members such as Laurie, clinicians, and disabled activists worked together to enact structural change, but not without tension across generations and identity categories.

In the 1970s, in tandem with the birth and growth of the independent living movement, Laurie was one of first polio service providers to expand services beyond diagnosis-specific supports to provide a cross-disability approach to the needs of children and emerging adults with complex support needs (such as technologies, skilled nursing, and personal assistance): "We can't let divisiveness happen. We must all work together. Visual impairments, hearing impairments, physically disabled, mentally retarded, mentally ill, the elderly."[14] Laurie became very involved as an ally in the independent living movement, though she "prefer[red] to think of the movement as an interdependent living movement rather than an independent living movement."[15] She was very focused on getting people out of hospitals and into the community:

> The [phone] calls usually start by asking for the name of a nursing home that will take people on ventilators. I react violently to the suggestion and remind them that they do not need nursing. They need a pair of hands that they can direct. They do not need to be buried alive in a nursing home. They need to continue to live their lives as they choose.[16]

Through the latter decades of the twentieth century until her death, Laurie continued to develop communication networks to keep polio survivors in touch with each other. She was also involved in identifying and understanding post-polio syndrome. She was central to disability rights coalition building in the United States and is referred to in some publications as a grandmother of the independent living movement.[17]

There were some misunderstandings between Laurie, independent living movement cofounder Ed Roberts, and other disabled activists who did not always agree with or welcome the activism of nondisabled service providers and family members,[18] but overall, Laurie's approach was prescient to issues and unmet needs still obvious in 2021—and made especially apparent by the COVID-19 pandemic.

> Beware of the edifice complex; people don't need buildings; they need improved systems.[19]
> Beware of UBI, universal bureaucratic idiocy—be careful you don't become what you were originally created to fight against. [20]

Laurie died of cancer in 1989; as she experienced terminal illness and became disabled herself, she modeled disability access strategies by continuing to attend conferences and giving her final speeches from a stretcher.

It is important to understand the vision Laurie shared with polio survivors and the disability rights activists of the 60s and 70s to reshape the world to allow polio survivors and other disabled people to have a place in it. She died in 1989, shortly before a key piece of United States disability rights legislation, the Americans with Disabilities Act (ADA), was passed.[21] The ADA ensures access to communication, transportation, higher education, and employment. As noted earlier, in the United States, starting in the 1970s, public education, personal assistance services, and a variety of other supports for disabled people were codified, funded, and put into practice. However, community access was never universally available for disabled people in all regions of the United States, especially for those with complex medical conditions. Taking advantage of new laws required time, expertise, and money that many disabled people did not have, especially disabled people of color, those living in rural areas, and those with complex medical conditions.[22] Disabled people in the United States also disproportionately lived in poverty and experienced barriers to education and employment.[23]

Twenty-First Century Activism

Jumping ahead several decades to a time when centers for independent living have existed for over forty years, I write this chapter in memory of three prominent twenty-first-century disability activists with complex medical conditions who fought to live in their communities and stay out of congregate care: Nick Dupree (February 23, 1982–February 18, 2017), Carrie Ann

Lucas (November 18, 1971–February 24, 2019), and Stacey Milbern (May 19, 1987–May 19, 2020), all of whom died in preventable ways. If Laurie was a grandmother of the independent living movement, then these were her grandchildren. Despite more than fifty years of disability rights and independent living movement activism—despite all the changes to policy that occurred in the twentieth century—these activists died of preventable causes: an insurance company refusing to cover medication, nursing-home staff incorrectly adjusting ventilator settings, parts for machinery not arriving, multiple infections overwhelming their bodies, and surgery for a fast-growing cancer postponed due to COVID-19 related delays. They died of the "frequent flyer" experience of moving back and forth between nursing home and hospital because of insufficient housing or support structures for disabled people of any age with complex medical conditions to safely live in noninstitutional settings. They died because institutional settings, popularly considered safe alternatives, were deadly for them. They died due to complications from delayed surgery. They are all survived by loved ones, and Lucas was survived by multiple disabled children she had adopted. But before this, they lived, and their survival depended on disability justice practices of mutual care, interdependence, and collective access.[24]

Nick Dupree,[25] the only of the three activists I knew personally, authored a chapter in *Occupying Disability: Critical Approaches to Community, Justice, and Decolonizing Disability*.[26] His activist endeavors[27] were documented by United States National Public Radio (NPR), and he was an award-winning artist.[28] Block with Diallo[29] give more details about his life, especially his final months. Carrie Ann Lucas was a lawyer and mother of several disabled children.[30] She was a beloved activist whose life was cut short due to arbitrary drug rationing by her insurance company. The medication her insurance allowed did not help her and led to cascading effects that weakened her body, resulting in several hospitalizations and eventually death. Queer Asian disability justice activist Stacey Milbern had a fast-growing cancer, and her treatment was delayed due to the pandemic. She died, too soon and unexpectedly, of surgical complications.[31]

Unfortunately, these experiences are all too common and have become even more so due to increased vulnerabilities engendered by the COVID-19 pandemic. Milbern herself wrote powerfully about death and legacy, discussing Lucas in her 2019 blog post for the Disability Visibility Project, "On the Ancestral Plane: Crip Hand Me Downs and the Legacy of Our Movements." These are just three examples of unplanned survival followed by preventable death.[32] These activists survived childhood and emerged into a world that, despite over fifty years of disability rights and independent living movement activism, did not create a safe or accessible place for them, resulting in lifelong struggles for housing, proper medical care, technologies, and staffing to allow them to live safely and productively outside of long-term congregate care settings.

As a youth activist, Nick Dupree led a campaign called Nick's Crusade to change the law in Alabama to allow him to live at home after reaching adulthood rather than being automatically transferred to a nursing home in another state at age twenty-one.[33] Evolving health technologies are keeping people (barely) alive, but structural supports allowing continued survival and meaningful life experiences—such as choice of where to live, learn, work, and play—are tenuous threads that too often snap.

Despite their shortened lives and preventable deaths, Dupree, Lucas, and Milbern represent powerful positive examples of disability activism. All had important intimate relationships with partners and children. All had meaningful work and people who loved them. All had parents or loved ones who fought for them, and Lucas fought for her own children as a parent. Most people living with complex medical conditions requiring 24/7 support and technologies such as continuous medical ventilation do not have these opportunities.

From the 1960s polio epidemic through the birth of the independent living movement, disability activists and allies such as Gini Laurie fought for community-based supports and transformed disability policy on a national level. The preventable and premature deaths of Nick Dupree, Carrie Ann Lucas, and Stacey Milbern show that a similar level of transformation is needed now, especially in the realities of the COVID-19 pandemic. People with complex medical conditions and their families are no longer satisfied with either a "shut-in" life at home or an institutionalized existence moving from children's hospital to geriatric nursing home, though the realities of the pandemic have made this reality more likely than ever. Nick Dupree struggled to stay out of institutions his entire life with variable success. He was forced to live in one for a year to establish residency in New York and be eligible for services there. The final months of his life in 2016 and 2017 were a desperate and unsuccessful scramble between nursing homes and the hospital because of the system's failure to ensure him a safe place to live. In those months, he expressed dreams of a small residence/day program where youth and adults with complex medical conditions could live, work, play, and create together. He imagined holding children's art classes there. Acknowledging that congregate care settings are not generally preferred, he tried to imagine a livable future for himself. The message from his story, dreams, and activism is that children and adults like him deserve more than just the technology to keep them alive. This technology needs to be accompanied by shifts in policy and practice to allow people with complex medical conditions to live in safe places and engage in community life and desired occupations across their lifespan.

Aging Out of Children's Hospitals

Aging Out of Children's Hospitals is a qualitative and exploratory research project based in the United States and Canada that I began in 2017 with disability activist Julie Maury to honor Nick Dupree's passing. Methodologies combine semistructured interviews, analysis of public discourses, archival research, and autobiographical narratives. Health conditions and geographical distance limited in-person data collection even before the COVID-19 pandemic. As of 2023, the project team has interviewed a total of twenty-one people in the United States. It is poised for a new phase, directed by graduate student Dima Kassem, to look at the experiences of Canadian youth with rare medical conditions. The American cohort includes eight people with complex medical conditions requiring extensive periods of time living in children's hospitals, including six twentieth-century polio survivors and two people who reached adulthood in the twenty-first century with a variety of conditions and diagnoses; eleven mothers of children with complex medical conditions who could not themselves be interviewed; one disabled mother interviewed along with her disabled daughter; and one NGO leader. Some interviews were conducted in-person, but most were done by phone or video call. The polio survivors in the project were recruited from locations across the United States with the assistance of IVUN and PPI.[34] The rest of the interviewees were recruited via a children's hospital and health system in the northeastern United States or through calls on social media. I also reviewed archival materials from 1955 to the present available via Polio Place[35] (a service of PPI) and analyzed ten autobiographical memoirs. In this chapter, I refer mainly to the interviews with the eleven mothers whose children had either intellectual and developmental disabilities or communication access barriers that did not allow them to participate in interviews.

In the United States, supports for disabled children change drastically after the age of twenty-one, when children age out of the public education system. This shift is true for both children living at home and those in congregate care settings. As noted earlier, with the options made available by the work of disability activists and allies like Gini Laurie, there are now lots of supports for disabled children and adults to live at home with their loved ones, but expansions of services and supports do not meet the needs of everyone. As Alice Wong writes, "for all the unpleasantness that can come from the medical industrial complex, hospitals, especially children's hospitals were a place where I felt like I belonged in a very weird way. No one batted an eye at a wheelchair user or someone who looked different or who needed help eating or using the bathroom."[36] Institutionalization is not the preferred choice for parents or the health professionals supporting them, but some conditions and situations do not allow for children to live at home. As recounted by the mothers interviewed in the pre–COVID-19 pandemic period between 2017–2020, life changes in major ways, often for the worse, for children with complex medical conditions as they transition from pediatric to adult services and supports. Access to transportation, skilled nursing, and community decreases. Children used to being transported to school settings, where they had individualized medical supports, either find they have nowhere to go or need to take risks with inferior health supports to attend congregate day settings. As a result, parents (usually mothers) have to choose between staying home to ensure quality of care for their children, sending their children to day programs with inferior health supports, which puts their children at risk in the advent of a medical emergency, or moving their children to residential long-term care. Again, such decisions are not based on choice or preference but due to lack of alternatives.

Families do not feel adequately prepared for the major changes imposed on them when their children reach adulthood. They report a lack of information about the transition process leading to anxiety and disappointment that services are not as imagined:

> She's 19, she looks 12, she looks 11, so the first thing you see is kind of scary, because when you walked in there and you see there's no age limit. It goes from 21 to a person who could be at my mother's age, 65. Those things I think should not be left out in the conversation. They should tell you: "Please anticipate it's not like the school." I think they keep it very limited, the information they give you, because they don't want you to panic without knowing it. But I don't think it's helpful. (Camila)

Children who resided in pediatric hospital settings are no longer eligible for residential support in the children's hospital, and sometimes the only alternative—or the only way to be close to family—is placement in a geriatric nursing home or an inaccessible family home, trapped and isolated:

> She has to leave [the residential children's hospital], though, because she's aged out. She's aged out a while, and they've been great with Sunny and myself, very supportive and understanding, but she has to go, that's a reality I mean. There's just so much they can do. (Ann)

Very few community-based assisted living or group-home settings exist for young adults with complex medical conditions, and they are almost exclusively available to those with diagnoses of developmental disability. Similarly, there is a lack of safe and age-appropriate day programs, vocational services, or pathways to postsecondary education.

The people I interviewed whose children lived at home reported that funding for skilled nursing drops precipitously after the age of twenty-one, and therefore retention of reliable and stable nursing staff (needed for people on ventilators) becomes difficult. While pediatric clinicians might be skilled and experienced in working with children with complex medical conditions, most practitioners who primarily treat adults have more experience with the conditions of geriatric patients. The needs of emerging adults with complex conditions are very different, and because many did not survive into adulthood until recent decades, clinicians lack training and experience with this population. Clinicians applying knowledge based on experience with geriatric vent users can have deadly consequences. For example, the rules related to ventilator settings in nursing homes are sometimes standardized to prevent clinician error, but settings needed for children and young adults are very different than those appropriate for those with geriatric conditions; a nuance the clinicians may not have been trained to recognize, as highlighted by Nick Dupree's 2016 conflicts with well-meaning but dangerously misinformed clinicians in at least one nursing home, which contributed to his deteriorating health and eventual death.

In the period before the COVID-19 pandemic, there was a lack of funding and access to in-home supports, such as medical supplies and communication and other assistive technologies, and access barriers to leaving the home. Supply-line shortages and delays in treatments in the years of the COVID-19 pandemic led to increased uncertainty and stress for families trying to ensure sufficient in-home supplies, medicines, and equipment. Even before the pandemic, keeping up with needs could be a full-time job for family members, contributing to mothers' inability to work outside the home and creating social isolation for both people with complex conditions and family members responsible for their care. This put a major strain on families' abilities to keep members with complex medical conditions at home.

Providing supports to their children may become impossible as parents age and become unable to lift and transfer adult children or handle the complexities of navigating service bureaucracies. Parents need to start thinking about what their adult child's life might be like when parents can no longer support them in their home:

> We still lift him, we don't have the Hoyer lift yet, we're still lifting him . . . He's about 90, 95 pounds now. At some point, I know in years to come, he's going to be placed in a home. I'm a realist, but I know at some point that will happen. And it's not going to be a bad thing, because he loves being with other people that are like him. He loved going to school, he loves going to program. It's just going to be a dif-

ferent place where he's going to sleep. He, you know, he just goes with the flow. So, he'll be fine. I know in my heart. (Andrea)

Despite significant barriers to quality of life in adulthood for their children, mothers persist in imagining good futures in small-scale, home-like settings once children can no longer live at home:

ANN: it would be some type of small home setting, where she has all her medical needs met, which means round the clock nursing, doctor care, OT, PT, extracurricular activities . . . just an environment, a home setting where she could grow, and be amongst her peers, and have people around her, that have the same interests.
JULIE MAURY: A good home and a good place.
ANN: A good home and a good place! (Ann and Julie Maury)

These life changes, which threaten quality of life and even survival, are inherent not in medical or disability conditions but rather in structural supports provided or denied.

Discussion and Conclusion

The interviews from which these quotes were taken all were completed prior to the COVID-19 pandemic. Experiences of this pandemic in the United States have emphasized the vulnerability of people with complex medical conditions and the protective strategies that can be adopted. Unfortunately, this period has been accompanied by both quiet and passionate resistance to such strategies as masking and social distancing; explicit and implicit beliefs and practices have individualized responsibility for staying safe and minimized the significance of preventable death at the expense of disabled people. Passionate resistance is particularly present in movements against vaccination and masking, and despite continued risk, it is rare to see people masking in public places in the United States. Even many health contexts no longer require masks.[37] According to anthropologist Emily Mendenhall,[38] if someone dies of COVID-19, it is common for her interlocutors (people in a "hotspot" community where many had died of COVID-19) to highlight whether the deceased had additional conditions that were potentially life-threatening on the short or long term—including complex medical conditions but also conditions like obesity and diabetes as a way to make the deaths more acceptable. In contrast to twentieth-century activist movements such as the independent living movement, which opened possibilities for disabled people in public life, twenty-first-century realities are pushing in the opposite direction. This trend is evident in the examples given here where parents see no possibility for their children to live safely outside of congregate care settings. Policymakers are not protecting people with complex medical conditions and disability from the dangers of the pandemic, instead enacting and enforcing policies that put them in increased and sustained danger.

I conclude this chapter with a discussion of the importance of not only a rights-based but also a disability-justice based approach for understanding experiences of unplanned survival, preventable death, and limits to living a community-based life. Though policy solutions are needed, rights-based approaches regularly leave entire groups of people behind.[39] People in the United States with complex medical conditions are currently being left behind, as are undocumented families and people with intersecting experiences of race, ethnicity, and disability. As outlined by Sins Invalid and Berne et al., disability justice is an approach to care and activism with a focus on the principles of intersectionality, leadership by those most impacted, anticapitalist politic, and commitment to cross-movement organizing, recognition of wholeness, sustainability, cross-disability solidarity, interdependence, collective access, and collective liberation.[40] As noted in the work of disability justice authors such as Mia Mingus, Leah Lakshmi Piepzna-Samarasinha, and Shayda Kafai,[41] focus is also on not only holding power structures accountable for providing supports and services but also finding ways to support and care for each other. It is important to acknowledge that much of this care work involves both disabled and nondisabled women, especially mothers and sisters.[42] Though the mothers quoted here may not identify as disability justice activists, it is through strategies of disability justice that disabled people and their loved ones survive in times of austerity and catastrophe.

A powerful example of parent activism in alliance with disability activists is the U.S. organization Little Lobbyists. Parent and child leaders of this organization have written their own chapter in this book (see Stone et al., Chapter 8). The organization Little Lobbyists was formed in 2017 in response to threatened policy changes in the United States that put people with complex medical needs and disabilities in increased jeopardy.[43] This activist lobbying organization is dedicated to ensuring U.S. children with complex medical conditions have community-based supports to not just survive but thrive. Lobbying work includes advocating for better access to health care and health insurance, affordable prescription medication, and continuity of care throughout the lifespan. This includes lobbying for ability to access public education and seek all needed social and health services for citizens; undocumented residents should be able to access services and supports without fear of deportation. The organization stands against any form of discrimination that children with complex medical conditions and disabilities and their families face.[44] Its focus is to keep children alive, with their families, in their communities.

As disabled writer and performer Neil Marcus (1954–2021), whose own disability issues emerged in childhood, stated: "Disability is not a 'brave struggle' or 'courage in the face of adversity.' Disability is an art. It's an ingenious way to live."[45] The stories of Gini Laurie and her family, the activism of groups such as Little Lobbyists, and the mothers I interviewed all show ingeniously creative ways of confronting life-threatening adversity. They provide disability expertise, vision, and innovation that allow people to survive despite adversity, address the most difficult of personal and structural challenges, dream of better futures, and make dreams happen.

In the twentieth century, policy shifts in the United States made community life attainable for many disabled people. A similar shift must happen now to achieve similar advances for children and emerging adults with complex medical conditions. Bare survival is not enough. Adequate supports throughout childhood are not enough. Policy solutions, such as those advanced by Little Lobbyists, are needed to ensure rights to what Julie Maury and Ann mentioned: "a good home and a good life" for people with complex medical conditions across the lifespan. There are roles for both parent/family activism and disabled activists in these efforts, bringing distinct and overlapping insights and expertise to the struggle. For further discussion of these roles and how parent activists and disabled activists (and sometimes parent-child teams) engage and learn from each other and collaborate, see the chapter by Stone et al.

NOTES

1. Liat Ben-Moshe, Chris Chapman, and Allison C. Carey, *Disability Incarcerated: Imprisonment and Disability in the United States and Canada* (New York: Palgrave Macmillan, 2014); Lauren Berlant, "Slow Death (Sovereignty, Obesity and Lateral Agency)," *Critical Inquiry* 33, no. 4 (2007): 754–80; Pamela Block and Sini Diallo, "Activism, Anthropology, and Disability Studies in Times of Austerity," *Current Anthropology* 61, no. S21 (2020), https://www.journals.uchicago.edu/doi/full/10.1086/705762; Jasbir K. Puar, "The 'Right' to Maim: Disablement and Inhumanist Biopolitics in Palestine," *Borderlands* 14, no. 1 (2015): 1–27; Margrit Shildrick, "Living On: Not Getting Better," *Feminist Review* 111 (2015): 10–24.

2. Judith Heumann, *Being Heumann* (Boston: Beacon Press, 2020).

3. "Joan Headley, Part 01 of 06: Gini Laurie and Rehabilitation Gazette," It's Our Story, July 21, 2010, https://www.youtube.com/watch?v=vDu1-vxlvvU; "Gini Laurie | Post Polio: Polio Place," Polio Place, 2011, http://www.polioplace.org/people/gini-laurie; "About Gini Laurie: American Activist (1913–1989) Biography, Facts, Career, Wiki, Life," People Pill, n.d., accessed December 20, 2023, https://peoplepill.com/people/gini-laurie.

4. James Tobin, *The Man He Became: How FDR Defied Polio to Win the Presidency* (Boston: Simon & Schuster, 2013).

5. "The Gazette | Post Polio: Polio Place," Polio Place, 2011, http://www.polioplace.org /GINI.

6. D. McGwinn, "The Article. Toomeyville Gazette," 1955, Polio Place, accessed December 20, 2023, https://www.polioplace.org/sites/default/files/files/Toomeyville_Gazette _September_1955.pdf.

7. "Individuals with Disabilities Education Act (IDEA)," IDEA, U.S. Department of Education, n.d., accessed November 12, 2021, https://sites.ed.gov/idea/.

8. ADA, "An Overview of the Americans with Disabilities Act," adata.org, 2017, https:// adata.org/factsheet/ADA-overview.

9. Susan Agrawal, "Home - Kids' Waivers," Kids' Waivers, accessed December 20, 2023, https://www.kidswaivers.org/; Clay Risen, "Julie Beckett, Who Helped Disabled Children Live at Home, Dies at 72," *New York Times*, May 25, 2022, https://www.nytimes.com /2022/05/25/us/julie-beckett-dead.html.

10. "Olmstead: Community Integration for Everyone," ada.gov, n.d., accessed December 20, 2023, https://www.ada.gov/olmstead/index.html.

11. Kathy Martinez, "Independent Living in the U.S. & Canada," Independent Living Institute, 2003, https://www.independentliving.org/docs6/martinez2003.html.

12. Heumann, *Being Heumann.*

13. Ibid.; Fred Pelka, *What We Have Done: An Oral History of the Disability Rights Movement* (Amherst: University of Massachusetts Press, 2012).

14. Joan Headley, "Independent Living: The Role of Gini Laurie," accessed December 2, 2024, https://post-polio.org/networking/advocacy/independent-living-the-role-of-gini -laurie/, https://www.independentliving.org/docs6/headley200103.html.

15. Ibid.

16. Ibid.

17. Ibid.

18. Allison C. Carey, Pamela Block, and Richard K. Scotch, *Allies and Obstacles: Parents of Children with Disabilities and Disability Rights* (Philadelphia: Temple University Press, 2020).

19. Headley, "Independent Living."

20. Ibid.

21. ADA, "An overview of the Americans with Disabilities Act," adata.org, 2017, https:// adata.org/factsheet/ADA-overview.

22. Carey, Block, and Scotch, *Allies and Obstacles.*

23. Annual Disability Statistics Compendium, "2020 Annual Disability Statistics Compendium," 2020, https://disabilitycompendium.org/compendium/2020-annual-disability -statistics-compendium.

24. Patricia Berne, Aurora Levins Morales, David Langstaff, and Sins Invalid, "2018 Ten Principles of Disability Justice," *WSQ: Women's Studies Quarterly* 46, no. 1 & 2 (2018): 227–30.

25. Nick Dupree, "My World, My Experiences with Occupy Wall Street and How We Can Go Further," in *Occupying Disability: Critical Approaches to Community, Justice, and Decolonizing Disability*, ed. Pamela Block, Devva Kasnitz, Akemi Nishida, and Nick Pollard (New York: Springer, 2016): 225–33, https://link.springer.com/chapter/10.1007/978 -94-017-9984-3_15.

26. Pamela Block, Devva Kasnitz, Akemi Nishida, and Nick Pollard, *Occupying Disability: Critical Approaches to Community, Justice, and Decolonizing Disability* (New York: Springer, 2016), https://link.springer.com/book/10.1007/978-94-017-9984-3.

27. Joseph Shapiro, "A Medicaid Victory," National Public Radio, 2003, https://www.npr.org/2003/02/12/974391/a-medicaid-victory.

28. "Nick Dupree," Wynn Newhouse Awards, n.d., accessed November 12, 2021, https://www.wnewhouseawards.com/nickdupree.html.

29. Block with Diallo, "Activism, Anthropology, and Disability Studies in Times of Austerity."

30. Sarah Kim, "Carrie Ann Lucas Dies at Age 47. You Probably Haven't Heard of Her and That's a Problem," *Forbes*, February 25, 2019, https://www.forbes.com/sites/sarahkim/2019/02/25/carrie-ann-lucas-dies/.

31. Alice Wong, *Year of the Tiger* (New York: Penguin Random House, 2022).

32. Block and Diallo, "Activism, Anthropology, and Disability Studies in Times of Austerity."

33. Dupree, "My World, My Experiences with Occupy Wall Street."

34. "Home," International Ventilator Users Network, ventnews.org, 2021, https://www.ventnews.org/; "Home," Post-Polio Health International, 2021, https://post-polio.org/.

35. "Home," Polio Place, polioplace.org, 2011, https://www.polioplace.org/.

36. Wong, *Year of the Tiger*, 58.

37. Pamela Block, E. Pereira, A. Mello, and D. Sakellariou, "Introduction to the Special Issue: Disability and Covid-19," *Disability Studies Quarterly* 41, no. 3 (2021), https://doi.org/10.18061/dsq.v41i3; Jordan Grunawalt, "The Villain Unmasked: COVID-19 and the Necropolitics of the Anti-mask Movement," *Disability Studies Quarterly* 41, no. 3 (2021), https://doi.org/10.18061/dsq.v41i3.8343; Joana Milan Lorandi and Pamela Block, "Social and Health Experiences of Disabled People with Complex Medical Conditions during the COVID-19 Pandemic," *Research in Social Science and Disability* 13 (2023): 113–34; Mia Mingus, "You Are Not Entitled to Our Deaths: COVID, Abled Supremacy & Interdependence," *Leaving Evidence* (blog), January 16, 2022, https://leavingevidence.wordpress.com/2022/01/16/you-are-not-entitled-to-our-deaths-covid-abled-supremacy-interdependence/.

38. Emily Mendenhall, *Unmasked: COVID, Community, and the Case of Okoboji* (Nashville: Vanderbilt University Press, 2023).

39. Berne, Levins Morales, Langstaff, and Invalid, "2018 Ten Principles of Disability Justice"; Carey, Block, and Scotch, *Allies and Obstacles*; Leah Lakshmi Piepzna-Samarasinha, *The Future Is Disabled* (Vancouver: Arsenal Pulp Press, 2022); Leah Lakshmi Piepzna-Samarasinha, *Care Work* (Vancouver: Arsenal Pulp Press, 2018); Wong, *Year of the Tiger*.

40. Berne, Levins Morales, Langstaff, and Invalid, "2018 Ten Principles of Disability Justice"; Sins Invalid, "10 Principles of Disability Justice," *sinsinvalid.org* (blog), 2015, https://www.sinsinvalid.org/blog/10-principles-of-disability-justice.

41. Mia Mingus, "Changing the Framework: Disability Justice. How Our Communities Can Move beyond Access to Wholeness," *Leaving Evidence* (blog), February 12, 2011, https://leavingevidence.wordpress.com/2011/02/12/changing-the-framework-disability-justice/; Piepzna-Samarasinha, *Care Work*; Shayda Kafai, *Crip Kinship* (Vancouver: Arsenal Pulp Press, 2021).

42. Allison C. Carey, "Parents and Professionals: Parents' Reflections on Professionals, the Support System, and the Family in the Twentieth-Century United States," in *Disability Histories*, ed. Susan Burch and Michael Rembis (Champaign: University of Illinois Press, 2014), 58–76; Carey, Block, and Scotch, *Allies and Obstacles*; Eva F. Kittay, *Love's*

Labor: Essays on Women, Equality, and Dependency (New York: Routledge, 1999); Eva F. Kittay, *Learning from My Daughter: The Value and Care of Disabled Minds* (New York: Oxford University Press, 2019); Headley, "Independent Living."

43. "Little Lobbyists," Little Lobbyists Action Network, 2021, https://littlelobbyists .org/.

44. Ibid.

45. Block, Kasnitz, Nishida, and Pollard, *Occupying Disability*.

8

SURVIVE AND THRIVE

*How Little Lobbyists Empowers Families to
Fight for Disability Justice*

JENEVA STONE, ELENA HUNG, LAURA LEBRUN HATCHER, AND
ROGER A. STONE

L ittle Lobbyists is a family-led nonprofit organization that advocates for
the needs of medically complex and disabled children. We are a disability rights organization, as our children with disabilities will become
adults with disabilities (and some already have). We believe health care, education, and community inclusion are human rights for all people with complex medical needs and disabilities. Inclusion is at the heart of all we do.

We are determined to course correct harmful narratives about disabled
children. First, we teach families the ethics of centering their disabled children
instead of parents. We introduce our children as people first, before discussing
their medical and other support needs. We advocate with our children, not
on their behalf. Second, we encourage families to see themselves and their
children as part of the disability community, working alongside and learning
from disabled adults. Third, we take charge of the narrative by insisting that
lived experience is expertise and must be considered when making policy.

Our advocacy priorities[1] include the right to health care, education, and
community inclusion—for all. Since our inception in 2017, we have advocated to preserve the Affordable Care Act (ACA), increase Medicaid funding
and protect it from block grant proposals and work requirements, lower prescription drug costs, and increase funding for Medicaid's Home and Community-Based Services (HCBS) waivers. During the COVID-19 pandemic,
we advocated to protect people with disabilities. We support the Individuals
with Disabilities Education Act (IDEA), the Americans with Disabilities Act
(ADA), and the 1999 U.S. Supreme Court Olmstead Decision, which, along

with the ADA, guarantees the right of people with disabilities to live in their communities. When we say "all means all," we mean it; there is no such thing as "other people's children." All people regardless of race, sex, gender identity, religion, ethnicity, disability, or country of origin deserve access to health care without fear of deportation or other penalties.

The Founding of Little Lobbyists

In the summer of 2017, Elena Hung and Michelle Morrison, parents of children with complex medical needs and disabilities (Xiomara and Timmy, respectively), were worried about the future of health care given threats from the newly elected Trump administration to repeal "Obamacare," a euphemism for the ACA.

The ACA was the first U.S. statute to address systemic health insurance inequality for those ineligible for Medicare or Medicaid. Prior to the ACA, most Americans relied on their employers for access to health insurance. Individuals who attempted to buy insurance on their own faced staggering premium costs and outright denial if they had even the most minor "preexisting condition."

The ACA requires Americans to purchase health insurance (the individual mandate), establishes an employer mandate, and sets requirements for health insurers that include ten essential health benefits, a prohibition on denying coverage or charging more for preexisting conditions, and removal of annual and lifetime caps on insurance coverage.[2] To lower costs, the ACA offers to expand Medicaid (a state-federal matching program established in 1965) in each state and establishes state health insurance exchanges with individual and family plans for direct purchase by consumers.

Since the ACA[3] was signed into law by President Barack Obama on March 23, 2010, the Republican Party has made its repeal a priority. On March 6, 2017, the American Health Care Act (AHCA) was introduced in the U.S. House of Representatives by House Republicans,[4] and Senate Republicans introduced versions of the House bill that summer. These Republican bills threatened to gut the ACA by eliminating (or allowing states to opt out of) the individual mandate, eliminating the employer mandate, altering or eliminating the ten essential health benefits, and allowing insurers to once again deny coverage for preexisting conditions and place annual and lifetime caps on insurance coverage. The bills also sought to slash federal Medicaid spending and replace it with a block grant program.

An ACA repeal would have put families like Elena's and Michelle's in jeopardy of medical bankruptcy, as had been the fate of many families prior to the ACA. Both Xiomara and Timmy were born after the ACA became law, and their mothers were concerned about their very survival should Republicans succeed.

At the time, Timmy was in kindergarten and fascinated by robots and pirates. Xiomara was almost three years old and loved Sesame Street and playing with her brother. Timmy was born just six days after the ACA provision went into effect banning lifetime caps on medical expenses. He was born seven weeks premature and spent six months in the neonatal intensive care unit (NICU) having multiple surgeries and treatments. A typical health insurance lifetime cap in 2017 was $1 million; Timmy's medical costs exceeded $1 million before he turned three months old.[5] His six-month stay in the NICU cost $2 million. Xiomara, whose name means "ready for battle," has a similar story, but her NICU stay cost $3 million.[6] For both children, ACA protections meant insurance covered nearly all their NICU stays and health care going forward.

While preserving the ACA meant saving the individual mandate, employer mandate, ten essential benefits, and more,[7] Little Lobbyists shrewdly stuck to the aspects of the ACA their families could most easily demonstrate: the negative impact on families if annual and lifetime insurance caps were reinstated, people with preexisting conditions were excluded, and cuts to Medicaid occurred.[8]

Both women recall that the idea for Little Lobbyists was sparked in June 2017. On May 4, the House passed the AHCA, sounding the alarm among health care advocates. Elena began making calls to pull together a meeting of her friends with medically complex and disabled children. At the time, Elena's and Michelle's impulse was to act quickly to protect their children's lives. They forged alliances with the disability community as they began their advocacy journey.

A simple plan was formed: collect photos and stories of children with complex medical needs and disabilities from around the country and take them directly to legislators. Because the group lived in the suburbs of Washington, DC, Capitol Hill was an easy train ride away, so group members could deliver these stories in person. They also decided to bring their children to the Hill (with their ventilators, oxygen, wheelchairs, walkers, leg braces, feeding tubes, and more in tow) so lawmakers could see firsthand who needed the protection of the laws and programs under threat. The children were encouraged to speak directly to lawmakers as well.

Elena and Michelle were members of an existing Facebook group founded by parents called National Action for Medically Complex Kids. Through that platform and personal contacts, they reached out to share their plan and request stories from families across the nation. In less than a week, the group collected over 150 stories:

Between Michelle and I, we had a small network of families already. They were mostly families with children with tracheostomies and feeding tubes because our kids have tracheostomies and feeding tubes. So we just reached out to our friends one-on-one and then created a Facebook group that said, "Hey there, tell us your story. Just write out a paragraph about your kid, what they like, what they don't like, and their hobbies. Then tell us a little bit about their medical history, and tell us about what health care means to your family. Send us a cute photo of your kid because we want to put a face on this." . . . It was very low budget. We had a Google document. People submitted stuff, and we were putting it together by hand. A lot of people were people we knew; some of them had reached out by word of mouth.[9] (Elena Hung)

The group's first visit to Capitol Hill was on June 20, 2017.[10] Five families from the DC metro area gathered for it. The message was simple: here are our children; they belong in their communities; they need quality health care to survive; they deserve to be heard by their elected officials.

How Little Lobbyists Got Its Name

In preparation for the June 20 visit, Elena and Michelle contacted the media. A *Vox* reporter, Sarah Kliff, had filed a story about Timmy in March,[11] so the two reached out to her again. The day after the visit, Kliff filed a story with the headline, "The Littlest Lobbyist: A 6-Year-Old, Whose Life Depends on ACA, Heads to Capitol Hill."[12] Petula Dvorak, a columnist for the *Washington Post*, filed a story about the group on June 22: "as they shared elevators with lobbyists from the liquid metal industry who smiled tightly at the elevator full of wheelchairs, they brought real life to this tidy enclave of lawmakers."[13]

During that first day of office visits, the group realized it needed a name:

[The receptionist] would say, "Oh, and which organization are you with?" and Michelle and I would always look at each other. We're like, "No, it's just us. It's Elena and Michelle." . . . We noted that these offices were looking for an organizational name, like that was the norm, and we were sort of just a bunch of moms and dads and kids walking in.[14] (Elena Hung)

When Kliff's article appeared the next day, the group decided to lean into the identity of "the little lobbyists" and began using the name to introduce itself to congressional offices,[15] despite the fact that neither the adults nor the children were professional, paid lobbyists. The sobriquet was simply catchy and made the group stand out.

The group's Twitter account debuted as Little Lobbyists on June 24 and immediately caught the attention of health care leaders with large social media followings, including Andy Slavitt, former acting administrator of the Centers for Medicare and Medicaid Services, and Ben Wikler, Washington director of MoveOn. MoveOn, The Arc, Center for American Progress, Family Voices, ADAPT, and numerous other organizations also elevated the group's message, as did countless individual disabled persons.[16]

That June and July, Little Lobbyists was everywhere—speaking at rallies and press conferences, posting on social media, and doing interviews with journalists. The group took off fast through the hard work of being present, speaking out, and having a clear message. Elena and Michelle's determination was everything.

Little Lobbyists was featured in national news outlets, including *Time* magazine,[17] the *New York Times*,[18] and the *Washington Post*.[19] The group also caught the attention of House Minority Leader Nancy Pelosi (D-CA), who began to acknowledge and thank Little Lobbyists in her public remarks.

Our name, "Little Lobbyists," was a happy accident, yet it stuck. It emphasizes our primary focus on advocating for medically complex and disabled children. We consider ourselves a disability rights organization for children and families.

The Founding Ethics of Little Lobbyists

From its first meeting, Little Lobbyists was determined to be different from other advocacy groups started by parents of disabled children. Elena and Michelle were fiercely protective of their children's privacy. If families were to go public with their children's stories, parents would need to control the media narrative in service of their children's dignity. Elena and Michelle agreed to center the children as kids first, medical diagnoses second, as in their instructions to families sending in stories through the National Action Facebook page. The two wanted to project an ethos that steered clear of seeking pity or using children for political stunts.

Michelle recalls those crucial early decisions:[20]

[There was] the cute kids factor [that we needed to address]. . . . We were really struggling with how we do this in a way that we keep our kids from being objectified? Where is that line? And that was a tricky one. We didn't want to become political eye candy: "Oh, look at these kids with this [legislator]." There were people [though] that were really looking for ways to personify the health care story. We were there at the right time for that to happen.

Elena provides additional context:[21]

I didn't want to bring our children to Capitol Hill and have it be a pity case like "Jerry's Kids" and all those telethons from years ago. I was very clear that I wanted to run as far in the opposite direction as possible, that we were not going to drag our kids to the Hill for pennies and to get people's sympathy. We wanted to humanize our children and help others to see them as their own children, see them as children in their neighborhoods and children in their communities, children that they could themselves love.

Elena and Michelle stayed true to their vision. Early news articles about the group emphasize the children's likes and dislikes alongside their medical conditions. They mention the children smiling, laughing, and playing, and the accompanying photos do the same. Timmy, one article notes, knew how to find the best frozen yogurt and popcorn on Capitol Hill.[22] In October, Little Lobbyists went trick-or-treating on the Hill, which became an annual event until the COVID-19 pandemic.

On Hill days, parents made sure kids had plenty of breaks and snack time. Children often sat next to their parents during meetings, literally having a seat at the table to discuss their health care. They were encouraged to interact with lawmakers on their own terms, whether simply greeting congresspersons and staff or delivering their own message, in their own words, about health care. Friendships developed among the children, and Hill days began to feel like playdates.

Robbie Jeanne, then a photographer for the Senate Democrats Media Center (SDMC), accompanied Little Lobbyists on Hill days, press conferences, and media appearances for several years. Because of the photos he took, both in a professional role and in a personal capacity, Little Lobbyists was able to accomplish its main goal of putting a face on health care. We shared those photos far and wide and humanized public policy through them. Robbie understood what Little Lobbyists was trying to do, and his visual images became a powerful tool to show the joy of disabled children living their lives, which has been underrepresented.

Identifying with the Disability Community

During the summer of 2017, protests led by disabled activists were featured on national news broadcasts, with images showing activists being dragged from their wheelchairs and arrested. Little Lobbyists was very vocal about its support for the disabled protestors, repeatedly drawing the connection that children with disabilities grow up to be adults with disabilities, the very same people being dragged from wheelchairs.

As Elena expanded her outreach to health care allies, she had more contact with disability rights groups. As she spoke to them, she learned and adjusted the way Little Lobbyists presented itself:[23]

> We can talk about health care as this broad stroke, but it didn't specifically address disability. [Other] people were saying the word "disabled." We were using the words "medically complex," or "children with complex medical needs" because we wanted to stress the urgency of that. And very quickly as we grew, we're, like, well, it's "complex medical needs and disabilities." . . . So I think in the first two weeks we started saying, it's complex medical needs and disabilities.

Jamie Davis Smith, mother to Claire, had been advocating with Moms-Rising when she met Elena on Capitol Hill. A writer and attorney, Jamie's *Washington Post* article, "My Daughter Doesn't Have 'Special' Needs. She's Disabled,"[24] summed up the Little Lobbyists approach:

> Listening to what people with disabilities say about the issue made me realize that it's important to consult them. Other disability advocates . . . emphasize the importance of saying a person is disabled. [Rebecca] Cokley says the term is powerful because it provides legal protections under the Americans With Disabilities Act. "Special" or "different" needs are not protected under the law, but disabilities are. She also says that parents need to advocate with their children rather than for them; this means paying attention to what their children, and people with disabilities, want rather than defaulting to terms they or their children's providers feel more comfortable using.

The juncture of adding "disabilities" to the group's tagline—"children with complex medical needs and disabilities"—was an inflection point. It marked a rejection of the condescending societal ableism of "special needs" and a turn toward the rights-based language necessary for political change.

Finding Our Place within the Disability Community

As they plunged into the world of advocacy, Elena and Michelle realized that *children* with complex medical needs and disabilities are rarely represented among disability and family advocacy groups. For example, ADAPT focuses on the needs of disabled adults; MomsRising focuses on the needs of children broadly. The majority of parent advocate groups focus on children with developmental disabilities or rare diseases, that is, either disability or medical needs, but not both. Little Lobbyists could step into that vacuum.

Additionally, in the United States, Medicaid rules treat disabled adults and children differently, meaning that policy solutions to disability and pediatric health issues are not always one-size-fits-all.[25] Little Lobbyists understood that it had a role to play in ensuring children and families were represented accurately in a loud and complex legislative conversation.

In service of these goals, Elena and Michelle retained their commitment to centering their children. They were so committed that Timmy's diminishing interest in going to Capitol Hill and sharing his story in public—after the ACA was rescued in 2017 and 2018—led Michelle and her family to pull back from the group:[26]

> We didn't want to be taking advantage of our kids, either. And so where is that line? That was a constant, constant struggle. That's why . . . when Timmy said he wasn't interested in going, we [said] okay, then we won't go. He needs to have [the] agency to be able to say no.

So Little Lobbyists found its path by learning to identify with the needs of disabled children, not by emphasizing the needs or goals of parent caregivers.

Strategizing to Save the ACA

Little Lobbyists' advocacy strategy was simple and effective. Elena and Michelle put those first 150 stories in a binder tabbed by state, which allowed them to quickly find family stories for each congressperson. They also printed off copies to hand directly to members or staff.

For their first Hill day, official meetings were secured with Senator Chris Van Hollen (D-MD), because both women were his constituents, and Senate Minority Leader Chuck Schumer (D-NY); both meetings were fruitful. Other congressional offices encouraged the group to drop by. Elena credits the advocacy group Family Voices with helping Little Lobbyists learn to navigate Capitol Hill physically and strategically. In preparation for June 20, Elena had googled "family health care organizations" and emailed Family Voices asking for help. A staff member from Family Voices accompanied Little Lobbyists as it navigated elevators and underground tunnels with children who were wheelchair and stroller users.

Part of the magic of advocacy is realizing that you *do* have a voice and that others *are* listening. Part of the opportunity of being in person on Capitol

Hill are chance encounters that enable grassroots organizers to form connections to build on later. Such meetings as one with Senator Elizabeth Warren (D-MA) really raised the group's spirits:[27]

> We were taking the underground train [that runs beneath the Senate office buildings,] and she was clearly in a hurry. And she saw our children, and she just rushed over to talk to them. . . . She had very encouraging words, and I think that gave us a boost. When you talk about families who have never been on the Hill, have never advocated, have never lobbied, and here is a recognizable face, right, we all know who Elizabeth Warren is. And for her to say you are doing a great thing, keep telling your stories as it's really important. Your children matter. To hear that on your first day on the Hill was an unexpected catalyst, that unexpected encouragement that really kept us going. After that we always went back to, "Hey if Elizabeth Warren who's running late for an important meeting took 5–10 minutes to stop and talk to us and tell us this was important, surely, we can get time with others and, and they should be listening to us." (Elena Hung)

The group had initially thought to make just one visit to Capitol Hill to influence senators. However, they realized that all one hundred offices—spread out over three different buildings—could not be visited in a single day. Bolstered by the positive feedback they received, they made a commitment to share what had, by then, become hundreds of family stories:[28]

> What was important to us that first week was actually following through on the promises we'd made to all the families that we would personally hand over their stories to their senators, or to their senators' offices at least. It wasn't possible to get to all the offices the first day. So, initially, the reason we came back was we'd promised all these families. . . . Then we realized that there were so many stories to tell, and that we were actually getting a lot of people to listen to us. (Michelle Morrison)

The families were a thirty-minute metro ride from the Capitol, and many parents had flexible work schedules. This recognition of privilege spurred the group to continue its activities.[29]

Elena and Michelle strategized, with the help of friends, to provide a bigger megaphone for their families. Little Lobbyists began its social media presence on Facebook because all the family support groups were there; however, Twitter was the breaking news social media platform where the disability and health care rights groups were. Some days, ACA news was breaking hour by hour; on Twitter, Elena and Michelle could get the most up-to-date information as well as share their own message.

Elena says that Twitter was key to the group's early success. Not only did the platform make it easier to connect with other activists, it also allowed the group to respond to political issues in real time. Unlike Facebook, on which widely used privacy settings can slow down messaging momentum, Twitter was entirely public. In addition to personal tags, hashtags allowed relevant content to come up in the feeds of politicians and advocacy organizations large and small, enabling spontaneous retweets and quote tweets as well as greater visibility.

Twitter, through practice, was also key to developing the "Little Lobbyists voice." Elena and Michelle were intent on introducing the children as people first, sharing their activities and interests, and discussing medical needs second. They developed an organizational diction that allowed for fierceness but centered respect and affection for their children and the disability community. At every turn, Little Lobbyists encouraged people with disabilities to speak for themselves rather than have allies speak for them.

As Little Lobbyists expanded its messaging through in-person visits to Capitol Hill offices, Facebook outreach to families, and on Twitter, Elena and Michelle began to forge alliances with the disability community, including ADAPT and other organizations. Our families participated in many rallies but not all the protests. The noise and confusion frightened several of our children, and many protests were held outside in extreme summer heat, which was a health consideration for some.[30]

By late June 2017, Laura LeBrun Hatcher, mother of Simon, had heard of Little Lobbyists. A friend had forwarded Sarah Kliff's June 21 article, knowing that Laura was worried about the possible ACA repeal. As Laura recalls,[31]

> I did some internet sleuthing, and tracked them down and found an email address. I said, "You know, I saw this article. I think this idea of showing up in person with stories of folks from other states so that you have a reason to go to [other legislators'] office[s] . . . it's brilliant. I don't live that far away. I'm in Maryland. Let me know what I can do to support [you]." And, 10 minutes later, they wrote back, "What are you doing tomorrow?"

Laura, her husband, Brian, and Simon began attending Hill days, telling Simon's story among the chorus of families desperate to preserve the ACA, Medicaid, and access to health care for their children.

Tension built throughout late June and into July 2017 as the U.S. Senate began deliberating bills to gut or eliminate the ACA; however, the Senate was unable to summon enough votes to support any of them. On July 25, the Senate approved a procedural motion to vote on the House-passed AHCA and scheduled a vote for July 28. This vote was known as the "skinny repeal" because Senator Mitch McConnell (R-KY) had proposed an amendment to the AHCA that would repeal rather than replace key aspects of the ACA.[32]

Throughout the day on July 28, huge numbers of activists gathered at the U.S. Capitol to protest the bill and await the vote. Laura was unable to be with the other Little Lobbyists that day. A graphic designer, she says she "stress designed" a logo for the group while waiting on the vote: the graphic incorporates the words "Little Lobbyists" with a child holding a star and a stripe, the U.S. flag, and a heart with an EKG line through it. This design became the official Little Lobbyists logo (see Figure 8.1).

As Elena recalls, the July 28 vote was "everything." The skinny repeal failed when Senator John McCain (R-AZ) famously turned down his thumb as a "no" vote at two A.M. on July 29. Little Lobbyists families had been visiting congressional offices all day and then held vigil outside the U.S. Capitol into the night, alongside thousands of other activists. This was the vote, the night, the everything that would determine whether the ACA would survive. Reporter Emma Roller of *Splinter* wrote that the protestors' voices were so loud that they "echoed off the side of the Capitol and reverberated back to us, making it sound like there was an identical group of protesters hiding in the portico."[33] Elena, Michelle, and Xiomara (Timmy was at home recovering from a hospital stay) were among those there until four A.M., talking to reporters and celebrating.

A few days later, Laura was able to join the rest of the group at the "Our Lives on the Line" rally.[34] By then, Laura had used her professional expertise to create full branding for Little Lobbyists. She brought buttons and signs with the logo to the rally, which the group used that day, and redesigned the Little Lobbyists website, set up in June. In addition, Laura designed story

Figure 8.1 Little Lobbyists Logo. (*Designed by Laura LeBrun Hatcher.*)

templates for the famous binder, as well as professional letterhead to give the group a polished look.

Meetings over the course of that summer with House Minority Leader Nancy Pelosi (D-CA) helped cement Little Lobbyists' influence on the Hill:[35]

> The first time [we met Nancy Pelosi] was in 2017, at one of the rallies that Move On organized. Most of the fight was in the Senate by the time we got involved. . . . We told her what we were doing in the Senate, we showed her the binder we were carrying . . . and [we said], look, these are all our children. And she took the time to flip through it and read. . . . She encouraged us, this is so important, please keep telling your stories. I did not realize then that we were going to have many more interactions with her. But that first interaction was meaningful. (Elena Hung)

In the 2018 midterm elections, House Democrats gained a majority. Pelosi was elected Speaker of the House, and in her acceptance speech, she credited "our Little Lobbyists [who] bravely came forward to tell their stories"[36] as one of the groups that had helped to save the ACA.

Challenges and Successes of Initial Organizing

Little Lobbyists got up and running in the moment, without funding or even politically savvy leaders. The group's parents had an unshakable human bond with their children, which was apparent to all who met them. As Elena has said, "What we're really doing is celebrating the joy of disabled children."

Robbie Jeanne zeroed in the group's appeal and success:[37]

> It was just, "Look my kid in the eye and see that they're human. We're here because this might get taken away. Remember my child's face." . . . That's the power of Little Lobbyists: People would be in a rush or in their own head about something else going on in the world, and then they get to talk to these kids and learn what they're into and learn that they're humans too. I had the privilege of being able to see them sort of break down senators, where they became less senator-like and more like aunts and uncles, like parents. They became friends of the Little Lobbyists.

Little Lobbyists' leadership made good use of social media, understanding which platforms were best for which type of engagement. Their use of social media and the press was entirely community based—working from their circle of contacts outward in larger circles. Early press coverage was considered "earned media," meaning that journalists wrote about Little Lobbyists because they found it newsworthy.

The group also made good use of in-person and online approaches to advocacy, developing and sharing best practices with one another. Finally, Little Lobbyists is fortunate that members who are lawyers, graphic designers, writers, editors, health care professionals, former lobbyists, and many more have been willing to volunteer special skills and expertise.

We are cognizant of the fact that parent-led groups are often conferred greater symbolic respect than groups led by people with disabilities. As an organization, we strive to balance the scales. During the 2017 ACA protests, we were aware that sympathy for disabled children made it easier for our organization to get Capitol Hill meetings. We leveraged that privilege to insist that congresspersons also meet with adult disabled activists if they were to meet with us.

In addition, we make efforts to prioritize full disability representation and diversity in our work and are especially mindful to include all disabilities. When invited to collaborate on a project or an event, we ask about the diversity of other participants and, if necessary, protest lack of diversity, equity, and inclusion. Our executive director has declined speaking invitations where she would be the only nonwhite, nonmale, disabled person onstage. We have also declined invitations when we, as parents of disabled children, are invited to lead on disability issues instead of disabled adults. We are mindful of the exclusionary history of advocacy by families like ours and are intentional about course correcting the narrative to center people with a disability by insisting organizers do the same.

Little Lobbyists Advocacy: 2018–Present

Establishing a Mission: Issues and Priorities

Little Lobbyists began its advocacy because of the immediate threat to health care; however, we quickly understood that our cause was greater than the preservation of the ACA. As an organization committed to those who are medically complex *and* disabled, it was natural to view issues through the lens of disability. For Little Lobbyists, *all* policy issues became disability issues.

2018 and 2020 Elections

Initially, Elena and Michelle hoped to change the health care narrative by emphasizing that it should not be a partisan issue and that party affiliation should not matter when the lives of medically complex and disabled children are at stake. In fact, some Little Lobbyists families identify as Republican or Independent. At first, Little Lobbyists was able to obtain meetings with congressional Republicans, but as the partisan landscape on Capitol Hill deepened during the first two years of the Trump administration, fewer Republicans were willing to meet.

In its efforts to preserve health care access, Little Lobbyists joined other advocacy groups in a federal lawsuit[38] filed in September 2017 to prevent the Trump administration from expanding the availability of short-term, limited-duration health plans, aka junk plans.

With the ACA still at stake, Little Lobbyists sprang into action during the 2018 midterm elections and the 2020 presidential election in favor of candidates who *would* support the ACA, Medicaid, and disability issues. These candidates were Democrats, and health care became one of the key issues in 2018 and 2020, allowing Democrats to regain control of the U.S. House of Representatives in 2019 and the U.S. Senate and presidency in 2021. During the election cycles, Little Lobbyists partnered with Health Care Voter, which, through its own story-sharing platform, broadcast Little Lobbyists family stories to a large audience.

Republican-led efforts to repeal the ACA continued through June 2021, when the U.S. Supreme Court issued a 7–2 ruling to uphold the ACA in Texas v. Azar.[39] Little Lobbyists worked with allies to ensure families' voices were heard, including joining other advocacy groups to file an amicus brief supporting the ACA.[40]

Community Living Rights Are Civil Rights

Throughout its advocacy, Little Lobbyists has urged politicians to protect the rights of persons with disabilities because our disabled children will one day grow into adults with disabilities. We want our children to survive and thrive.

In addition to the ACA, state/federal partnership programs under Medicaid are a critical source of support for people who are poor, disabled, and/or elderly. Medicaid was established by President Lyndon Baines Johnson in the Social Security Act of 1965, part of his Great Society initiative. The 1965 law entitled people who need 24/7 or nursing-level care to receive care in an institutional setting without a waiting period. This stipulation is frequently referred to as Medicaid's "institutional bias."

Prior to the 1980s, disabled people in the United States were routinely institutionalized despite efforts of disability and parent activists during the 1950s, 1960s, and 1970s to keep loved ones at home, where they belong. The advocacy of Julie and Katie Beckett became a tipping point for the development of Medicaid's HCBS waivers, which provided the community integration services—including home health aides, nurses, and personal assistants—the disability community had long sought. Living in the community of your choice is a civil right.[41]

Little Lobbyists wholeheartedly takes up the cause of increasing access to HCBS, which enables our loved ones to remain in their communities throughout their lifetimes. Because Medicaid is a state/federal partnership program, waiting lists for HCBS vary by state. As of 2022, there were over eight hundred thousand people on waiting lists nationwide,[42] and many thousands more need community supports but do not meet waiver eligibility requirements. We also condemn state and federal efforts to turn Medicaid into block grants.[43] Medicaid is a state/federal partnership program in which the federal government's funding share is flexible and may expand with state needs. Under block grant proposals, the federal government would provide a capped annual amount to states, typically far less than required to operate current programming.

In 2019, Tennessee became the final state to enact a "Katie Beckett" waiver, which provides HCBS supports to minor children and waives the family income requirement, nearly forty years after the Centers for Medicare and Medicaid made these waivers available to states. This effort was led by various Little Lobbyists families who live in Tennessee.

In 2021, President Joe Biden announced plans for a massive infrastructure bill known as Build Back Better (BBB). In it, the administration proposed a $400 billion investment in HCBS, originally introduced as part of the Better Care Better Jobs Act introduced by Senator Bob Casey (D-PA) and Representative Debbie Dingell (D-MI). Along with many other health care and disability rights organizations, Little Lobbyists allied with the Care Coalition, which has advocated relentlessly for increased HCBS funding.[44]

While the Biden administration's plans to invest in human infrastructure were bogged down in Congress, Little Lobbyists worked alongside its allies to support the administration's COVID-19 relief package, the American Rescue Plan,[45] which included funds for HCBS workers, medical care, and personal protective equipment.

The COVID-19 Pandemic

Little Lobbyists saw the onset of the pandemic in 2020 as yet another component of its mission to increase awareness of the needs of our community: health, education, and community inclusion, all of which have been threatened during the pandemic.

The unchecked spread of the virus threatens disabled lives. Hasty and poorly executed swings between remote learning services and in-classroom learning jeopardize the protections afforded disabled students under IDEA.[46] The disability community has been forced into far greater isolation—first due to the virus itself and subsequently due to a complex and rocky vaccine rollout, followed by irresponsible social policies at the local, state, and national levels.

Disability rights activist Imani Barbarin started the Twitter hashtag #MyDisabledLifeIsWorthy[47] during the pandemic in response to ableism of all political stripes that devalued disabled lives as inevitable casualties of COVID-19. That sentiment became a rallying cry for the disability community as many state and local governments ignored and deprioritized mask mandates and as the Centers for Disease Control and Prevention (CDC) began loosening restrictions and liberalizing guidance, even as disabled people continued to become seriously ill and die.

When, in 2022, CDC director Rochelle Walensky said on national television that it was "really encouraging news" that the majority of people dying from COVID-19 were "unwell to begin with,"[48] Little Lobbyists immediately released a statement:[49]

> Her cruel remarks tell people with complex medical needs and disabilities, including our children, that their lives do not matter. It erroneously gives the dangerous implication that COVID-19 is not something most people should be concerned about, further marginalizing our families. It weakens critical attempts to mitigate the surging pandemic currently overwhelming our hospitals, increasing the harm to disabled people who rely on medical care.

Efforts by disability groups including Little Lobbyists prompted a meeting with and eventual apology from Walensky.[50]

The pandemic also shifted the manner in which Little Lobbyists operated. As both the pandemic and the January 6, 2021, insurrection eliminated in-person access to members of Congress, Little Lobbyists shifted its activities online, increasing use of our Facebook page, Twitter account, and website (including our blog[51] and our statements[52] pages) to share information on critical issues affecting our community and encourage our members to reach out to representatives by phone, email, social media, and video call.

Throughout the pandemic, Little Lobbyists has joined with allies in the disability community—American Association of People with Disabilities (AAPD), The Arc, the Autistic Self Advocacy Network (ASAN), and others—to advocate for continued public masking mandates, prioritization of those with complex medical needs and disabilities for vaccines, justice for disabled school children, and increased Medicaid funding for those with disabilities.

Family Empowerment

At the heart of Little Lobbyists is a strong sense of community. We began by collecting family stories to bring to Congress in order to save the ACA. We are experts on our own lives; our lived experience is as valid as, and should be presented alongside, statistics and policy analysis.

Elena describes a huge part of her job as "passing the mic." She takes issue with a common practice she has observed in which personal stories are not heard, and if they are, they are shared by someone other than the person directly affected. She feels strongly that everyone should be empowered and have the opportunity to tell their own story. This practice includes not just passing the mic to Little Lobbyists families but also, whenever possible, to disabled adults and activists who are more qualified to speak than parents of disabled children.

Behind the scenes, Little Lobbyists' leadership works to develop relationships with politicians and other advocacy groups to enable members to have a platform. Calls from reporters to speak with families are regularly shared on the Little Lobbyists private Facebook pages. When families are tapped individually to speak at press conferences, hearings, and other events, leadership provides support to craft remarks. Opportunities to write for our blog are regularly posted.

As a result, Little Lobbyists families have testified at congressional hearings, shared stories with reporters, and written op-eds and articles for both local and national publications, including the *Washington Post*, *New York Magazine*, *Scary Mommy* blog, and *Today*.[53] Our families have been invited to attend the State of the Union address as guests of Congress to bring awareness to health care and children with complex medical needs and disabilities.[54]

The Little Lobbyists blog is dedicated to empowering families and people with disabilities to share their stories about health care and disability rights at the federal and state levels. We want to hear about families' engagement with their state legislatures and communities. Between 2018 and 2022, our blog featured over seventy different voices.

At the heart of Little Lobbyists' family empowerment mission is a drive to educate families on disability, disability history,[55] and the preferences of the disability community in terms of language and representation.[56] We are the recent recipient of a Ford Foundation grant to develop a curriculum and program to do just that. For most families of disabled children, understanding disability is a learning curve. We meet families where they are but discourage the use of "special needs" in favor of "disabled" (among other words and phrases), encourage parents to center their children instead of themselves, and encourage families to refrain from oversharing private aspects of their children's care.

Challenges of Maintaining an Ongoing
Advocacy Organization

Little Lobbyists is entirely volunteer run. On top of that, our organization faces the same challenges of any advocacy group—funding, obtaining non-profit status, allocating leadership roles—and deals with these issues in the context of members whose lives are already stretched for time due to the innumerable tasks associated with the medical, educational, and community service needs of children with disabilities. It is not uncommon for families to spend twenty or more hours a week on caregiving tasks in addition to full or part-time jobs plus other responsibilities. As is a focal point of our advocacy, families face incredible barriers to state and federal support programs.

We refer to our work as a relay, not a marathon. Our leadership reminds everyone that when someone needs to tap out, they need only pass the baton. Our group is like a chorus: a choir can sustain a note indefinitely because each individual singer can drop out to breathe as necessary and then join back in.[57]

We remind ourselves that we are volunteers—we set goals and work toward them, but we are still fallible. We make use of contemporary tools for collaboration such as Google Docs, Slack, and others that can be accessed online at any time of day or night. Burnout, of course, is a real problem no matter how we try to ease the workload. If those who hold leadership roles must step down (and some have), we redistribute roles and responsibilities.

Conclusion and Future Directions

Little Lobbyists has developed strong ties with disability, health care, and congressional allies, as well as a robust social media presence, to advance policies and legislation at the federal, state, and local levels that support civil rights for all persons, especially those who are medically complex and disabled. Through our work, we reach and empower thousands of families every day. One day, we hope to have a chapter in every state.

Little Lobbyists' success is a testament to the democratic process. Through peaceful protests and rallies, meetings with federal and state legislators, congressional testimony and press conferences, media interviews and op-eds/letters to the editor, Little Lobbyists has, against the odds, been part of a coalition that helped secure the ACA and Medicaid. We have a voice. Democracy works when we use our voices constructively to create change.

While our mission is advocacy (policy and legislation), the heart of our work, the dream goal, is changing the narrative about disability and negative cultural perceptions of it. We seek to normalize disability and the accommodations disabled people require and are entitled to by law. Our work is to make change happen not only in the halls of Congress but in our everyday lives.

In these troubled days of 2022, we stand with our allies to protect the bodily autonomy, self-determination, and well-being of everyone, particularly women, people of color, LGBTQ+ individuals, and people with complex medical needs and disabilities. We continue to believe that "all means all" and that there is no such thing as "other people's children."

The June 2022 U.S. Supreme Court decision to overturn Roe v. Wade dramatically limits the Fourteenth Amendment's protection of civil rights: to make personal decisions without government interference. It also upends previous rulings on personal rights including bodily autonomy, marriage, intimacy, sterilization, medical care, housing, speech, and more. People with disabilities have historically been denied the right to make these fundamental decisions about their own lives.

Our goal is for the United States to become a place where the government champions policies and laws that protect civil rights for all. We are working to map a path to better health care, education, and community inclusion for every person with complex medical needs and disabilities.

Our chapter was finalized prior to the November 2024 U.S. presidential election. Little Lobbyists remains committed to advocating for children with complex medical needs and disabilities. We are cognizant of the challenges ahead in the United States.

NOTES

1. "Our Advocacy Priorities," Little Lobbyists, 2021, https://littlelobbyists.org/advocacy.

2. The ACA's individual mandate requires all persons to purchase health insurance or pay a fine. The employer mandate requires "employers with 50 or more full-time equivalent employees to provide health coverage to at least 95% of full-time employees and sets a minimum baseline of coverage and affordability" (Louise Norris, "Employer Mandate," HealthInsurance.org, 2024, https://www.healthinsurance.org/glossary/employer-mandate/). The ten essential health benefits are ambulatory patient services; emergency services; hospitalization; maternity and newborn care; mental health and substance use disorder services; prescription drugs; rehabilitative and habilitative services and devices; laboratory services; preventive and wellness services and chronic disease management; and pediatric services including oral and vision care ("10 Essential Health Benefits Insurance Plans Must Cover under the Affordable Care Act," Insights Column, Families USA, February 9, 2018, https://familiesusa.org/resources/10-essential-health-benefits-insurance-plans-must-cover-under-the-affordable-care-act/).

3. "About the Affordable Care Act," Health Care Home, U.S. Department of Health and Human Services, last reviewed March 17, 2022, https://www.hhs.gov/healthcare/about-the-aca/index.html.

4. "Timeline of ACA Repeal and Replace Efforts," Ballotpedia: The Digital Encyclopedia of American Politics, n.d., accessed December 19, 2023, https://ballotpedia.org/Timeline_of_ACA_repeal_and_replace_efforts.

5. Sarah Kliff, "The Obamacare Provision That Saved Thousands from Bankruptcy," *Vox*, March 2, 2017, https://www.vox.com/policy-and-politics/2017/2/15/14563182/obamacare-lifetime-limits-ban.

6. Meghan Holohan, "For These Moms, the Health Care Debate Is Personal," Parents, *Today*, July 7, 2017, https://www.today.com/parents/health-care-debate-these-moms-it-s-personal-t113375.

7. The ACA's individual mandate requires all persons to purchase health insurance or pay a fine. The employer mandate requires "employers with 50 or more full-time equivalent employees to provide health coverage to at least 95% of full-time employees and sets a minimum baseline of coverage and affordability" (Louise Norris, "Employer Mandate," HealthInsurance.org, 2024, https://www.healthinsurance.org/glossary/employer-mandate/). The ten essential health benefits are ambulatory patient services; emergency services; hospitalization; maternity and newborn care; mental health and substance use disorder services; prescription drugs; rehabilitative and habilitative services and devices; laboratory services; preventive and wellness services and chronic disease management; and pediatric services including oral and vision care ("10 Essential Health Benefits Insurance Plans Must Cover under the Affordable Care Act," Families USA, September 2, 2018, https://familiesusa.org/resources/10-essential-health-benefits-insurance-plans-must-cover-under-the-affordable-care-act/).

8. Because state waiting lists for Medicaid home services are so long and institutional care is so dangerous and of such poor quality, families of medically complex children in particular rely on private insurance plans. Pre-ACA, these plans were mostly obtained through employers. Pre-ACA, employers could block new employees with preexisting conditions (or family members with preexisting conditions) from receiving employer health benefits. As a result, the majority of families with disabled and medically complex children have become highly dependent on the ACA to retain health coverage altogether. Without such insurance, families would end up in medical bankruptcy.

9. Elena Hung, interview by Roger A. Stone, February 23, 2022, video transcript, 11:45:38 to 11:46:37.

10. Sarah Kliff, "The Littlest Lobbyist: A 6-Year-Old, Whose Life Depends on ACA, Heads to Capitol Hill," *Vox*, June 21, 2017, https://www.vox.com/policy-and-politics/2017/6/21/15842780/senate-health-care-lifetime-limits.

11. Kliff, "The Obamacare Provision That Saved Thousands."

12. Kliff, "The Littlest Lobbyist."

13. Petula Dvorak, "Parents of Sick Kids Try to Remind Congress What the Health-Care Debate Should Be About," Local Perspective, *Washington Post*, June 22, 2017, https://www.washingtonpost.com/local/parents-of-sick-kids-try-to-remind-congress-what-the-health-care-debate-should-be-about/2017/06/22/784231b2-574e-11e7-ba90-f5875b7d1876_story.html.

14. Elena Hung interview, 13:34:51 to 13:35:23.

15. Heather Mason, "The Little Lobbyists Continue to Fight for Health Care Access," Amy Poehler's Smart Girls, *Medium*, July 19, 2017, https://amysmartgirls.com/the-little-lobbyists-continue-to-fight-for-health-care-access-c51fddbaf20c.

16. Little Lobbyists turned to so many individuals and organizations for support and advice that summer that it is difficult to name them all, and doing so risks leaving some-

one out. We are eternally grateful to all those who worked so hard to save the ACA and who helped Little Lobbyists along on its own journey.

17. Charlotte Alter and Haley Sweetland Edwards, "The United Patients of America," *Time*, July 13, 2017, https://time.com/4856231/the-united-patients-of-america/; Charlotte Alter, "How Women Helped Save Obamacare," *Time*, July 29, 2017, https://time.com/4878 724/donald-trump-gop-health-care-women/.

18. Robert Pear, "'Little Lobbyists' Help Save the Health Care Law, for Now," *New York Times*, September 30, 2017, https://www.nytimes.com/2017/09/30/us/politics/little-lob byists-obamacare.html?_r=0.

19. Jamie Davis Smith, "My Daughter Doesn't Have 'Special' Needs. She's Disabled," On Parenting, *Washington Post*, September 28, 2017, https://www.washingtonpost.com /news/parenting/wp/2017/09/28/my-daughter-doesnt-have-special-needs-shes-dis abled/.

20. Michelle Morrison, interview by Roger A. Stone, March 24, 2022, video transcript, 20:01:26 to 20:02:09.

21. Elena Hung interview, 11:40:27 to 11:41:03.

22. Eric March, "They're Tiny. They Just Helped Save Obamacare. And They're Not Done Yet," *Upworthy*, July 28, 2017, https://www.upworthy.com/theyre-tiny-they-helped -save-obamacare-and-theyre-not-done-yet.

23. Elena Hung interview, 14:02:10 to 14:02:55.

24. Davis Smith, "My Daughter Doesn't Have 'Special' Needs."

25. In the United States, disabled children and adults are fighting for the civil right to live in their communities. Medicaid (a U.S. public health insurance program) offers HBCS waivers for disabled children and adults. What is "waived" is Medicaid entitlement to care in an institution—under the current Medicaid statute, home care is considered optional. Medicaid is a state-federal matching grant program, and states are free to design their own HCBS waivers, with varied rules, populations served, and waiting lists (which often number in the tens of thousands). HCBS waivers for medically complex and disabled children end between the ages of eighteen and twenty-one, with no guarantee of further home services. States typically have an HCBS waiver for developmentally disabled adults; however, these waivers are often designed to exclude disabled adults who have complex medical needs. Disabled adults without developmental disabilities find it difficult to obtain funding for home care at all. In addition to health care and home services, disabled adults have a necessary focus on housing and employment, while disabled children and their families have a necessary focus on education.

26. Michelle Morrison interview, 20:04:29 to 20:04:44.

27. Elena Hung interview, 11:53:57 to 11:55:24.

28. Michelle Morrison interview, 19:58:27 to 19:59:01.

29. Today, Little Lobbyists' board and staff are diverse, and it is led by a disabled woman of color (Elena Hung identifies as a disabled person); however, our organization still relies on families with time and resources to volunteer long, unpaid hours. These families are skewed white and higher income. Promoting diversity, equity, and inclusion remains a challenge.

30. While disabled adults are free to make their own decisions to risk their health and safety, parents of disabled children in the U.S. can be held legally responsible for such decisions by child protective services. Children can even be removed from the care of parents whose actions are deemed unsafe, whether or not the parent was following the wishes of the child to begin with.

31. Laura LeBrun Hatcher, interview by Roger A. Stone, March 10, 2022, video transcript, 15:08:47 to 15:09:14.

32. "Timeline of ACA Repeal and Replace Efforts."

33. Emma Roller, "At the Capitol with Those for Whom Last Night Mattered the Most," *Splinter*, July 28, 2017, https://splinternews.com/last-night-mattered-for-them-1797330480.

34. Perry Stein, "Liberal Groups Plan Saturday Protests around the County to Save Obamacare," Local, *Washington Post*, July 28, 2017, https://www.washingtonpost.com /local/liberal-groups-plan-protests-around-the-country-saturday-to-save-obamacare /2017/07/28/94daad12-739c-11e7-8839-ec48ec4cae25_story.html.

35. Elena Hung interview, 13:45:20 to 13:46:27.

36. "Speaker Nancy Pelosi (D-CA) Addresses House of Representatives—FULL SPEECH," C-SPAN official YouTube channel, January 3, 2019, https://www.youtube.com /watch?v=dnH7O99d6S0; Gina Martinez, "Nancy Pelosi Just Outlined Her Agenda for the Most Diverse Congress Ever," *Time*, January 3, 2019, https://time.com/5493191/pelosi -house-speaker-speech-transcript/.

37. Robbie Jeanne, interview by Roger A. Stone, February 28, 2022, video transcript, 13:42:13 to 13:43:24.

38. Noam N. Levy, "Patient Advocates, Healthcare Groups Sue Trump Administration to Preserve Insurance Protections," Politics, *Los Angeles Times*, September 14, 2018, https://www.latimes.com/politics/la-na-pol-health-plans-lawsuit-20180914-story.html.

39. Greg Stohr, "Supreme Court Rejects GOP Challenge to Affordable Care Act," *Bloomberg* (U.S. edition), June 17, 2021, https://www.bloomberg.com/news/articles/2021 -06-17/u-s-supreme-court-upholds-affordable-care-act.

40. "Little Lobbyists Files Brief in Defense of the Affordable Care Act in the Supreme Court," Statements and Press Releases, News & Media, Little Lobbyists, May 14, 2020, https://littlelobbyists.org/statements-and-press-releases/2020/5/14/little-lobbyists-files -amicus-brief-in-defense-of-the-affordable-care-act-in-the-supreme-court.

41. Jeneva Stone and Laura LeBrun Hatcher, "Medicaid 101: Human Infrastructure & Civil Rights," *Little Lobbyists* (blog), August 26, 2021, https://littlelobbyists.org/blog /2021/8/26/medicaid-101-human-infrastructure-amp-civil-rightsnbsp-by-jeneva-stone -amp-laura-hatcher.

42. "How American Families Benefit: Better Care Better Jobs Act, S.2210," National Fact Sheet, United States Senate Special Committee on Aging, August 20, 2021, https:// www.aging.senate.gov/imo/media/doc/How%20American%20Families%20Benefit.pdf.

43. "Little Lobbyists Statement Opposing Medicaid Block Grants," Statements and Press Releases, News & Media, Little Lobbyists, October 3, 2019, https://littlelobbyists.org /statements-and-press-releases/2019/10/3/little-lobbyists-statement-opposing-medicaid -block-grants.

44. Kimberley Leonard, "Democrats Just Unveiled a $400 Billion Caregiving Bill That Would Supercharge Home Care and Boost Pay for Workers as 820,000 People Wait for Help," *Business Insider*, June 24, 2021, https://www.businessinsider.com/biden-400-billion -plan-for-families-with-disabilities-infrastructure-talks-2021-6.

45. "Little Lobbyists Need Home and Community Based Services Funding in a Covid Relief Package," Statements and Press Releases, News & Media, Little Lobbyists, December 3, 2020, https://littlelobbyists.org/statements-and-press-releases/2020/12/3/little -lobbyists-need-home-and-community-based-services-funding-in-a-covid-relief-package.

46. Anna North, "We Need to Talk about What School Closures Mean for Kids with Disabilities," *Vox*, August 6, 2020, https://www.vox.com/2020/8/6/21353154/schools-re opening-covid-19-special-education-disabilities.

47. Imani Barbarin, "I Started #MyDisabledLifeIsWorthy, Here's Why the Response from Nondisabled People and Medical Professionals Should Alarm You," *Crutches & Spice* (blog), January 26, 2022, https://crutchesandspice.com/2022/01/26/%EF%BF%BCi-started -mydisabledlifeisworthy-heres-why-the-response-from-nondisabled-people-and-medical -professionals-should-alarm-you/.

48. "CDC Director Responds to Criticisms on COVID-19 Guidance," video, GMA, January 10, 2022, https://www.goodmorningamerica.com/news/video/cdc-director-re sponds-criticisms-covid-19-guidance-82131389?fbclid=IwAR3gx_97-iZAqbdlJ2QVQ3 CkGJQx2MAomM4gwZCBZKvE2P-RiW8BE3dMtmA.

49. "Disabled Lives Are Worth Saving," Statements and Press Releases, News & Media, Little Lobbyists, January 10, 2022, https://littlelobbyists.org/statements-and-press -releases/2022/1/10/disabled-lives-are-worth-saving.

50. Eric Garcia, "CDC Director Apologises in Meeting with Disability Rights Activists after Frustration with Policy Response," *Independent*, January 15, 2022, https://www .independent.co.uk/news/world/americas/us-politics/cdc-disability-rights-covid-policy -b1993651.html.

51. Blog Index, Little Lobbyists, n.d., https://littlelobbyists.org/posts.

52. Statements & Press Releases Index, Little Lobbyists, n.d., https://littlelobbyists.org /statements-and-press-releases.

53. News & Media Articles Index, Little Lobbyists, n.d., https://littlelobbyists.org/news -media.

54. "Wexton Invites Loudon Woman to State of the Union to Highlight Healthcare," *Loudon Now*, February 4, 2020, https://www.loudounnow.com/2020/02/04/wexton-invites -loudoun-woman-to-state-of-the-union-to-highlight-healthcare/; Zack Budryk, "Pelosi Invites Head of Disability Advocacy Group to State of the Union," *The Hill*, February 4, 2020, https://thehill.com/homenews/house/481505-pelosi-invites-head-of-disability-ad vocacy-group-to-state-of-the-union/.

55. Stone and LeBrun Hatcher, "Medicaid 101."

56. Jeneva Stone, "Using Our Words: Being a Better Disability Ally," *Little Lobbyists* (blog), April 29, 2021, https://littlelobbyists.org/blog/2021/4/29/hq7b4b077ge3xw5i0x4 wrootb1f0gh.

57. From "the parable of the choir," a meme used frequently in social justice circles without definitive attribution.

9

How to Do Limitless Lifelong Self-Determination

Erin Compton and Diane Compton

Guardianship is one of the biggest self-determination decisions parents of children with intellectual disabilities have to make. Often, parents begin considering guardianship options shortly before their child's eighteenth birthday. For many, guardianship is seen as a rite of passage, with parents being judged negatively if they do not legally protect their children. What if, instead, parents were supported in developing self-determination from the child's birth? Would giving children with intellectual disabilities opportunities for leadership and advocacy skills reduce the number of people who have restrictive guardianships and provide greater self-determination for those who do? This chapter is written by a self-advocate and parent team; it begins with a self-advocate perspective on how self-determination can be developed as early as infancy. The chapter then examines obstacles that prevent the development of self-determination:

- Societal definitions and expectations for the parent role
- Schools teaching conformity to neurotypical ideals
- Segregated schools leading to segregated communities
- Effects of seclusion and restraint

The chapter concludes with suggestions for change so that children and parents are better prepared for independence and self-determination and require less restrictive guardianship protections.

Erin's Turn

Self-determination means people get to decide how to live their lives in a way that leads to the brightest and fullest tomorrows possible. I was born in 2004 with Down syndrome, which means I have pretty severe health issues and an intellectual disability with expressive language challenges. Having a disability doesn't mean people can't be leaders and self-advocates, but they have to step up and fight against discrimination to do so.

Here's a quiz question:

My disability is
(a) Good—this is me
(b) A struggle
(c) Getting ignored by people
(d) Getting included in state government
(e) All of the above

The right answer is "(e), All of the above." I am all of these things, but I also have disability pride, which means there is no stopping me. I am not alone in this leadership journey. I have mentors—some on the ground and some in heaven. Even some presidents of the United States had disabilities.

Self-determination means all of us having the right amount of leadership opportunities. Leaders come in all ages—some young and some very old. Everybody is a leader of their rights and choices.

In 1969, Bengt Nirje wrote about the normalization principle, which says that the choices, wishes, and desires of people with intellectual disabilities have to be respected and taken into consideration as nearly as possible.[1] However, it was not until the 1990s that laws were passed to help make this so. When George W. Bush signed the Americans with Disabilities Act (ADA) into law, he said, "Let the walls of discrimination come tumbling down," prohibiting by law the discrimination of all people with disabilities. At the same time, people were recognizing that those with intellectual disabilities should have a voice in deciding how they live now and in the future. Others saw the potential in people like me, who have intellectual disabilities.

According to Michael Wehmeyer, self-determination is defined as "acting as the primary causal agent in one's life and making choices and decisions regarding one's quality of life free from undue external influence of interference."[2] To me, that means that I can learn and be smart and still have a disability. I may be different, but different is normal.

Alex Gorz, who uses they and them pronouns, is a good friend, is kind, funny, and cool, and has physical and intellectual disabilities, said:

Self-determination means I can make decisions based on my own opinion, not someone else's. Self-determination is important to me. I have a lot of self-determination. Self-determination in school can be complicated. In some special education classrooms, teachers think that disabled students can't think for themselves or make their own decisions. This is frustrating. It is good to be able to make your own choices. Self-determination is hard when my choice isn't an option, when the right choice is the hard choice, and when the right choice is unpopular. Self-determination in school can be good, even when it is hard, because I can advocate for myself and be proud of myself. Self-determination can also help me accomplish a lot.[3]

This quote shows that people with disabilities can work hard and make their own decisions. Alex is a leader, but some people don't see that they can speak up and speak out. Alex has a voice and can advocate for themselves—people just need to listen differently. Angie Gorz, Alex's mom, added, "Transition has been a petri-dish of internalized ableism, with a hierarchy of students based on the level of support needed," showing the challenges that families face in many segregated educational programs.[4]

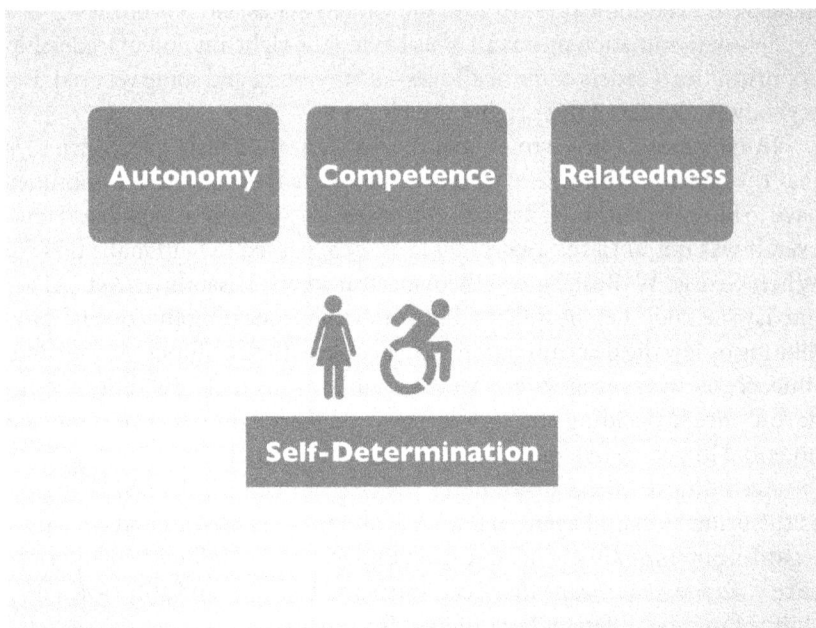

Figure 9.1 Developing Self-Determination through Autonomy, Competence, and Relatedness

Bryce Giron, an outgoing seventeen-year-old who enjoys gymnastics and swimming and also has Down syndrome, said self-determination means "having confidence and people not underestimating what I can do."[5] Edward L. Deci and Richard Ryan said that for self-determination to happen, people must have autonomy or control, competence, and relatedness (see Figure 9.1).[6]

Autonomy means people can make decisions and have control to live their best lives. Competence means people should presume competence instead of incompetence and should be given the chance to be educated and develop competence. If schools decide that a student can't learn math and refuse to teach math in a way the student can understand, then the student will never have competence of math. Relatedness means that students have friends and relationships with people who can help them achieve their goals—people to hang out with and mentors who can help them with school and careers. Everyone needs people.

Tables and graphic organizers are a good way for people with intellectual disabilities to organize and communicate their ideas. Here are some ideas for developing self-determination in newborns, preschoolers, and teens. They won't be the same for everyone, but these ideas can help people think differently about people with disabilities and their limitless self-determination.

Self-Determination in Children Ages Zero to Three

Self-determination for babies???!! Say what?? Babies with disabilities are their own people and are developing their mindsets. Susan Hoekstra, my first reading teacher when I was three, said, "When children are born into an orphanage, they cry, but their needs are not met. They learn to stop crying, because no one answers them."[7] Caregivers and families need to make sure they support their baby's needs so that babies don't lose their voice. Susan continued that for students with disabilities, "early intervention is huge—you must start as early as possible when the brain is pliable." Table 9.1 shows some ways to develop self-determination in babies and toddlers.

As students grow into elementary schoolers, leadership and self-determination are even more important. I had the chance to ask disability advocate Judy Heumann about self-determination, and she said, "We have to talk to parents who have kids who are 2 or 3 years old. Kids should not be put in a place where they aren't going to learn. We have to get rid of the expectation that kids can't learn. We have to fight for integration in schools, so the kids can get ready for college programs."[8] Heumann shows how important it is to educate and prepare kids for the future. Table 9.2 shows ways to develop self-determination in elementary school.

TABLE 9.1 SELF-DETERMINATION AND DEVELOPMENT FOR BABIES AND TODDLERS	
Self-Determination Example	Ways to Develop Self-Determination
Autonomy	
Decision making	People with disabilities need to be able to decide which toys and food they want. They need food that is good for their bodies. Understanding why they might not like something can help with sensory issues. For example, my body can't handle a lot of fiber in food. It took fifteen years for doctors to finally figure out this wasn't a sensory issue but an "I don't want to throw up" issue.
Competence	
Sleeping	Babies with disabilities are often like babies without disabilities. Sometimes babies have to spend more time in the NICU, and parents have to advocate for their child's self-determination and maybe even their life. Doctors need to understand that babies with disabilities are people who they can help make healthy and survive. Babies can be included in self-determination, and doctors need to understand that all kids need a chance to grow and develop their limitless minds.
Eating	
Self-comforting	
Walking	Sometimes people with disabilities can't walk, or they may take longer to learn how to walk. But a lot of people still like to get around and interact with people. Just because people can't walk, doesn't mean they can't have movement—just like the civil rights movement. Walking is limited, but movement is limitless. All people can have movement.
Talking	Instead of limiting people to talking, think of limitless communicating. People can use AAC devices and sign language to communicate. Even hand gestures, dance movements, behavior, and facial expressions can help people communicate. Self-determination does not rely on talking.
Relatedness	
Caregivers	Caregivers can develop self-determination by respecting and taking care of the child, just like they would any other child.
Medical professionals	Babies with disabilities sometimes have medical crises, and they need medical professionals to give the very best treatment. Babies might have rare medical conditions, and consequences may occur if doctors and nurses don't provide proper treatment.
Therapists	Therapists need to honor and respect the energy and self-determination of people with disabilities and their families. Therapists have to listen to behavior and body language.

Building Self-Determination in High School Students

People with disabilities in high school sometimes struggle to have self-determination. Schools and teachers have bias against self-determination and don't let us make our own choices. Some adults treat us like little children—it is annoying.

TABLE 9.2 SELF-DETERMINATION AND DEVELOPMENT FOR ELEMENTARY SCHOOL CHILDREN	
Self-Determination Example	Ways to Develop Self-Determination
Autonomy	
Learning to speak up and speak out	This is so important. Self-advocacy skills can't be limited to asking for help. Self-advocacy means people can make the world better for everyone.
Disability pride	People with disabilities need to be who they are and be proud of their disabilities. Schools need to teach disability pride, disability culture, and be passion ignitors.
Competence	
Learning to read and write	People with disabilities may have to learn to read and write differently than their friends. Technology helps by reading the text out loud if needed. Some people need help—that's normal. It's not normal to not help them learn, because they need an education. Speech to text can help them write. Eye gaze technology can help students use the computer or match words with pictures and definitions.
Learn the practice of learning	Kids need to learn how to learn. Any testing done should help people figure out how the school can help the kids learn. If people with disabilities are segregated, they will be in isolation and not learn what they are supposed to learn.
Relatedness	
Working together	If you separate people with disabilities from other students, no one learns how to work together. Sometimes students without disabilities teach things, and other times students with disabilities teach things.
Cooperation, not compliance	Cooperation is the process of working together to the same end. Compliance means a person does what they are told. Students with disabilities are taught to be compliant, not to make their own decisions. If students don't comply, they can be sent to the principal or expelled from school, and they don't learn.
Including a friend	Including people is an important skill for people's whole lives. Why not get started learning it right away?

Cindy Bickman, a coach from Atlanta, Georgia, says, "I see athletes with disabilities the same way I see typical athletes. They want to have fun, work hard, learn new skills, and enjoy success. The pace may be a little slower than typical athletes. Skills may need to be broken down into smaller parts. Safety has to come first, which may mean adaptive equipment and extra help. But the sport is the same and the technique and skill progressions should follow the same program as typical athletes."[9]

Cindy has built a very successful team that regularly travels around the world for competitions. On building self-determination in athletes, Cindy said,

TABLE 9.3 SELF-DETERMINATION AND DEVELOPMENT IN HIGH SCHOOL STUDENTS

Self-Determination Example	Ways to Develop Self-Determination
Autonomy	
Self-advocating for self-determination	Self-advocating is more than asking for help. It's trusting in your instincts and believing in yourself. It's stepping up and speaking out. Schools need to listen to students and help them succeed.
Independent living	Parents can help their children by teaching them how to cook, get meals, find a place to live, and care for themselves. Help can be unified, meaning the community can help people live their best lives. Everybody needs help from their community—people with disabilities do, too. People with disabilities aren't broken people in a regular world. We are regular people in a broken world.
Universal design is for everyone	People with disabilities have dreams they can create and have a right to make come true. Universal design makes it possible for everyone to create their futures by helping them learn and making information understandable. Even jobs and colleges can use universal design to create career paths that don't discriminate against people with disabilities.
Competence	
Learning how to speak up against discrimination	Schools shouldn't teach students that they can't learn. All students with disabilities need to speak up and speak out to change this. If schools don't educate students, then it is harder for students to succeed.
Find your talents and your dreams	Everyone has talents, and they should believe in and be proud of that. The school has talents to teach students, and they should help students achieve their dreams, especially after graduation. If the school has separate classes for people with disabilities, it is called segregation—that is not who we are. Students can be powerful, strong self-advocates, and school should not be a fight. Schools need to listen that people like me need an education. That is why I'm using my will and my might to create inclusion.
Foundation of all classes working together	Segregating students from one or more classes takes away that foundation of learning. English classes tell the stories of history classes. Math class lessons are used in consumer economics. Respect accommodations for intellectual disabilities as much as those for physical disabilities. Just because someone dictates what they are writing, doesn't mean they didn't write it independently. Don't use grammar and spelling to hold a student back. If we want to give people a voice, then people need to listen, even if commas and periods aren't in the right place.
Relatedness	
Group projects	Students with disabilities can be limitless in group projects by relying on one another. All students can make new friends and be social in the group. Working together helps build trust in each other. Schools need inclusionaters who are willing to lead and trust in each other.
Teachers become mentors	Teachers can help students get in their career path by teaching and helping them fulfill their potential.
Parents	Parents can help their children be successful and independent and point guiding lights toward the child. Parents can help their children make independent decisions and support those decisions. This is a good time to practice decision making.

The most important key to self-determination and confidence is setting the athlete up for success. The coach has to choose skills, progressions, and competitions which the athlete is prepared to perform. Setting goals is great, but they must be realistic and achievable in a short period of time. Athletes with disabilities take a long time to master a sport, so it is important to set short term, measurable goals the athlete can understand and appreciate.

Cindy said that as a coach, she focuses first on the athlete but involves the family whenever she can:

In my program, we do many performances which include everyone—Gymnastics for All. When a child is born with a disability, the parents have to dedicate many hours to teaching that child. When the whole family performs together, they are all working toward a common goal, and the relationship changes. Often, the child with the disability has to teach the parents skills or choreography. This gives family members a new appreciation of the abilities of the athlete with disABILITIES.[10]

Table 9.3 shows some other ways to develop self-determination in high school students with disabilities.

Diane's Turn: Self-Determination Challenges Facing Self-Advocates and Families

"Everything starts and ends with the family for those with high support needs," said family advocate Laurie Jerue: "The parents can either be the biggest allies or the biggest obstacles to self-determination."[11] Jerue is cofounder of Illinois Parents of Adults with Developmental Disabilities United, a resource Facebook page with over six thousand members.

As for all children, nature and nurture play a crucial role in development for children with disabilities. However, societal expectations, cultural traditions, and parent support systems are often constructed with biases against children with disabilities, particularly intellectual disabilities. Parents themselves may be contending with post-traumatic stress disorder (PTSD) from medical battles or chronic stress. A 2009 study in the National Library of Medicine estimated the rate of PTSD in parents of children with disabilities to be 18.9%.[12] A study conducted in Australia showed that 18.6 percent of parents of children with autism met the criteria for a provisional diagnosis of PTSD.[13] These rates, combined with the findings of a 2022 study showing that "youth of parents with PTSD were nearly three times more likely to have parent-reported physical and emotional abuse,"[14] put children with disabilities at greater risk.

Families Are Expected to Inspire Others, Not Fight for Access

Parents are often expected to simultaneously conform to and defy societal norms while defining and responding to their child's needs. Stella Young, the late Australian disability rights activist, created a TED Talk in 2014 defining "inspiration porn" as "objectifying disabled people for the benefit of non-disabled people."[15] Examples of inspiration porn include sayings like "The only disability is a bad attitude," often paired with a picture of a disabled person. Young said that while she is inspired by others, it is because "we are learning from each other's endurance and strength. Not against our bodies and diagnoses, but against a world that exceptionalizes and objectifies us." Families experiencing disability can, by extension, also experience objectification and confusing contradictions:

- Overcoming their children's challenges but not challenging the biases of medical or educational professionals
- Enduring hardships but not complaining when the hardships are caused by a system completely inaccessible to their child
- Accepting being called "difficult" or "that parent" when trying to obtain services their child needs to succeed

Parents who have low expectations for systems that are supposed to educate their children are rewarded and complimented for accepting segregation and a lower quality of education. Just as compliance is often an expectation for special education students, it can be even more so for parents. Schools hire attorneys, ignore issues, and use gaslighting to intimidate parents into compliance. And while defendants in criminal cases do not have to argue that laws like the Fifth Amendment exist, school administrations often pretend that the Individuals with Disabilities Education Act (IDEA) does not exist or does not apply to them, with enforcement of these laws left to the parents. Legal battles are expensive, and schools control access to students' social and academic experiences. The fear of retaliation is strong, especially to a parent who may be experiencing chronic stress or PTSD.

Parent involvement is considered valuable for student success, yet schools are not always welcoming of involvement, especially when it comes to students who have both intellectual disabilities and chronic health conditions. A 2013 study reported that in 2009–2010, there were more than 11 million children in the United States with special health care needs, including 1.3 million adolescents (age 12–17) who had a chronic health condition and developmental, emotional, or behavioral needs for which they received special education services. In a national survey only 29% of adolescents with both health and developmental needs were receiving the full spectrum of the recommended transition services.

The study found that parental advocacy served three primary functions: "(a) advocating for services to meet the child's needs; (b) acting as an expert on their own child; and (c) protecting the child from incompetent or uninformed professionals."[16]

Schools Teach Conformity to Neurotypical Ideals

Building self-determination is difficult in an educational system created for typical students. Goals built around preventing and extinguishing neurodiverse adaptations, such as self-talk, stimming, and avoiding eye contact, are justified as improving peer assimilation but may make learning more difficult. For example, self-talk can be very useful for people with Down syndrome. A study conducted by the Adult Down Syndrome Center of Lutheran General Hospital including five hundred patients ranging in age from eleven to eighty-three showed "that 81 percent of those studied engage in conversations with themselves or imaginary companions."[17] While self-talk is a valuable way of organizing thoughts and ideas and is especially useful for test taking and essay writing, professionals often attempt to silence self-talk, concerned that it is distracting or a sign of mental illness. While prohibiting students from using self-talk in school may spare ridicule from classmates and teachers, it may also eliminate independent critical thinking strategies and limit academic success. Many parents' greatest fear is that their child will not be accepted or have friends, and they may continue extinguishing neurodiverse adaptations at home in an attempt to provide better opportunities for socialization and acceptance.

Furthermore, some schools use test results to limit access to education rather than to help make grade-appropriate curriculum and materials accessible. If a student tests below grade level, they will often be taught at a lower grade level; repeat testing shows that students—understandably—do not learn the higher grade level material that was not taught. Low test results become a self-fulfilling prophecy, leading to segregated classrooms with separate curriculum and compounding the effects of learning and intellectual disabilities with educational disadvantages. This cycle is often hidden from parents, as they are not in the classroom. COVID lockdowns allowed many parents to see this cycle in action for the first time. Parents who accept school personnel as experts may not question why their child is falling behind and may attribute lack of education to the student's ability rather than the teaching methods.

Segregated Schools Lead to Community Segregation

Furthermore, segregated classrooms lead to segregated communities. Illinois, where Erin and I live, is a state that still uses state-operated institutions to house people with disabilities. According to Going Home Coalition data compiled by Carole Rosen for The Arc of Illinois, *The State of the States in Intellectual and Developmental Disabilities* report concluded that costs had risen to $286,000 per person for approximately 1,640[18] people per year in 2019.[19]

While a higher level of care is needed for some, outdated ideas and stereotypes—especially in the medical and education fields—may inadvertently reduce self-determination and increase dependency on higher care levels. If schools continue under-assessing abilities and refusing to provide meaningful education or transition activities, families will have fewer post-graduation options and seek higher care and more restrictive guardianship options rather than building independence or choice into their decisions.

Seclusion and Restraint Take Away Self-Determination

Another issue that greatly affects self-determination is seclusion and restraint, which impact students with disabilities at much higher rates than nondisabled students. Seclusion refers not to well-designed sensory rooms students access by choice but instead to rooms used to isolate. According to the 2017/2018 *Civil Rights Data Report*, of the 50,992,401 students enrolled in schools across the country, 101,990 students were subjected to restraint and seclusion, with a breakdown shown in Table 9.4.

The counts for students subjected to physical restraint, mechanical restraint, and seclusion are not mutually exclusive. If a student was physically

TABLE 9.4 THE NUMBER OF INCIDENTS IN TOTAL AND FOR STUDENTS WITH DISABILITIES		
	Number of Incidents	Incidents Involving Students with Disabilities
Physical Restraint	70,833	56,905
Mechanical Restraint	3,619	1,494
Seclusion	27,538	21,277
Total	**101,990**	**79,676**

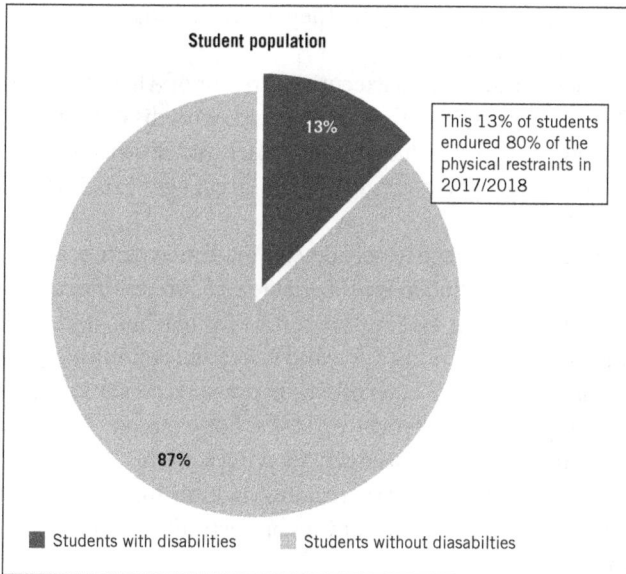

Figure 9.2 Students with Disabilities Are Disproportionately Physically Restrained

restrained and secluded, they would be counted once in each category. Thus, the total of 101,990 may not represent the number of individual students affected. However, of the 101,990 incidents of restraint and seclusion, 78 percent involved students with disabilities, an alarming number considering these students only composed 13 percent of the total student population (see Figure 9.2).[20]

In some cases, families have accepted this treatment and fight for the right to access seclusion and restraint. The Judge Rotenberg Center (JRC) in Massachusetts requires students to wear backpacks so that staff members can administer shocks to students. Although this treatment has been banned in the rest of the country, parents lobbied for JRC to continue shocking their children. According to the Civil Rights Data Collection, while federal law does not specifically prohibit use of restraint and seclusion, "there are circumstances under Section 504 and Title II in which the use of restraint and seclusion may constitute discrimination against students with disabilities. More specifically, in some cases, the use of restraint and seclusion may result in unlawful discrimination against individual students with disabilities in violation of Federal civil rights laws."[21]

If we continue to expose people with intellectual disabilities to this treatment at young ages, how do we ever move forward? Education and medical personnel have normalized abuse as treatment to such an extent that parents do not see other options. If, as a society, we offered parents and self-advocates alternatives to shock therapy, would they be advocating for potentially trauma-inducing treatment?

Guy Stephens, founder and executive director of Alliance Against Seclusion and Restraint, explained that "individuals with disabilities are far more likely to be restrained and secluded, as are Black and Brown children and kids with a trauma history. It is often young children, ages 5, 6, 7 who are being restrained and secluded."[22]

The trauma and damage to self-determination experienced by students who are restrained or secluded is undeniable and can result in student death. Restraining students can also be dangerous for teachers and staff. Understanding behavior as communication and using that communication to allow students to have greater self-determination prevents escalation and develops decision-making and self-advocating skills. For example, for students who elope, understanding why the student is leaving activities can have long-term benefits, instead of immediately segregating, restraining, or expelling—strategies that deny students with disabilities opportunities to learn and practice self-determination.

According to Stephens,

> There's a power dynamic involved with seclusion and restraint, and that power dynamic goes against self-determination. Kids with disabilities may get punished for things that are perfectly natural to them and may even be self-regulating. It's all the things that lead up to the restraint and seclusion that are taking away someone's right to be who they are. When people are restrained or secluded, they lose their autonomy. When other people are controlling of us, it is harder for us to act on our own behalf. We give up something when we are being controlled by others. Physical interventions prevent students from exercising their own free will.

However, Stephens noted that the power dynamic may be even more harmful to students who have self-determination and self-advocacy skills.

> I remember teaching my son, who is neurodivergent, to advocate for himself. I was really proud of him. There were certainly people who appreciated that, but some people didn't. Some people wanted to have control. And that puts you at odds of having self-determination and autonomy. I think in our world, sometimes there is too much focus on compliance and control and not enough on connection and compassion. Sometimes when people are self-advocating or really trying to make determinations for their own well-being or futures, there are people who aren't receptive to it.

Highlighting minority groups' struggles, Stephens added, "The mindset that needs to change, is not the mindset of the individual who is having things done to them—it is the mindset of the individuals who are doing the things to them."

Two key components to self-determination, autonomy and relationships, are harmed by seclusion and restraint, as Stephens said:

> We are not collaborating. A lot of behavior change is based around rewards and consequences. We really need to stop doing things to kids and work with them. If we want to help solve problems that might be causing difficulty for a kid, we should collaborate—we should work together. The most important thing is relationships. With those relationships, you will more than likely find people who are supporting self-determination, more than likely being a part of students helping to come up with their goals. There's a mindset out there that kids don't have the same rights as other people—and if you look at kids with disabilities, that's even stronger—adults think that we need to decide everything for them.

Stephens concluded by saying, "Using seclusion and restraint is harmful to self-determination—it's harmful to autonomy and the freedom to be who we are. The voice of self-advocates is at the top of finding solutions to this problem. If students don't feel safe, it's very hard for them to connect with people. It's very hard to regulate. It's very hard to learn if you don't feel you're safe, if you don't feel you are in an environment where your voice matters."

Tricia Giron and her son Bryce dealt with a school's use of seclusion and restraint. Tricia is a strong proponent of self-determination and created a free preschool program for families with arts and crafts, snack preparation, and clean-up stations to share her ideas for independence. She also is the leader of an inclusive 4-H Club, with many members with disabilities holding leadership positions, and a parent adviser for the local high school. On building independence and self-determination, Tricia said,

> We've always tried to instill confidence in Bryce by assuming he CAN do something. We gave him the same opportunities we gave his siblings, modifying/helping just enough for him to be successful. It is a delicate balance: the concept of providing just enough and not too much. That's where we had conflict with the school, as they wanted to throw all the tools at him before they saw what he was capable of. In our opinion, that limits progress and creates a child who assumes he cannot do something. We continually challenge him with age-ap-

propriate tasks, encouraging him if he has difficulties. He knows we believe he can do it.[23]

However, the school used an Applied Behavioral Analysis (ABA) approach. As Tricia described, "I've never been a fan of the ABA approach. I've seen it, tried it, and it might work well for some situations, but not all. Sadly, behavior therapists like to use it across the board. They fail to fully observe the behavior—they see what they need to see clinically." Tricia continued by describing Bryce's reaction to restraint and seclusion:

> Restraint in 8-year-old Bryce only made him angrier. It was not a successful de-escalation tool, yet the school used it over and over. When his reaction finally peaked, they moved him to a padded room and shut the door, holding it closed. When the staff opened the door, he would get up, as I think any child would do, and they shut the door again. Trained behavior experts expected an 8-year-old with intellectual disabilities to sit for 10 more seconds before getting up, which made no sense. He was simply getting more frustrated and angrier. His education was suffering because he spent most of day in some sort of disciplinary action.

Tricia removed Bryce from public school and began homeschooling, finding inclusion in a co-op where Bryce was able to see positive behavior modeled by other homeschool students, close the gap with his peers, and return to public school for high school.

For parents who understand the importance of self-determination, schools can create many problems, Tricia explained.

> I think we parents just want to keep giving Bryce the best we can in life. School can make that more difficult for us or they can be partners with us. The former certainly takes an emotional toll and increased stress. In our case, they made it harder, but that did not deter us from finding another way to develop self-determination. When a school partners, truly partners, the outcome can be so incredibly positive for everyone. That partnership makes it easier to push onward. We now have a partner in the high school who sees self-determination as we do, with a very positive outcome.

Moving forward to the Third Generation of Special Education

With all the challenges, is it possible for schools to help create self-determination in students with disabilities?

Michael Wehmeyer proposes that current thinking about intellectual disabilities, self-determination, and self-directed learning have created a third generation of inclusive practices. Wehmeyer writes that educators need "to reconsider our historical approaches and intervention models and to move from creating programs for students based upon their label to the design of truly individualized supports; from creating separate, congregate services to implementing inclusive practices; and from a focus on student incapacities and deficits to a focus on individual strengths."[24]

While first-generation inclusive practices focused on moving students from congregate settings to inclusive classrooms and the second generation focused on supporting students in those inclusive classrooms, the third generation focuses less on where a student is educated and more on what the student is taught. Wehmeyer writes,

> At the core of the third generation inclusive practices are a focus on promoting and enhancing the self-determination of all students, including students with disabilities and special educational needs; ensuring that the curriculum is universally designed and instruction is flexible for all students; implementing schoolwide interventions that benefit all students, such as positive behavior supports; and creating a vision for schools that include all students. Research suggests that implementing third generation inclusive practices enables students to achieve greater access to the general education curriculum and will lead to more positive educational and adult outcomes, empowering students by enabling them to direct their own lives more effectively.

Wehmeyer's research ultimately shows "that students who leave school as self-determined young people achieve more positive adult outcomes and attain a better quality of life and higher lifestyle satisfaction."[25]

The challenge is that not all schools have reached the third generation, and many remain in the first generation. The level of inclusion changes even at individual schools within a district based on biases and attitudes of teachers and administrators. Legal actions are time consuming and expensive and may not result in prompt or suitable remediations.

Mitchell Robins, a recent high school graduate, autistic blogger (mitchellslifewithautism.com), and self-advocate for people who use spelling as a form of communication, shared, "School was crushing for my self-determination. They put me in the traditional special education box and neglected my strengths. I needed to be built up, but I was pushed down. School could be the basis for self-determination, but instead, it led me to question my abilities." Mitchell continued, "The person who most helped me was my mom. She was always letting me show others what I am capable of doing, and she fought for me. The letterboard training she got me changed my life. Most non-speaking autistic people would benefit from this training. It allowed me to communicate self-determination."[26]

Susan Robins, parent of Mitchell, said, "For people like my son, the goal is not independence, but the ability to ask for accommodations and to have agency in planning one's life in both the short and long term." She expressed a concern felt by many parents of people who are nonspeaking, and continued, "I think independence needs to be replaced with respected interdependence. We all are interdependent to some degree. Those with expressive communication disabilities due to apraxia need to depend on others. The trouble is making sure that others respect the views of the apraxic individual and provide accommodations." Susan uses power of attorney rather than full guardianship: "I speak with Mitchell about every decision. His sister and others whom we designate will do the same one day. I don't know if this is enough protection, but at this time, guardianship seemed wrong. It is a conversation we will revisit, as we want him protected."[27]

The Effects on Guardianship Decisions

While guardianship decisions are ultimately made by parents, biases, opportunities, and actions of others—including societal definitions and expectations for the parent role, conformity to neurotypical ideals, school segregation, and usage of seclusion and restraint—affect the decision. If we, as individuals and as a society, want to decrease reliance on most-restrictive guardianship, opportunities to change the level of support and messages parents receive exist in many areas, including early family resources, medical care, state supports, therapists, and school administration. This diagram, created by the authors, highlights influences that affect the guardianship decision (see Figure 9.3).

Cindy Montgomery, cofounder and CEO of Teachability, a company that matches employment and candidates with disabilities, said,

> If we don't start developing self-determination skills early, it becomes difficult for students with disabilities to work. They need to practice decision making and failing. That's right. That's how we learn to cope with failure and that's how we learn to ultimately thrive in the workplace. It's terrifying to give a young person the dignity of risk, but it's worth it. Each parent needs to determine the level of risk that makes the most sense for their child.

Cindy continued, "Vocational rehab services are available to anyone in the U.S. from age 14–24. There is federal law, CFR 361.48, that states exactly

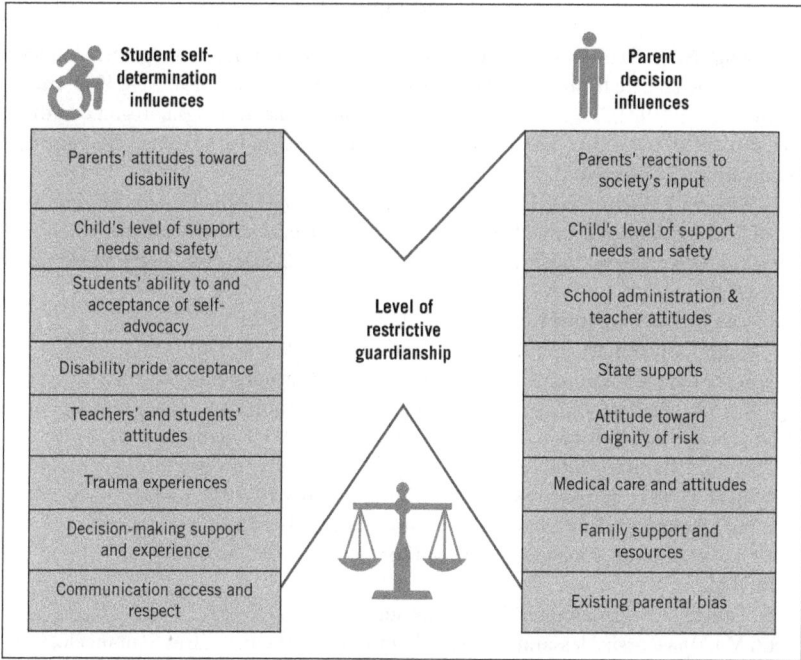

Figure 9.3 Influences That Affect Guardianship Decisions

what Voc Rehab will cover in support of employment. If people tell you employment and self-determination aren't possible, they are uninformed or may have outdated thinking. If you are informed and think self-determination is possible, it will be."[28]

Erin's Turn: Conclusion

Because the voice of self-advocates is key to success, this conclusion is by Erin.

Instead of guardianship, I am doing supported decision making to help me become a self-advocate adult and so I have a better understanding of what being an adult means. For me, I'm happy with supported decision making because I can decide what to do next. I have been preparing my whole entire life for this moment, and I am ready to take on this responsibility. Now is the time to speak up against discrimination and for self-determination. Schools need to listen and to understand all types of communication. The ADA helps us choose our own stories and our journeys. We must use our voices to become uniters. We especially need to listen to the voices of people who need technology to help them speak the unspoken. In a limitless world, we cannot limit ourselves to one way to speak, write, or lead. We just can't.

NOTES

1. Bengt Nirje, "The Normalization Principle and Its Human Management Implications: Classic Article from 1969," *SRV-VRS: The International Social Role Valorization Journal* 1, no. 2 (1994): 19–23, https://bpb-us-e1.wpmucdn.com/blogs.uoregon.edu/dist/d/16656/files/2018/11/Nirje-The-Normalization-Principle-and-Its-Human-Management-Implications-2f3t9mm.pdf.

2. Michael L. Wehmeyer, "The Importance of Self-Determination to the Quality of Life of People with Intellectual Disability: A Perspective," *International Journal of Environmental Research and Public Health* 17, no. 19 (2020): 2, https://doi.org/10.3390/ijerph17197121.

3. Alex Gorz, email interview by the authors, June 9, 2022.

4. Angie Gorz, email interview by the authors, June 9, 2022.

5. Bryce Giron, video-conference interview by the authors, June 24, 2022.

6. Ryan M. Richard and Deci L. Edward, "Self-Determination Theory and the Facilitation of Intrinsic Motivation, Social Development, and Well-Being," *American Psychologist* 55, no. 1 (January 2000): 68.

7. Susan Hoekstra, interview by the authors, October 29, 2022.

8. Judy Heumann, interview by the authors, September 23, 2021.

9. Cindy Bickman, interview by the authors, October 23, 2022.

10. Ibid.

11. Laurie Jerue, email interview by the authors, June 15, 2022.

12. Martina Corsi, Alessandro Orsini, Virginia Pedrinelli, Andrea Santangelo, Carlo Antonio Bertelloni, Niccolò Carli, Rodolfo Buselli, Diego Peroni, Pasquale Striano, Liliana Dell'Osso, and Claudia Carmassi, "PTSD in Parents of Children with Severe Diseases: A Systematic Review to Face Covid-19 Impact," *Italian Journal of Pediatrics* 47, no. 8 (2021), https://doi.org/10.1186/s13052-021-00957-1.

13. Michelle Stewart, Alexandra Schnabel, David J. Hallford, Jane A. McGillivray, David Forbes, Madeline Foster, Kerrie Shandley, Madeleine Gardam, and David W. Austin, "Challenging Child Behaviours Positively Predict Symptoms of Posttraumatic Stress Disorder in Parents of Children with Autism Spectrum Disorder and Rare Diseases," *Research in Autism Spectrum Disorders* 69 (2020), https://doi.org/10.1016/j.rasd.2019.101467.

14. Christina G. Macdonnell, Theresa Andrezejewski, and Janey Dike, "Intergenerational Trauma: Parental PTSD and Parent-Reported Child Abuse Subtypes Differentially Relate to Admission Characteristics in the Autism Inpatient Collection," *Autism Research* 15, no. 4 (2022): 665–76, https://doi.org/10.1002/aur.2669.

15. Stella Young, "I'm Not Your Inspiration, Thank You Very Much," TED Talk, June 9, 2014, https://www.ted.com/talks/stella_young_i_m_not_your_inspiration_thank_you_very_much.

16. Roberta S. Rehm, Lucille T. Fisher, Elena Fuentes-Afflick, and Catherine A. Chesla, "Parental Advocacy Styles for Special Education Students during the Transition to Adulthood," *Qualitative Health Research* 23, no. 10 (2013): 1377–87, https://doi.org/10.1177/1049732313505915.

17. Dennis McGuire, Brian A. Chicoine, and Elaine Greenbaum, "'Self-Talk' in Adults with Down Syndrome," Children's Hospital of Philadelphia, March 1, 2013, https://www.chop.edu/news/self-talk-adults-down-syndrome.

18. "Transition Report by SODC," Illinois Department of Human Services, 2023, https://www.dhs.state.il.us/page.aspx?item=82095.

19. Emily S. Tanis, Amie Lulinski, Joy Wu, David L. Braddock, and Richard Hemp, *The State of the States in Intellectual and Developmental Disabilities: 2019*, 12th ed. (Lawrence, Kansas: University of Kansas, in preparation).

20. Department of Education and the Office for Civil Rights, "2017–18: The Use of Restraint and Seclusion on Children with Disabilities in K-12 Schools," Civil Rights Data Collection, October 2020, https://www2.ed.gov/about/offices/list/ocr/docs/restraint-and -seclusion.pdf.

21. Ibid.

22. Guy Stephens, video interview by the authors, June 22, 2022.

23. Tricia Giron, video interview by the authors, June 24, 2022.

24. Michael L. Wehmeyer, "Self-Determination and the Third Generation of Inclusive Practices," *Revista de Educacion* 349, no. 3 (May–August 2009): 45, https://www.educa cionyfp.gob.es/revista-de-educacion/dam/jcr:cdb14e14-b97e-436c-a4f6-acb21b01a027 /re34903ing-pdf.pdf.

25. Ibid.

26. Mitchell Robins, email interview by the authors, June 16, 2022.

27. Susan Robins, email interview by the authors, June 16, 2022.

28. Cindy Montgomery, email interview by the authors, July 2022.

Contributors

Dr. Pamela Block (she/her) is professor of anthropology at Western University. She is a fellow of the Society for Applied Anthropology and former president of the Society for Disability Studies (2009–2010). Her books include *Allies and Obstacles: Disability Activism and Parents of Children with Disabilities* with Allison C. Carey and Richard K. Scotch, Temple University Press (2020), which won awards from the North Central Sociological Association and the American Sociological Association Disability and Society Section, and *Occupying Disability: Critical Approaches to Community, Justice, and Decolonizing Disability* with coeditors Devva Kasnitz, Akemi Nishida, and Nick Pollard, Springer (2020). She publishes about disability culture, cultural perceptions of disability, and scholarly intersections of disability and anthropology. She studies disability experience on individual, organizational, and community levels, with particular interest in intersections of gender, race, economic status, sexuality, and disability in movements for disability liberation (justice and rights) and disability oppression (eugenics, sterilization, mass incarceration, and killing) in Brazil, the United States, and Canada. Her current research involves sibling care relationships, the experiences of people with complex medical conditions who rely on technologies such as mechanical ventilation and 24/7 skilled nursing for survival, and Retratos Defiças: Disability Portraits from Brazil. She actively supports initiatives related to the cultural, activist, and scholarly emergence of neurodivergence and disability identities in Brazil and other Global South countries.

Allison C. Carey (she/her) is professor of sociology and chair of the Department of Sociology and Anthropology at Shippensburg University in Pennsylvania. She also directs the master's program in organizational development and leadership and teaches disability studies courses. Her research focuses on disability rights and activism. Her books include *On the Margins of Citizenship: Civil Rights and Intellectual Disability in 20th Century America* (2009), *Allies and Obstacles: Disability Activism and Parents of Children with Disabilities* (cowritten with Pam Block and Richard Scotch, 2020), and *Disability and the*

Sociological Imagination (2022). She coedited three volumes of *Research in Social Science and Disability—Community and Disability* (vol. 6, with Richard Scotch, 2011); *Disability Allies and Alliances: Opportunities and Challenges* (vol. 12, with Joan Ostrove and Tara Fannon, 2020); *Disability in the Time of Pandemic* (vol. 13, with Sara Green and Laura Mauldin, 2023); and *Disability Incarcerated: Disability and Imprisonment in the US and Canada* (with Liat Ben-Moshe and Chris Chapman, 2014). In 2021, she was awarded the Distinguished Career in the Sociology of Disability Award from the Disability and Society Section of the American Sociological Association, and she was awarded Scholarly Achievement awards in 2010 and 2021 from the North Central Sociological Association.

Diane Compton (she/her) is a parent advocate and mom of three, including her coauthor, Erin. Diane is a member of the IL Council of Developmental Disabilities and a coadministrator of the IL Parents of Developmental Disabilities, a Facebook advocacy and support page with over six thousand members. She copresents with Erin and Erin's first reading teacher, sharing the parent perspective on the importance of inclusion.

Erin Compton (she/her) is a proud self-advocate who is finishing her senior year at the IL Virtual School and Academy. One of the youngest members of the IL State Rehabilitation Council, she represents students who, like her, are transitioning from school to the rest of their lives. Erin was awarded an Inclusion Champion Award from the IL Association of Rehabilitation Facilities. She dances professionally with a group called Unfolding Disability Futures. She also plays hockey with the Chicago Storm and performs on a circus wheel for Cirque Experience in Chicago. Erin works for the Chicago Cubs in a competitively paid job she obtained thanks to the recruiting organization Angels for Higher.

Jaclyn Ellis (they/them). My name is Manidoomakwakwe (MAN-i-dou ma-Kwa Kway). My English name is Jacky. I'm from London, Ontario, and I'm from the Wolf clan on my bio dad's side and Robertson on my bio mom's side. I'm in the sociocultural anthropology Ph.D. program at Western University. My research is mainly doing participatory research with autistic adults. I am also autistic.

Laura LeBrun Hatcher (she/her), with her husband, Brian, daughter Olivia, and son Simon, is a founding member of Little Lobbyists. As part of the Little Lobbyists' leadership, Laura oversees communication, content creation, media development, and technical support. She also engages in direct advocacy at federal and state levels with legislators, members of the administration, family caregivers, and individuals with disabilities. Laura has testified in the U.S. Congress and Maryland state legislature; been interviewed by the *Washington Post*, *New York Times*, *Politico*, *New York Magazine*, and *Univision*; and spoken at many rallies and press conferences, most notably at the invitation of Speaker Nancy Pelosi and Vice President Kamala Harris. In addition to her work with Little Lobbyists, Laura is a professor of graphic design at Towson University, an award-winning creative consultant, and co-owner of Hatcher Design Office, LLC, which specializes in human-centered design solutions to help organizations do good, better.

Elena Hung (she/her) is executive director and cofounder of Little Lobbyists, a family-led organization that advocates for children with complex medical needs and disabilities. Elena, her daughter Xiomara, and families like them visit Capitol Hill and offices across the country to speak with lawmakers and staffers about what is possible when disabled children have access to the health care, education, and community inclusion they need to survive and thrive. Her opinion pieces have been published in the *New York Times, Baltimore Sun, Vox, HuffPost,* and other publications. She was honored with the inaugural Speak Up for Better Health Award by the Center for Consumer Engagement in Health Innovation at Community Catalyst and recognized as Ally of the Year by the Autistic Self-Advocacy Network (2018). She is a frequent speaker at conferences (including Families USA, Netroots, and RESULTS International), as well as press conferences and rallies. She has testified before Congress twice on health matters related to disabled children with complex medical needs. Elena is also a national cochair of Health Care Voter, a campaign to mobilize voters and hold elected officials accountable for their votes on health care.

Bridget Liang (they/them) is a mixed race, queer, transfeminine, neurodiverse, disabled, fat fangirl. They came into their queerness in Hamilton, Ontario, and cofounded RADAR Youth Group at the LGBTQ Wellness Centre (the Well), the first queer group in a high school in Hamilton, and was instrumental in the passing of an equity policy in the HWDSB. They are a Ph.D. candidate in the Gender, Feminist, and Women's Studies Program at York University, a community researcher, workshop and group facilitator, performance artist, and fiction writer. Much of their work revolves around intersectionality and arts-based research.

Jenelle Rouse (she/her), Ph.D., is a culturally Deaf, independent, nontraditional researcher and body-movement dance artist. Born and raised in Canada, she has more than a decade of teaching experience under her belt as a classroom teacher at a bilingual school for the Deaf in Ontario. She currently brings a B.A. with honors (Toronto), B.Ed. as a member of the President's List (Oshawa), M.A., and Ph.D. (London) into her passion of learning, collaborating, creating, and writing. In addition to being a "behind the scenes" voluntary member of change-making organizations, she has worked part-time as an adjunct professor at several postsecondary institutions for at least three years in different provinces to engage candidates in their respective fields. Working in a variety of roles does not stop her from codirecting various groundbreaking projects such as Black Deaf Canada (Research), Multi-Lens Existence, and Just Keep Going Reel. Although American Sign Language is a focal theme, Jenelle is a firm believer that having sign language as a base is of utmost importance for every Deaf child to access contextual resources that recognize and promote sign language acquisition.

Richard K. Scotch (he/him) is professor of sociology and public policy at the University of Texas at Dallas, where he chairs programs in sociology and public health. His research interests include social policy reform and social movements in disability, health care, education, and human services. His books include *Allies and Obstacles: Disability Activism and Parents of Children with Disabilities* (with Pam Block and Allison C. Carey), *From Good Will to Civil Rights: Transforming Federal Disability Policy, Disability Protests: Contentious Politics 1970–1999* (with Sharon Barnartt), and *Disability and Community* (with Allison C. Carey). Dr. Scotch is past president of the Society for Disability Studies and past chair of the Section on Disability and Society of the American Sociological Association (ASA). He was named a 1999 Switzer Fellow by the National Rehabilitation Association, served on the Advisory Committee on Disability Studies in the Twenty-First Century of the National Institute of Disability, Independent Living, and Rehabilitation Research, was awarded the 2013 Senior Scholar Award by the Society for Disability Studies, and in 2014 received the inaugural Distinguished Contribution Award of the ASA Section on Disability and Society. His current research projects include interviews with political candidates with disabilities and a study of social and community barriers experienced by burn injury survivors.

Cheryl Najarian Souza (she/her) received her Ph.D. in sociology from Syracuse University. She is associate professor of sociology and faculty associate at the Center for Women and Work at the University of Massachusetts, Lowell. Her research and teaching interests include looking at concepts of disability and ability from intersectional, interdisciplinary, and feminist perspectives. She has written extensively about the Deaf community and the challenges Deaf women in particular face in paid work, mothering, and education. She has also explored cultural representations of Helen Keller. Currently, she is working on a project that looks at the discourses of (dis)ability in educational and family environments. In addition to several articles, she is the author of the book *"Between Worlds": Deaf Women, Work, and Intersections of Gender and Ability* (Routledge, 2006).

Jeneva Stone (she/her), Ph.D., M.F.A., is a writer advocate. Her essays and poems have appeared in many literary journals. She is the recipient of fellowships from MacDowell, Millay Arts, and Virginia Center for the Creative Arts. Jeneva and her son Rob volunteer for several health care and disability rights groups. They are members of Little Lobbyists, a family-led organization that advocates for the health care needs of children with complex medical needs and disabilities. Jeneva is the Little Lobbyists blog manager and serves on the Montgomery County, Maryland, Commission on People with Disabilities. She also volunteers for the Rare Action Network, part of the National Organization for Rare Disorders. Both she and Rob are members of the Self-Directed Advocacy Network (SDAN). Jeneva and Rob have delivered remarks at U.S. Senate press conferences and health care rallies and testified before the Maryland General Assembly. Jeneva's opinion writing has been featured in the *Washington Post* and *CNN Digital*. She and Rob are 2020 graduates of The Arc of Maryland's Partners in Policymaking program.

Roger A. Stone (he/him) (J.D., Columbia University) is a political Internet pioneer, entrepreneur, and author. He is founder and president of Advocacy Data. He has combined his knowledge of campaigns with cutting-edge technology to invent techniques used throughout U.S. politics. His work on the first political online video advertisement won the American Association of Political Consultant's Pollie Award. Campaigns & Elections named him a Rising Star of American Politics. His work has appeared in the *Washington Post, Politico, Campaigns & Elections, Columbia Journal of Law and Social Problems, Candy Wholesaler Magazine*, and numerous other publications. He is the father of a child with an ultrarare condition and member of Little Lobbyists.

Dr. Lisette E. Torres (she/her/ella) is a trained scientist and disabled scholar-activist who is a senior researcher at TERC, a nonprofit made up of teams of math and science education and research experts. She is also director of operations and communication for the new national NSF AISL equity resource center called the Reimagining Equity and Values in Informal STEM Education (REVISE) Center. Dr. Torres has a doctorate with a certificate in social justice from the School of Education at Iowa State University and a M.S. in zoology with a certificate in ecology from Miami University. Her academic research focuses on racialized gender justice and disability in science and higher education. She is an active member of Science for the People, a cofounder of Sines of Disability: Dismantling Ableism in Mathematics and Beyond, and a cofounder and former executive board member of the National Coalition for Latinxs with Disabilities (CNLD). Dr. Torres is also an advisory board member of Science Friday's Breakthrough Dialogues program and the Invisible Disability Project (IDP). She has been identified as an AERA/Spencer Foundation Early-Career Scholar and a Kavli Foundation Sponsored Network Leader for Inclusive Science Communication.

Grace Tsao (she/her) has spent her career working in higher education, nonprofit, and state government in various capacities including teaching, research, and grant writing. Over the years, she has been involved in many organizations that center social justice and served on multiple boards including the Disabilities Fund at the Chicago Community Trust and the State Rehabilitation Council in Illinois. She was also a grant-making committee member of the Asian Giving Circle, which funds nonprofits that support the Asian American community. Grace has a B.S. in news-editorial journalism from the University of Illinois at Urbana-Champaign, an M.S. in cultural foundations of education with a concentration in multicultural education from the University of Wisconsin at Milwaukee, and an M.A. in sociology from Loyola University Chicago, where her focus was on race, gender, and disability. She is the chairperson and advocacy chair of the Statewide Independent Living Council of Illinois. Grace has muscular dystrophy and uses a power wheelchair.

INDEX